Social Investment and Social Welfare

NEW HORIZONS IN SOCIAL POLICY

Series Editors: Patricia Kennett and Misa Izuhara, *University of Bristol, UK*

The New Horizons in Social Policy series captures contemporary issues and debates in social policy and encourages critical, innovative and thought-provoking approaches to understanding and explaining current trends and developments in the field. With its emphasis on original contributions from established and emerging researchers on a diverse range of topics, books in the series are essential reading for keeping up to date with the latest research and developments in the area.

Titles in the series include:

Housing Wealth and Welfare
Edited by Caroline Dewilde and Richard Ronald

Social Investment and Social Welfare
International and Critical Perspectives
Edited by James Midgley, Espen Dahl and Amy Conley Wright

Social Investment and Social Welfare

International and Critical Perspectives

Edited by

James Midgley

Harry and Riva Specht Professor Emeritus and Professor of the Graduate School, School of Social Welfare, University of California, Berkeley, USA

Espen Dahl

Professor of Health and Social Policy, Oslo and Akershus University College of Applied Sciences, Norway

Amy Conley Wright

Associate Professor of Social Work and Director of the Institute of Open Adoption Studies, University of Sydney, Australia

NEW HORIZONS IN SOCIAL POLICY

EE Edward Elgar
PUBLISHING

Cheltenham, UK • Northampton, MA, USA

Published by
Edward Elgar Publishing Limited
The Lypiatts
15 Lansdown Road
Cheltenham
Glos GL50 2JA
UK

Edward Elgar Publishing, Inc.
William Pratt House
9 Dewey Court
Northampton
Massachusetts 01060
USA

A catalogue record for this book
is available from the British Library

Library of Congress Control Number: 2016959928

This book is available electronically in the **Elgar**online
Social and Political Science subject collection
DOI 10.4337/9781785367830

ISBN 978 1 78536 782 3 (cased)
ISBN 978 1 78536 783 0 (eBook)

Printed and bound in Great Britain by TJ International Ltd, Padstow

Contents

Contributors

Sarah Cook is the Director of the United Nations Children's Fund (UNICEF) Innocenti Research Centre and was formerly Director of the United Nations Research Institute for Social Development (UNRISD) from 2009 to 2015. She was a Fellow at the Institute of Development Studies (IDS), UK (1996–2009) and has also worked for the Ford Foundation in China. She has undertaken extensive research on social and economic transformations in China, on social protection, labour markets and gender. Her publications include *Social Protection as Development Policy – Asian Perspectives*, Routledge, 2010 (edited with Naila Kabeer); 'Harsh Choices: Chinese Women's Paid Work and Unpaid Care Responsibilities under Economic Reform', *Development and Change*, 2012 (with Xiao-yuan Dong); and recent papers on social policy in China's response to crisis.

Espen Dahl is Professor of Health and Social Policy at Oslo and Akershus University College of Applied Sciences, Norway. He earned his PhD in sociology at the University of Oslo in 1994. His current research interests are social policy, health inequity, labour markets and work inclusion. At Oslo and Akershus University College of Applied Sciences he has served as research director of the interdisciplinary research programme on Care, Health and Welfare, the research group on Health and Social Policy, and of the Centre for Work Inclusion. He serves as an advisor on health inequity on the advisory board of the Directorate of Health. He has authored numerous reports and journal articles. The articles have appeared in journals including *Social Science and Medicine*, *European Sociological Review*, *Journal of Epidemiology and Community Health*, *International Journal of Social Welfare* and *Journal of European Social Policy*.

Amy Østertun Geirdal is Professor in Social Work and head of the PhD programme in Social Work and Social Policy at Oslo and Akershus University College of Applied Sciences, Norway. She holds a bachelor's degree in social work from Oslo and Akershus University College of Applied Sciences and a master's degree in health science from the University of Oslo. She has a doctoral degree from the PhD programme in medicine, University of Oslo. She has worked as a medical social worker and genetic counsellor and has taught in the bachelor programme in social work and the master's programme in mental health. Her main research interests are mental health and quality of life among persons with rare and/or hereditary diseases and among students, social inequality and health, and the importance of relations in mental health care. Her recent publications in English include 'Satisfaction with Life in Adults with Marfan Syndrome (MFS): Associations with Health-related Consequences of MFS, Pain, Fatigue and Demographic Factors', *Quality of Life Research*, 2016; and 'Systematic Review of Chronic Pain in Persons with Marfan Syndrome', *Systematic Clinical Genetics*, 2015 (both articles with Gry Velvin, Trine Bathen and Sven Rand-Hendriksen).

Anthony Hall is Professor of Social Policy at the London School of Economics, UK. During 2003–2005 he worked for the World Bank in Washington, DC, USA as Senior Social Development Specialist for Latin America. His recent books are: *Forests and Climate Change: The Social Dimensions of REDD in Latin America*, Edward Elgar Publishing, 2012; *Global Impact, Local Action: New Environmental Policy in Latin America*, Institute for the Study of the Americas, 2005; *Social Policy for Development*, Sage Publications, 2004 (with James Midgley); *Amazonia at the Crossroads: the Challenge of Sustainable Development*, Institute of Latin America Studies, 2000; and *Sustaining Amazonia: Grassroots Action for Productive Conservation*, Manchester University Press, 1997. He has published a number of papers on the impacts of conditional cash transfers in Brazil, focusing on political dimensions. His latest research concerns Brazil's programme of South–South development cooperation in the areas of cash transfers and nutritional security since the early 2000s, focusing on relationships with Africa as a strategy of soft foreign policy.

Knut Halvorsen is Professor Emeritus of Social Policy at Oslo and Akershus University College of Applied Sciences, Norway. He completed his doctoral dissertation in sociology. He was the first director of the Social Welfare Research Centre at the Institute of Social Work, as well as course director of a master's programme in International Social Welfare and Health Policy. His main research interests are unemployment, early retirement, marginalization and comparative social policy. He has published several textbooks in social policy and social research methods. Among books published in English is *Work, Oil and Welfare, The Norwegian Welfare State*, Universitetsforlaget, 2008 (with Steinar Stjernø). Among articles and chapters published in English are: 'Work

Orientations in Scandinavia: Employment Commitment and Organizational Commitment in Denmark, Norway and Sweden', *Acta Sociologica*, 2001 (with Stefan Svallfors and Jørgen Goul Andersen); 'Changing Labour Markets, Unemployment and Unemployment Policies in a Citizenship Perspective', in J.G. Andersen, J. Clasen, W. van Oorschot and K. Halvorsen (eds), *Europe's New State of Welfare*, Policy Press, 2003; and 'Legitimacy of Welfare States in Transitions from Homogeneity to Multiculturality: A Matter of Trust', in S. Mau and B. Veghte (eds), *Social Justice and Legitimacy and the Welfare State*, Ashgate, 2007.

James Lee is former Professor and Head of the Department of Applied Social Sciences at the Hong Kong Polytechnic University. He specializes in comparative housing studies and social policy in East Asia. His research focuses largely on housing policy, social policy and social development, with a special interest in institutional arrangements facilitating the attainment of both social and economic objectives. He publishes in international journals such as *Housing Studies*, *Pacific Review*, *Policy and Politics*, *Environment and Planning* and *Economic Geography*. He has also published and co-edited a number of books, including *Social Policy and Change in East Asia*, Lexington Books, 2014 (with James Midgley and Yapeng Zhu); *The Crisis of Welfare in East Asia*, Lexington Books, 2007 (with K.W. Chan); *Housing and Social Change: East West Perspectives*, Routledge, 2003 (with Ray Forrest); and *Housing, Home Ownership and Social Change in Hong Kong*, Ashgate, 1999.

Joe C.B. Leung is Honorary Professor, Department of Social Work and Social Administration, University of Hong Kong, and Visiting Professor, Institute of Social Development and Public Policy, Beijing Normal University, China. His research and publications focus on social welfare reforms both in Hong Kong and in mainland China. Specific research areas include pension reforms, social assistance, care of older people, social development, social work education, community building, human service management, programme evaluation and family services. His most recent book is *China's Social Welfare: The Third Turning Point*, Polity Press, 2015 (with Yuebin Xu).

Thomas Lorentzen is a Professor at the Department of Sociology at the University of Bergen, Norway. He works with longitudinal analyses of register data focusing on labour market outcomes and welfare receipt. He also teaches quantitative methods for the social sciences. He is currently involved in several comparative register data-based analyses of the Nordic welfare states.

James Midgley is Harry and Riva Specht Professor Emeritus and Professor of the Graduate School at the School of Social Welfare, University of California, Berkeley, USA. He has published widely on issues of social development, international social welfare and social policy. Among his most recent books are *Poverty, Incomes and Social Protection: International Policy Perspectives*, Routledge, 2013 (with Richard Hoefer); *Social Protection, Economic Growth and Social Change: Goals, Issues and Trajectories in China, India, Brazil and South Africa*, Edward Elgar Publishing, 2013 (co-editor with David Piachaud); *Social Policy and Social Change in East Asia*, Lexington Books, 2014 (with James Lee and Yapeng Zhu); *Social Development: Theory and Practice*, Sage, 2014; and *Social Welfare for a Global Era: International Perspectives on Policy and Practice*, Sage, 2017. He is a Fellow of the American Academy of Social Work and Social Welfare and has held honorary professorial appointments at Nihon Fukishi University in Japan, the University of Johannesburg in South Africa, Hong Kong Polytechnic University, and Sun Yat-sen University in China.

Leila Patel is the South African Research Chair in Welfare and Social Development and Director of the Centre for Social Development in Africa at the University of Johannesburg, South Africa. She was previously the Director General for Social Welfare in the Mandela government and played a leading role in the development of South Africa's welfare policy. Some of her notable publications include her book *Restructuring of Social Welfare: Options for South Africa*, Ravan Press, 1993; the *White Paper for Social Welfare*, Department of Welfare, Republic of South Africa, 1997; *Social Welfare and Social Development in South Africa*, Oxford University Press, 2005; *Social Protection in Southern Africa New Opportunities for Social Development* (co-editor), Routledge, 2013; and a second edition of *Social Welfare and Social Development*, Oxford University Press Southern Africa, 2015. She has published widely in the field of social welfare and social development in the African context. Currently she leads a range of social development research projects relating to social protection, gender and care; children and youth development innovations; and developmental social work and the transformation of social welfare services in South Africa. She received the Distinguished Woman in Science (Humanities and the Social Sciences) Award from the Ministry of Science and Technology, Republic of South Africa, in 2013.

Sony Pellissery is Associate Professor and Director of the master's programme in Public Policy at the National Law School of India University, Bangalore, India. His primary area of interest is to learn how the politics of markets interacts with the politics of welfare state. He aims to understand the nature of the state in the Global South, where the disciplines of social policy and of development studies use their respective lenses to comprehend the predicament of human welfare. He has previously published in the *Journal of Social Policy*, *Social Policy and Administration*, *Journal of Human Development* and *International Social Security Review*. His recent book is *Shame of It: Global Perspectives on Anti-Poverty Policies*, Polity Press, 2013 (co-editor, with Erika Gubrium and Ivar Lødemel). He was awarded the India Social Science Research Award by the International Development Research Centre (IDRC) Canada in 2009, and the Ram Reddy Social Scientist Award by the Prof. G. Ram Reddy Memorial Trust in 2015.

Steinar Stjernø is Professor Emeritus of Social Policy at Oslo and Akershus University College of Applied Sciences, Norway. He has been Rector/President at the Norwegian State College of Social Work and Local Government Administration and Oslo University College. He has headed the Norway Commission on Higher Education, the Norwegian National Research Programme on Welfare, and served on a number of boards in higher education and research institutes. He has published books on social policy, social assistance and poverty. Among his books published in English are *Solidarity in Europe, The History of an Idea*, Cambridge University Press, 2004; and *Work, Oil and Welfare, The Norwegian Welfare State,* Universitetsforlaget, 2008 (with Knut Halvorsen). Other publications in English include 'Social Democratic Values', in Michael Opielka, Wim van Orschot and Birgit Pfau-Effinger (eds), *Culture and the Welfare State: Values and Social Policy in Comparative Perspective*, Edward Elgar Publishing, 2008; and 'Solidarity Beyond Europe', in Lester Salamon (ed.), *Solidarity Beyond Borders: Ethics in a Globalising World*, Bloomsbury Publishing, 2015.

Anne Grete Tøge is a PhD candidate in Social Work and Social Policy at Oslo and Akershus University of Applied Sciences, Norway. She holds a bachelor's degree in social work and a master's degree in welfare studies from the University of Agder, Norway. She has conducted a number of studies on the health effects of the 2008 economic recession and individual unemployment experience in Europe. She is also engaged in several cluster-randomized trials in Norway, investigating the effects of complex interventions aimed at improving follow up of active labour market programme participants, reducing school drop-outs and reducing intergenerational transmission of poverty. Among articles published in English are 'Health Effects of Unemployment in Europe (2008–2011): A Longitudinal Analysis of Income and Financial Strain as Mediating

Factors', *International Journal for Equity in Health*, 2016; 'Effects of Individualised Follow-up on Activation Programme Participants' Self-sufficiency: A Cluster-Randomised Study', *International Journal of Social Welfare*, 2015 (with Ira Malmberg-Heimonen); and 'Unemployment Transitions and Self-rated Health in Europe: A Longitudinal Analysis of EU-SILC from 2008 to 2011', *Social Science and Medicine*, 2015 (with Morten Blekesaune).

Amy Conley Wright is an Associate Professor of Social Work and Director of the Institute of Open Adoption Studies at the University of Sydney, Australia. She formerly held positions as Senior Lecturer in Social Work and Member of the Early Start Research Institute at the University of Wollongong, Australia and Assistant Professor of Child & Adolescent Development at San Francisco State University, USA. Her publications include peer-reviewed journal articles on the topics of social investment in children, child maltreatment prevention, parent peer support and policy advocacy. This work has been featured in journals including *Policy Studies Journal, International Journal of Social Welfare, Journal of Social Services Research* and *Children and Youth Services Review*. She is co-author of *Six Steps to Successful Child Advocacy: Changing the World for Children*, Sage Publications, 2013 (with Ken Jaffe); and co-editor of *Developmental Social Work: Investment Strategies and Professional Practice*, Oxford University Press, 2010 (with James Midgley).

Yuebin Xu is Professor at the School of Social Development and Public Policy, Beijing Normal University, China. His field of research has been focused on social assistance and elderly care. His recent publications (in English) include *China's Social Welfare: the Third Turning Point*, Polity Press, 2015 (with Joe C.B. Leung); 'Poverty and Quality of Life of Chinese Children: From the Perspective of Deprivation', *International Journal of Social Welfare*, 2015 (with Yu-Cheung Wong and Ting-Yan Wang); 'Pensions and Social Assistance: The Development of Income Security Policies for Old People in China', in S. Chen and J.L. Powell (eds), *Aging in China: Implications to Social Policy of a Changing Economic State*, Springer Science+Business Media, 2012 (with Zhang Xiulan); and 'From Social Insurance to Social Assistance: Process and Development in China's Urban Social Welfare Policy', *Asia Pacific Journal of Social Work and Development*, 2010 (with Zhang Xiulan).

Preface

We are immensely grateful to everyone who participated for making this book possible. Thanks to Espen and his colleagues in the Health and Social Policy Research Group at the Oslo and Akershus University College of Applied Sciences, Norway for providing an opportunity for the authors to come together. We are also very grateful for the support provided by the University. Thanks to Amy for working so diligently with our authors to standardize the book's chapters and for preparing the manuscript for submission to Edward Elgar Publishing. Each of the contributors deserves special thanks for their informative chapters: James Lee for his contribution on housing and social investment in Hong Kong and Singapore, Sony Pellissery for his chapter on the Indian government's investments in child care and rural employment, Leila Patel for her chapter on social investment and the Child Support Grant in South Africa, Anthony Hall for his account of the investment function of the Brazilian conditional cash transfer programme, Joe Leung and Yuebin Xu for their chapter on pensions and social investment in China, Knut Halvorsen, Amy Østertun Geirdal and Anne Grete Tøge for their critical assessment of child care as social investment in Norway, Steinar Stjernø for his chapter on the potential of social investment policies to promote the integration of immigrants in Europe and Sarah Cook for her analysis of the contribution of the international agencies to promoting social investment worldwide. Of course, the editors also contributed chapters, so thanks to Amy for her chapter on early childhood investments in Australia, Espen and Thomas Lorentzen for the chapter on employment policy in Norway, and Jim for his overview chapter and the chapter on community investment in the United States.

Finally, our thanks go to Emily Mew and Alex Pettifer at Edward Elgar Publishing who enthusiastically supported the idea for the book and to Tori Raven who handled the initial contract discussions. Emily has since provided wonderful support and it has been a joy to work with her, and many thanks to Karissa Venne for her excellent editorial oversight. Madhubanti Bhattacharyya managed the book's production with great efficiency and Cathrin Vaughn was a proficient and helpful copy-editor. Thanks also to Sue Sharp and her colleagues for marketing the book. We are also grateful to Patricia Kennett and Misa Izuhara for including this book in their series on New Horizons in Social Policy.

Introduction

James Midgley, Espen Dahl and Amy Conley Wright

The notion of social investment has attracted widespread interest among Western and especially European social policy scholars in recent years. Generally, they regard social investment as a new approach to social welfare in which governments prioritize policies and programmes that promote employment, prepare people for productive work through education and job training, and support employment through family leave and similar policies. They often contrast the social investment approach with the traditional 'welfare state' approach that emerged in Western countries in the years following the Second World War; this approach prioritizes resources transfers through comprehensive social and income maintenance services to people in need, and in this way seeks to reduce poverty, redistribute resources, foster social solidarity and promote altruism. However, many social policy scholars believe that the traditional welfare state approach is no longer viable. Faced with new economic and social pressures such as population ageing, deindustrialization, increased economic competition arising from globalization and intense budgetary constraints, a new and dynamic alternative such as social investment is needed to address current economic, social and political realities. By shifting the focus from welfare transfers to social investments, they claim that governments will be better able to deal with current challenges and ensure the well-being of their citizens.

The academic literature on social investment has proliferated and addressed both the analytical and normative dimensions of the subject. Several social policy writers (Bonoli, 2013; Esping-Andersen, 2002; Giddens, 1998; Hemerijck, 2012, 2013; Morel et al., 2012; Midgley, 1999, 2015; Sherraden, 1991) have sought to analyse and define social investment and describe its features. This has been accompanied by attempts to conceptualize social investment with reference to other established theoretical frameworks in social policy. Generally, social investment is viewed as paradigmatic in that it amounts to a distinctive

1

ordering of interventions and budgetary allocations to comprise a unique approach that differs not only from the traditional welfare state approach but also from the neoliberal approach which prioritizes individual responsibility and the utilization of the market for welfare purposes. Social investment is also distinctive because of its productive function. Unlike the welfare state approach which fosters consumption transfers that market liberal economists believe impede economic development, Midgley and Tang (2001) contend that social investment promotes economic participation and generates positive rates of return to the economy.

Some scholars have documented and conceptualized social investment's historical evolution. This scholarship is often cast in stadial terms, viewing social investment as the most recent of a series of sequential stages in the evolution of government welfare. According to this historical schema, the first was the welfare state stage, based on Keynesian and Beveridgean ideas, which emerged after the Second World War to provide comprehensive social services and income transfers which would eradicate need and foster greater equality. The second neoliberal stage emerged in the 1980s as radical right-wing governments opposed to welfare statism were elected in the United States, Britain and other Western countries. This stage was marked by retrenchment, the privatization of statutory programmes, outsourcing and greater use of means testing when determining eligibility for benefits. Social investment is the latest stage, which is replacing the neoliberal stage. Unlike the neoliberal stage, it accords a key role for the state as the initiator of social investments and active welfare policies. Since social investment challenges neoliberalism, it is said to comprise a new, post-neoliberal stage in the history of social policy (Jenson, 2009).

At the normative level, many social policy scholars commend social investment's electoral promise, policy applicability and relevance to current economic and political realities. Although various positive assessments of its policy usefulness have been articulated, the normative advocacy of social investment has also been influenced by debates in progressive political circles about the limitations of the traditional welfare state approach. An important influence was the British Labour Party's Commission on Social Justice, which reviewed the Party's economic and social policies in the wake of its unexpected electoral defeat in 1992 (Commission on Social Justice, 1994). Questioning the assumptions on which the Party's social policies had long been based, the Commission proposed a radical reformulation of its approach in order to enhance its relevance to a post-industrial society in which traditional proletarian occupations and class loyalties had given way to middle-class individualism, consumerism and scepticism about welfarism. A new emphasis on social investment would, it was argued, have greater electoral appeal. It was in this context that the term 'social investment state' was coined by Anthony Giddens (1998), the respected sociologist and an adviser to Prime Minister Tony Blair, to contrast the Party's new approach with its traditional welfare state approach and to promote its wider 'Third Way' agenda. In Europe, several Social Democratic parties followed by embracing policy changes that would increase labour flexibility and impose work requirements on the recipients of unemployment benefits, yet pursuing an agenda characterized by 'active protection' and 'enabling to work' (Bonoli, 2013; Huo, 2009). In the United States, social policy debates among the New Democrats inspired presidential candidate Bill Clinton to adopt an electoral platform that downplayed the Democratic Party's traditional welfarism. Michael Sherraden's (1991) writing on promoting financial asset accumulation among low-income families was particularly influential in popularizing social investment ideas among American social policy-makers and academics.

Another relevant and important development was the European Union's Lisbon Treaty of 2000, which was primarily concerned with modifying the Union's constitutional provisions, but also directed member states to refocus policy in a number of fields including justice, security and welfare in order to achieve greater standardization and coordination and to promote approaches better suited to changing needs and realities. The Treaty's Social Agenda raised a number of issues concerning the limitations of the traditional welfare system which needed to be addressed if the social challenges facing the Union and its member states were to be met (Vandenbroucke and Vleminckx, 2011). Mindful of the high rates of unemployment and particularly youth unemployment in many European countries, the Social Agenda urged that greater emphasis be placed on job creation, new forms of work organization, education and skills development, new employment opportunities for youth, and policies to promote social inclusion and eradicate poverty; all of which were linked to the notion of social investment as an organizing social policy framework. As in Britain and the United States, these developments inspired several European social policy scholars to commend the positive features of the social investment approach and to advocate for its adoption.

As may be expected, the normative advocacy of social investment has provoked vigorous debates. Perhaps the most forceful criticisms have come from scholars committed to the traditional welfare state approach who believe that social investment's emphasis on employment and

knowledge and skills development affronts social policy's historic commitment to meet social needs through services and income transfers
(Cantillon, 2011; Cantillon and Van Lancker, 2013; Nolan, 2013). Welfare, they contend, should not be concerned with promoting work but
with delivering services to people in need and fulfilling their social
rights. They are also critical of what they perceive as social investment's
instrumentalism, which uses investments to promote economic growth
rather than meeting basic human needs. Instead of treating people as ends
in themselves, social investment uses them as a means of achieving
economic development. A related problem is that the emphasis on
economic development has negative social consequences. Instead of
promoting well-being, the drive for growth has damaging consequences
both for the environment and for social life, where rampant consumerism
fosters acquisitive values and undermines the social fabric. Additionally,
concerns have been expressed about the behavioural compliance required
by conditional cash transfers and the social control this exerts on
populations dependent on government assistance.

Critics also point out that social investment's emphasis on work cannot
address the complex financial and social challenges facing many families
and especially those with low incomes. Similarly, it is not clear how the
needs of elders and people with disabilities, who are not able to work,
will be met by social investment policies that are more concerned with
economic participation than with providing benefits. They also contend
that advocates of social investment seldom refer to social rights, redistribution or the promotion of social solidarity, which are the key, historic
features of state welfare. In this regard, they reject the idea that social
investment is a new and distinctive social policy paradigm and claim that
it amounts to little more than a revisionist form of neoliberalism. Social
investment may ameliorate the excesses of neoliberalism but that does
not alter its fundamental commitment to individualism and self-
responsibility.

A major limitation of current scholarship into social investment, which
this book explicitly addresses, is its Eurocentric focus. The current
literature is predominantly concerned with Europe and the way European
governments are implementing social investment policies and programmes. Apart from occasional references to conditional cash transfer
programmes such as *Bolsa Família* in Brazil and developments in welfare
policies in Australia, the social investment literature is decidedly Eurocentric. The long and extensive experience of implementing social
investment policies in the nations of the Global South has been largely
ignored. Even the work of scholars in the United States who have made

a major contribution by formulating an asset-based approach to social investment is given little attention.

There are other limitations of social policy scholarship into social investment that will be raised in the following chapters of this book. In particular, the diverse types of social investment policies that have been introduced in different countries will be examined in a series of case study chapters which contend that it is more useful to focus on these policies than to utilize paradigmatic policy frameworks or stadial interpretations when studying social investment. Accordingly, these chapters focus on particular policies and programmes that have an investment function rather than on national-level policy frameworks. Although these are discussed within national contexts, they suggest that scholarly inquiry into social investment will benefit from documenting and interpreting the way these policies and programmes have evolved and function in different countries. As will be seen, these programmes include early childhood policies in Australia, employment-focused social policies in Norway, community development in the United States, preschool and employment policies in India, pension policy in China and housing policy in Singapore. In analysing these policies and programmes, the authors transcend description by examining the issues attending the implementation of social investment policies and discussing their limitations. Some of the book chapters are primarily concerned with a critical analysis of social investment policy programmes. The collection is augmented by chapters that range more broadly over related issues such as the contribution of international organizations to social investment, the gender dimensions of cash transfers in South Africa and the potential of social investment programmes to respond to immigration in Europe.

The editors and contributors to this book believe that scholarship into social investment will be enhanced by an appreciation of social investment policies and their history and functioning in different countries. While the European experience has insights to offer, these can be appreciated alongside a broader range of international examples that expand understanding of the potential and complexities of social investment. The book's editors contend that openness to learning from the experiences of other nations not only has intrinsic value since it enriches the field, but also fosters constructive policy learning and policy exchanges. By documenting and analysing the way social investment policies function in different parts of the world, academics and policy-makers will be able to examine local initiatives in the light of comparative experiences. They will also be able to assess their usefulness and judiciously adapt policy innovations originating elsewhere, contributing to the emergence of what Midgley (2017) calls a One World perspective that can address the pressing problems facing the global community today.

THE PLAN OF THIS BOOK

As noted earlier, this book seeks to contribute to the expanding literature on social investment by showing how social investment ideas have found application in a variety of programmes introduced by governments in different countries over the years. The book does not, as is common, focus on national-level interventions and comparative typologies but examines different, discrete social policies and programmes that have an investment function. These are described within the context of national welfare policy, and their strengths and limitations are examined. By showing how social investment policies and programmes have been adopted in different parts of the world, the book hopes to provide a comparative perspective that will enhance the largely Eurocentric analyses that characterize much of the literature on the subject. In addition to these case studies of social investment interventions, the book contains chapters that discuss the role of the international agencies in promoting social investment, the way social investment policies may promote the integration of migrants and refugees in Europe, and the role of gender in social protection in South Africa.

Chapter 1 by James Midgley provides a broad introduction to the concept of social investment and the way it is used in different academic and professional fields. Noting that the term 'social investment' is poorly defined, he offers a definition and examines the meaning of terms such as 'investment', 'consumption', 'income', 'assets' and 'capital' which are widely used in economics. The chapter then reviews the different ways in which the term 'social investment' has been used in four academic and professional fields, namely social policy, nonprofit management, community studies and development studies, where investment ideas have been influential since the 1950s. The chapter contends that scholars will benefit from understanding the way the concept of social investment has been employed in these different academic and professional fields. It concludes by suggesting that it may be possible to synthesize these different approaches to promote a comprehensive and globally relevant interpretation that will enhance the academic and policy relevance of social investment ideas.

Chapter 2 by Amy Conley Wright discusses social investment in early childhood in Australia. She presents arguments for social investment in young children and potential benefits for families, children and the broader society. The chapter then examines the Australian national early childhood development strategy, called *Investing in the Early Years* (Council of Australian Governments, 2009), to analyse strengths, gaps and challenges. This strategy is designed to promote the best possible outcomes for children, and by extension the nation. Policies in the areas of early childhood care and education, social transfers and parental leave are described and contextualized through a comparison with the averages provided by the Organisation for Economic Co-operation and Development (OECD), to identify strengths, gaps and challenges.

In Chapter 3, James Lee discusses the role of housing in social investment with reference to Singapore and other East Asian countries where housing serves not only to meet shelter needs but also as a powerful investment tool that has major long-term welfare effects. Traditional social policy theories have been vague on the social investment impact of social policy, especially with regard to housing policy. Its dual nature, as both consumption and investment, has made it difficult to align with other social policies such as health care and education. This chapter examines its role as social investment in two contrasting high-growth urban economies in East Asia: Singapore and Hong Kong. First, it tackles a gap in contemporary social policy debates and explains why the social investment aspect has been neglected. Second, through the case studies of Hong Kong and Singapore, it explains the important relationship between housing policy and social security. The purpose is to look beyond the residential dimension of housing and to establish a connection between housing policy and asset building. Given its enormous potentials on investment and returns, and its impact on life quality, wealth and social justice, a thorough understanding of the role of housing policy is vital to realizing the social investment potentials of contemporary social policy.

Next, in Chapter 4, Sony Pellissery discusses social investment policies in India, focusing on employment and early childhood programmes and the way they seek to meet the needs of poor families in India and provide them with resources that have an investment function. The Integrated Child Development Scheme (ICDS), since its beginning in the 1970s, has focused on providing nutrition to pregnant women and children up to the age of formal schooling. In contexts where poverty is pervasive, the chances of welfare loss through neglect as well as affordability are very high. The long-term impact of such neglect on human capital is immense. Similarly, India passed the National Rural Employment Guarantee Act (NREGA) in 2005 (based on an initiative introduced in 1972 in one of the states of India, Maharashtra) with an aim to provide employment opportunities in lean agricultural seasons as well as to build community assets through such labour. The chapter offers an overview and analysis of these two programmes and shows how a social investment approach was an essential component of development expenditure in the Global South.

Chapter 5 by Espen Dahl and Thomas Lorentzen examines labour market policy and related social policies in Norway, focusing on a selected set of recent reforms as well as their outcomes such as work participation and earnings, in particular for disadvantaged groups that are often targets of the reforms. A rather mixed picture emerges. Some reforms and parts of larger reforms carry the stamp of a true social investment approach, for example the reform in the Welfare and Labour Administration, and the Qualification programme targeted at social assistance recipients. Other reforms, such as changes in the Work Environment Act, cuts in benefits for disability beneficiaries with low pre-disability earnings, and stricter conditions for receiving social assistance benefit, fit poorly with a social investment strategy. Yet, it should be added that these reforms mostly tend to be carefully designed, are rather moderate in nature and restricted in scope. As these reforms are of recent date, their consequences are still unknown.

Next, in Chapter 6, Leila Patel discusses the gender dimensions of the Child Support Grant (CSG) in South Africa. This is one of the country's largest social protection programmes reaching almost 40 per cent of poor children. The grant is cited as a social investment in social care in the family and households, yielding positive outcomes through the empowerment of women, which in turn contributes to improved child well-being. The author draws on national and community-level data on gender and care in South Africa. The data however also point to the limitations of social investment policies in promoting gender justice, especially where such social policies fail to challenge the gendered nature of care in the family, community and social service sector.

In Chapter 7, James Midgley discusses social investment at the community level in the United States, where community development programmes have a long history and have prioritized inventions that transcend traditional welfare approaches. Noting that the literature on social investment has paid little if any attention to investments at the community level, the chapter examines the way the federal and state governments of the United States, supported by nonprofit organizations, have sought to invest in low-income communities by mobilizing assets, expanding employment, increasing access to education and affordable housing, and raising standards of living. It begins by tracing the origins of the community social investment approach in the late nineteenth century, when the settlement house movement introduced a number of initiatives designed to deal with urban poverty and deprivation brought about by industrialization, urbanization and mass migration into the United States. These activities were subsequently augmented by programmes introduced during the War on Poverty in the 1960s. The chapter discusses the way these programmes have evolved and now comprise a variety of community and asset building initiatives throughout the country. It concludes by assessing the achievements as well as limitations of the community social investment approach in the United States.

Chapter 8 by Anthony Hall takes a critical look at cash transfers in Brazil and assesses their strengths and limitations as promoting social investments. Brazil's conditional cash transfer (CCT) scheme, known as *Bolsa Família* – the world's largest, which benefits more than a quarter of the country's total population of more than 200 million – appears to embrace certain elements of a social investment approach, at least in principle. The programme aims to strengthen human capital formation by boosting school attendance and encouraging mothers' participation in vaccination and other preventive health care campaigns. Although the government has announced plans to make the programme more production-oriented, there are few direct links with employment creation, which have remained largely hypothetical. Furthermore, in the quest to maximize electoral gains through a focus on widening cash benefits, there has been a noticeable failure to make any significant headway with broader and longer-term social investments in health, basic sanitation, education and housing, for example. Such broad-based infrastructure support would serve to underpin the process of economic growth in a more sustainable fashion. This underlying tension will continue to frustrate any pretensions that Brazil might harbour towards developing an authentic social investment model, at least for the foreseeable future.

Next, in Chapter 9, Joe C. B. Leung and Yuebin Xu discuss pension reform in China and question whether the government's pension policies effectively promote social investments that produce future benefits to elders. Facing the challenges of an ageing population, escalating pension payments and imminent declining workforce, China has to formulate a sustainable, adequate and affordable pension system. Using pension reforms as an example, this chapter illustrates that harmonizing pension reforms are regarded as the key instrument of social investment strategy to promote economic performance. Pension reforms are pivotal to restructure the labour market, to facilitate labour mobility and integration across regions, occupational sectors, and rural and urban areas, as well as to enhance the quality of human capital. In short, a modernized economy has to be accompanied by a universal and equitable social security system.

In Chapter 10, Knut Halvorsen, Amy Østertun Geirdal and Anne Grete Tøge critically examine child care policies and programmes in Norway. The experiences of Norwegian children in preschools, schools and families, and the impact on their happiness and mental health, are examined, in relation to other European and Western children. The assumption that social investments in children and parents are always in the best interests of the well-being of children is questioned. Drawing on the United Nations Convention on the Rights of the Child of 1989, the authors contend that human rights, capabilities and citizens' perspective should be considered as an alternative to the social investment perspective. It is argued that the child's present experience (being) should be balanced with future-oriented investments (becoming).

Chapter 11 by Steinar Stjernø discusses the role of social investment as a means of integrating immigrants in Europe. The total foreign-born population of the European Union now constitutes 21 million persons, and in recent years, more than 1 million persons have been seeking asylum every year. A large number of immigrants are young people of working age. The author discusses the idea of social investment in European Union immigration policy. First, the chapter describes the number and distribution of immigrants from non-European Union countries. Second, the development of the role of the idea of social investment in the Union's normative framework is analysed with a particular focus on immigrants and the integration of immigrants into the labour market. Finally, the chapter concludes with a discussion of the relationship between declarations and actions.

Next, in Chapter 12, Sarah Cook reviews the role of international organizations in promoting social investment. This chapter explores the ways in which the social investment approach and its terminology have been adopted and promoted by selected international development organizations, as well as some international non-governmental organizations. It focuses on the period since the 1990s, when it is argued that a 'social turn' in development policy emerged as a reaction to the devastating social consequences of Washington Consensus adjustment policies, foreshadowing the global commitment to poverty reduction through the Millennium Development Goals and the evolution of a range of new policy instruments to deliver on this social agenda, most notably through targeted and conditional cash transfers. International organizations have played a significant role in the spread of such ideas and practices which can be identified with the social investment approach, if not always labelled as such. The promotion of these new instruments in development contexts, however, tends to obscure significant differences in goals, values and approaches among organizations. While often justified in social investment terms, a strong theoretical case for the use of such instruments as development policy is lacking. Instead, the case is largely grounded in evidence of 'what works' for short-term results linked to organizational priorities, notably poverty alleviation, impacts on specific groups (women, children) and behavioural change (such as use of health and education services).

The final, brief concluding chapter by the editors, Chapter 13, offers a short summary of the book and its chapters, drawing attention to the major lessons learned and discussing some of the future directions that scholarly research in the field should take. They point out that although the book offers a critique of the Western literature, it is not intended primarily to critique this literature, but rather to enhance its international relevance and contribute to the emergence of a globally relevant body of knowledge on social investment that will be helpful to policy-makers and practitioners seeking to promote social welfare around the world.

REFERENCES

Bonoli, G. (2013). *The Origins of Active Social Policy: Labour Market and Childcare Policies in Comparative Perspective*. New York: Oxford University Press.

Cantillon, B. (2011). The Paradox of the Social Investment State: Growth, Employment and Poverty in the Lisbon Era. *Journal of European Social Policy*, 21 (5), 432–449.

Cantillon, B. and Van Lancker, W. (2013). Three Shortcomings of the Social Investment Perspective. *Social Policy and Society*, 12 (4), 553–564.

Commission on Social Justice (1994). *Social Justice: Strategies for National Renewal*. London: Vintage Books.

Council of Australian Governments (COAG) (2009). *Investing in the Early Years – A National Early Childhood Development Strategy*. Retrieved from https://www.coag.gov.au/sites/default/files/national_ECD_strategy.pdf.

Esping-Andersen, G. (2002). A Child-Centered Social Investment Strategy. In G. Esping-Andersen, D. Gallie, A. Hemerijck and J. Meyers (eds), *Why We Need a New Welfare State*. New York: Oxford University Press, pp 26–67.

Giddens, A. (1998). *The Third Way: The Renewal of Social Democracy*. Cambridge: Polity Press.

Hemerijck, A. (2012). Two or Three Waves of Welfare State Transformation?. In N. Morel, B. Pallier and J. Palme (eds), *Towards a Social Investment Welfare State? Ideas, Policies and Challenges*. Bristol: Policy Press, pp. 33–60.

Hemerijck, A. (2013). *Changing Welfare States*. New York: Oxford University Press.

Huo, J. (2009). *Third Way Reforms: Social Democracy after the Golden Age*. Cambridge: Cambridge University Press.

Jenson, J. (2009). Redesigning Citizenship Regimes After Neoliberalism: Moving Towards Social Investment. In N. Morel, B. Palier and J. Palme (eds). *What Future for Social Investment?*. Stockholm: Institute for Future Studies, pp. 27–44.

Midgley, J. (1999). Growth, Redistribution and Welfare: Towards Social Investment. *Social Service Review*, 77 (1), 3–21.

Midgley, J. (2015). Social Investment, Inclusive Growth and the State. In R. Hasmath (ed.), *Inclusive Growth, Development and Welfare Policy: A Critical Assessment*. New York: Routledge, pp. 91–107.

Midgley, J. (2017). *Social Welfare for a Global Era: International Perspectives on Policy and Practice*. Los Angeles, CA: Sage Publications.

Midgley, J. and Tang, K.L. (2001). Social Policy, Economic Growth and Developmental Welfare. *International Journal of Social Welfare*, 10 (4), 242–250.

Morel, N., Pallier, B. and Palme, J. (eds) (2012). Beyond the Welfare State as We Knew it? In N. Morel, B. Pallier and J. Palme (eds), *Towards a Social Investment Welfare State? Ideas, Policies and Challenges*. Bristol: Policy Press, pp. 1–32.

Nolan, B. (2013). What Use is 'Social Investment'?. *Journal of European Social Policy*, 23 (5), 459–468.

Sherraden, M. (1991). *Assets and the Poor: A New American Welfare Policy*. Armonk, NY: M.E. Sharpe.

Vandenbroucke, F. and Vleminckx, K. (2011). Disappointing Poverty Trends: Is the Social Investment State to Blame? *Journal of European Social Policy*, 21 (5), 450–471.

1. Social investment: concepts, uses and theoretical perspectives

James Midgley

The concept of social investment has attracted a good deal of attention in Western social policy circles in recent times. The literature on the subject has expanded rapidly, offering both analytical and normative insights of value to academics, practitioners and policy-makers. In turn, policy developments in various countries – and especially the member states of the European Union – have influenced the way social investment has been defined in the social policy literature. Generally, the normative thrust of this literature is that social investment offers a viable alternative to what are perceived to be the drawbacks of the traditional 'welfare state'. Although social investment advocates recognize that the welfare state has raised standards of living, they claim that its focus on meeting consumption needs through cash transfers and social services is of limited value to governments facing new economic, political and demographic pressures. Social investment, it is argued, provides an alternative that is better able to cope with these pressures.

Despite its promise, the social investment approach has limitations, some of which were mentioned in the book's Introduction. It was noted that the paradigmatic conceptualization of social investment by Western social policy scholars as a new 'welfare state regime' fails to capture the nuances and complexities of the issues. Their approach also reflects a narrow Eurocentric focus that ignores the role of social investment in other parts of the world. The way the concept has been used in other academic fields has also been disregarded. For example, the contribution of scholars working in the interdisciplinary field of development studies has been overlooked even through social investment features prominently in their writing.

This chapter argues that the social policy literature can be enriched by incorporating contributions from different academic and professional fields into social investment discourse. It also provides a background to the other chapters of this book which, as noted earlier, review and critically assess social investment policies and programmes in different countries. The chapter begins by observing that the term is not only used in academic circles but has also been employed by the financial investment industry and in politics. It then discusses the way the concept has been employed in social policy, development studies, nonprofit management and community studies. It concludes by offering some thoughts on how an appreciation of these different definitions and conceptual approaches can inform the social policy literature on social investment. It suggests that it may be possible to synthesize these different approaches to promote a comprehensive and globally relevant interpretation that will enhance the academic and policy relevance of social investment ideas.

It should be noted that although widely used, the term 'social investment' is poorly defined and its meaning is often assumed to be self-evident. In addition, few writers have addressed the meaning of related terms such as 'consumption', 'income', 'assets' and 'capital', among others. Although space limitations preclude a detailed discussion of these concepts, this chapter offers some tentative thoughts on definitions. First, it defines investment as the allocation of resources in ways that produce additional, future, value-added resources. These additional resources are also known as returns. The rate of return is the percentage of the original investment that accrues over time. Social investments may be defined as allocations to social programmes that produce returns and promote future social well-being. In addition to accruing to individuals, households and communities, these returns benefit society as a whole. A distinctive feature of social investment is its 'productivist' character: in addition to benefiting people, social investment policies and programmes make a positive contribution to development. Next, consumption may be defined as the use of resources to meet immediate needs and wants for goods and services. Consumption is closely related to income, which is the flow of resources to individuals, households, groups or organizations. Income that exceeds basic consumption needs is often saved to create assets. Assets may be defined as accumulated or 'stored' resources which may be utilized for either consumption or investment. Finally, capital is one of the key factors of production which, together with labour, land, technology, knowledge and skill, comprise the resource allocations that initiate and facilitate the productive process.

DIVERSE INTERPRETATIONS AND PERSPECTIVES

It was mentioned earlier that the term 'social investment' is not only employed in academic circles. For example it is increasingly used by

mutual funds and financial investment firms that offer 'socially responsible' investment opportunities. One example is the American firm Domini
Investments which explicitly describes its financial products as social
investments. Founded by social reformer and activist Amy Domini
(2001), it regularly advertises in progressive left magazines in the United
States, hoping to attract clients who wish to invest in funds that have
positive social and environmental outcomes. As Landler and Nair (2008)
point out, financial investments of this kind differ from the social
responsibility practices of many businesses in that they permit individual
investors to seek returns in ways that are compatible with their social and
political preferences.

Politicians have also used the term to refer to government budgetary
allocations. While in office, British Prime Minister Tony Blair regularly
described his government's budgetary outlays as investments. Members
of the Conservative opposition loudly derided this practice, claiming that
the Prime Minister's attempts to conceal his party's traditional tax and
spend policies by describing public spending as investments would not
deceive the electorate. Although this criticism has somewhat tempered
the use of the term in political circles, it does not detract from the fact
that public spending which promotes future well-being may legitimately
be described as social investment. Indeed, Waldfogel (2010) reports that
the Blair government allocated significant resources to social investments
with positive consequences for social welfare.

However, it is primarily in established academic fields that the concept
of social investment has been popularized. To illustrate, the chapter
examines the use of the term in Western social policy or welfare state
studies, development studies and its subfield of social development, and
nonprofit and community studies. It also contrasts the way scholars in
these different fields employ the term, noting in particular that the
paradigmatic approach adopted by Western social policy writers differs
significantly from its use in the other fields. For example, in social
development, social investment is conceptualized not as a new paradigm
but as discrete interventions that have an investment function. The use of
the term in nonprofit management and community studies reflects a
similar approach.

Social Investment, the Welfare State and Social Policy

The concept of social investment has been widely discussed in the
interdisciplinary field of social policy in recent years. As noted earlier,
some social policy scholars believe that the traditional consumption-
based 'welfare state' is unsuited to the economic, demographic and social

changes that have taken place in Western countries since the 1980s, when deindustrialization, rising unemployment, ageing populations, changing attitudes and globalization limited the ability of governments to meet the needs of their citizens through comprehensive social services and income transfers. Questioning the relevance of the traditional welfare state, they contend that a more dynamic approach is needed that invests in people's capabilities to participate fully in the productive economy.

Several social policy writers contributed to the emergence of the social investment approach. Gilbert (Gilbert and Gilbert, 1989) was among the first to explicitly address the issue by arguing that the state should function as an enabler rather than a provider of welfare services. Another formative contribution came from Sherraden (1991) who criticized the traditional consumption-based welfare system, arguing for an asset-based approach that promotes savings and investments through matched savings accounts known as individual development accounts (or IDAs). Giddens (1998, 2000) made a major contribution by arguing that the traditional welfare state, with its focus on consumption, unconditional income transfers and the provision of social services to passive welfare recipients, should be replaced by the social investment state. In the new social investment state, governments would prioritize education and skill development which would prepare people to participate actively in the productive economy rather than relying on social benefits. These developments were augmented by Esping-Andersen et al. (2002) whose proposal for a 'New Welfare State' sought to refocus social policy's commitment to income transfers and social services by promoting 'child-centred' human capital investments, affordable daycare, family leave and other employed-focused policies.

Since then, the social policy literature on social investment has proliferated, and while different views on the subject have emerged, this literature shares common features. First, it is exclusively statist, focusing on statutory welfare and neglecting the contribution of nonprofits and faith-based organizations, markets and families, and particularly women. Another feature is the idea that social investment is a new and distinctive paradigm that differs from the traditional welfare state paradigm. What Giddens (1998) calls the 'social investment state' is qualitatively different from the welfare state. Morel et al. (2012) agree and explicitly contrast the emerging social investment paradigm with the Keynesian and neoliberal paradigms. Although they are not certain that social investment will in fact evolve into a fully fledged paradigm, they believe that its growing acceptance, especially in Europe, suggests that this will be the case. However, not all writers explicitly employ the term 'social investment' to characterize this new welfare paradigm and other terms such as 'active social policy' (Bonoli, 2013; Giddens, 1998), 'Third Way' reforms (Huo, 2009; Surender, 2004) and 'New Welfare' (Taylor-Gooby et al., 2014) have also been used.

Some social investment scholars offer a stadial, historic interpretation of the emergence of social investment, contending that the adoption of the European Union's Lisbon Treaty heralds the emergence of a new social investment phase in the history of social policy. Hemerijck (2012, 2013) argues that this shift, which he dubs the social investment 'turn', is a profound development involving a gestalt switch from traditional welfare transfers to empowering investments (Hemerijck, 2013, p. 39). Similarly, Jenson (2012) claims that the advent of the social investment stage signifies the end of the neoliberal era and its emphasis on individual responsibility, unfettered markets and minimal state involvement. Although the stadial interpretation views the emergence of social investment as a recent development, Morel et al. (2012) believe that formative social investment ideas can be traced back to the 1930s when Gunnar Myrdal first argued that social welfare programmes contribute positively to the economy. However, Midgley (2015) observes that social investment has an earlier provenance. An important precursor was a concern with what was called 'national efficiency' in Britain in the early twentieth century when social reformers argued that the country's low standards of nutrition, health care and education had lowered 'population quality' with negative consequences for Britain's position as a major imperial power. By expanding the social services, the population's fitness to compete successfully against rival imperial powers would be enhanced.

Augmenting the idea that social investment is a distinctive paradigm, differences between policies that promote social investments and those that perpetuate consumption are usually emphasized. As noted earlier, critics of the consumption-based welfare state emphasize the need for new policies and programmes that invest in human capabilities rather than transferring resources to passive welfare recipients. Morel et al. (2012) offer a helpful schematic representation of this difference, showing that social investments promote labour market participation and prepare people for employment, while consumption-based welfare is concerned with income transfers, social services and decommodification. They also draw a distinction between repairing and preparing social programmes. While the former seek to meet social needs and solve problems, the latter facilitate participation in the productive economy. Other epithets such as productive versus protective welfare and promotive rather than supportive welfare have also been used.

   This distinction has led some scholars to conclude that many governments are shifting their spending priorities from meeting social needs to
investing in education, job training and employment activation, with
deleterious consequences for those who are not able to participate in the
productive economy (Cantillon, 2014; Cantillon and Van Lancker, 2013).
As social services and income transfers are replaced by social investments, critics believe that the incidence of poverty and deprivation will
increase. However, as De Deken (2014) points out, there are formidable
problems in measuring expenditure shifts and assessing their impact. In
fact, analyses by scholars such as Hudson and Kühner (2009, 2012) find
little evidence that budgetary allocations have shifted from welfare
services to investments in OECD countries.

   Finally, the social policy literature on social investment is essentially
Eurocentric in that it is concerned with developments in Europe and other
Western countries. Few writers have examined the emergence of social
investment policies and programmes in other countries, and particularly
the developing countries of the Global South where, as will be shown
later, social investment ideas have featured prominently for many years.
One exception is Jenson (2010) who believes that social investment
diffused from Europe to Latin American countries fostering the creation
of conditional cash transfers and similar programmes. However, there is
little evidence that these programmes owe their origins to European
thinking. In fact, the inspiration for the Mexican *Prospera* programme
(originally known as *Progressa*) came from Santiago Levy, Mexico's
Minister of Finance, who introduced conditionalities into the country's
social assistance programme to meet the concerns of officials at the
World Bank who were critical of income transfer programmes (Levy,
2006). Similarly, there is no evidence that the introduction of Brazil's
Bolsa Família programme was influenced by European social investment
thinking.

   However, Western scholars are becoming more interested in the
adoption of social investment policies in the developing world and some
have launched research initiatives to study these developments. One
example is the ZiF research project into social welfare in the Global
South at Bielefeld University in Germany. Another is the World Politics
of Social Investment Project sponsored by a group of European scholars.
Of course, Western ideas have played a role in the emergence of the
concept of developmental welfare and its emphasis on social investment.
Some scholars schooled in Western social policy have combined the
developmental state concept invented by Johnson (1982) with welfare
state thinking to argue that the emphasis placed on employment and
education by East Asian governments has fostered a unique approach to

social policy which can be described as developmental or productivist welfare, or more generally as 'welfare developmentalism' (Holliday, 2000; Kwon, 2005; Midgley and Tang, 2001). Similar ideas have emerged in Latin American countries (Draibe and Riesco, 2007) and South Africa (Patel, 2015).

Development Studies, Social Development and Social Investment

Social investment ideas have played an important role in the inter-disciplinary field of development studies and its subfield of social development for many years. Development studies emerged after the Second World War when many former colonial territories secured inde-pendence from European imperial rule. In addition to training econo-mists, administrators and planners from the newly independent countries, scholars working in the field speculated on how the governments of these countries could modernize their economies and raise the standard of living of their predominantly rural populations. Together with inter-national agencies such as the United Nations and World Bank, they concluded that the key to prosperity lay in industrialization which, it was argued, would transfer labour from the agricultural subsistence sector into modern wage employment, raising incomes and initiating an upward trajectory of growth that would eventually result in the creation of a modern, mass-consumption society.

Many governments embraced this approach and mobilized investments for industrial development, primarily through international aid and bor-rowing but also through domestic capital. Hall and Midgley (2004) point out that although they were urged to defer consumption, most increased budgetary allocations to medical services, education and other social programmes. Livingstone (1969) notes that it was in this context that attempts were made to rationalize social spending as investments. A major initiative involved the creation of national community development programmes which established village-level agricultural and crafts pro-jects, as well as schools, adult literacy projects, clinics and community centres. These programmes expanded rapidly in the Global South in the 1950s and became a defining feature of the social development approach (Midgley, 2014).

Another major initiative came from development economists who argued that social spending should not be viewed as promoting consump-tion but as contributing positively to economic development. Myrdal (1957, 1970) was among the first to argue that social spending should be prioritized on developmental grounds, proposing that national plans integrate economic and social objectives through what he described as

unified socio-economic planning (Midgley, 1995). These ideas were very
influential in shaping development thinking at the United Nations (1971),
which urged member states to transcend the limited focus on industrial
investments by expanding social programmes. Schultz (1959, 1962,
1981) played a particularly important role by demonstrating that public
spending on health care, nutrition and education are investments that
contribute positively to economic development. Unlike Becker (1964),
his fellow Nobel prizewinning colleague at the University of Chicago,
Schultz focused on the social rather than private rates of return that
accrue through human capital investments.

These ideas were welcomed by staff at the World Bank who produced
a series of Sector Policy Papers in the early 1970s which used social
investment ideas to frame the Bank's lending policies in education, health
care, housing, nutrition and rural development. In 1975, these papers
were republished in book form and provided an economic rationale for
Bank President McNamara's efforts to focus the Bank's lending policies
on poverty reduction (World Bank, 1975). Although his efforts were
subsequently eclipsed by the Bank's adoption of neoliberal thinking, the
social investment approach continued to feature in its lending policies.
This is evident in Psacharopoulos's (1973, 1992) work on educational
investments which the Bank employed to determine which types of
investments produce the highest rates of return in countries at different
levels of development. A similar logic was employed by Abel-Smith
(1976) who advised the World Health Organization that spending on
preventive and primary health produced higher rates of return than
allocations to hospitals and curative services.

The adoption of social investment ideas in the developing world gave
expression to the principle that people who are healthy, well fed and
knowledgeable are far more likely to contribute to economic development
than those who are poorly educated, live in poverty, are ill-nourished and
suffer from debilitating illnesses. However, with the ascendancy of
neoliberalism in the 1980s and the imposition of structural adjustment
programmes by the International Monetary Fund and the World Bank,
social spending was severely reduced in many developing countries, with
negative social and economic consequences. Although the situation has
eased, these developments fostered a sceptical attitude towards governments which resulted in international aid being increasingly directed
towards nonprofits rather than government agencies. As Lewis and Kanji
(2009) observe, this fostered a very rapid expansion of the nonprofit
sector in the Global South.

The result is a pluralist approach to social investment that contrasts
sharply with social policy's welfare statism and reliance on government

provision. Although it was originally believed that the development process should rely exclusively on government investments, the expansion of nonprofits, grassroots community level organizations and even commercial providers has institutionalized pluralism within the field (Midgley, 2014). In addition to providing conventional social services, many nonprofits are engaged in development activities that enhance people's participation in local projects and raise the standard of living. Grassroots and indigenous organizations have also expanded rapidly in the Global South. Prominent examples include the Bangladesh Rural Advancement Committee (BRAC) and the Self Employed Women's Association (SEWA) in India which direct social investments primarily at women in order to increase their financial independence and well-being (Chen, 2008; Smillie, 2009). Indeed, it is often claimed that these and similar social investment programmes empower women, challenging entrenched patriarchial beliefs and practices.

While social policy scholars are exclusively concerned with national-level interventions, the social development literature reveals that social investment policies and programmes are implemented at multiple levels. The expansion of community development in the 1950s focused on the local level, but as public spending on education, health care and nutrition by national government increased, national-level social investments became prominent. These two levels were subsequently augmented by a focus on the household through what is called the livelihoods approach. Inspired largely by Sen's (1985, 1999) capability approach and its advocacy by the United Nations Development Programme (UNDP), investments are directed at families, and particularly those engaged in smallholding agriculture, to enhance their productive capabilities so that they can compete effectively in the economy and improve their standard of living (Helmore and Singh, 2001; Polak, 2008). These ideas have been accompanied by the growing influence of individualism and the adoption of market liberalism in the field. One example is the commercialization of microfinance, which was previously the prerogative of nonprofits and directly tied to the promotion of small-scale business activities, particularly by women (Bateman, 2010).

Social development writers do not draw a clear distinction between investment and consumption, and social investment is not conceptualized in paradigmatic or stadial terms. Also, Midgley (2014) points out that the development process is no longer defined in narrow economic terms but as a multidimensional process that combines economic, social, cultural, political, gender and ecological components. This has complicated the way the concept of social investment is used in the field. Many investments that may be regarded as having a predominantly productive function are also viewed as having a social welfare function. For example, many co-operatives engaged in production are simultaneously engaged in providing social services to their members. Similarly, the United Nations Millennium Development Goals initiative (United Nations, 2000) is generally believed to be concerned with meeting consumption needs, but Sachs (2005) points out that meeting basic income, health, housing and nutritional requirements may be viewed as investments that contribute to economic development. As will be apparent, this has confused matters and, unlike social policy with its paradigmatic distinction between investment and consumption, the use of social investment ideas in social development lacks the clarity and coherence of the social policy approach.

Philanthropy, Nonprofits and Social Investment

Although the nonprofit sector has historically been associated with charitable giving, the situation is changing rapidly as nonprofits adopt business methods, improve managerial efficiency and compete on commercial markets for resources. Today, few rely on traditional donations and many now utilize new sources of funding such as user fees and contracts. Many also compete with commercial providers to bid for government contracts and many are funded by foundations that require outcome evaluations to determine whether specified deliverables have been met. Many foundations also evaluate outcomes by calculating the rate of return that accrues to their lending allocations. Grant (2012) observes that the concept of social investment is now being used to characterize these developments in the nonprofit sector. The importance of generating returns is emphasized and the importance of assessing the impact of services on clients is given high priority. New terms such as 'impact investing' and 'mission investing' are now widely employed (Nicholls, 2014).

The new emphasis on social investment has been fostered by the belief that nonprofits should function as social enterprises that not only utilize business methods but also generate income from their services and other funding sources (Nyssens et al., 2006; Kerlin, 2014). Of course, private universities and hospitals have relied on user fees for many years, and in some cases they have accrued surpluses that fund sizeable endowments. These practices have been widely emulated by many nonprofits, and today some also generate resources by selling goods and services on commercial markets. Yunus and Weber (2010) describe these nonprofits as social businesses since they share many similarities with commercial providers except that they do not pay shareholder dividends. Although surpluses may be used to improve the quality of services, pay competitive salaries and create endowments, they and other social enterprises remain nonprofits.

A related development is the involvement of private investors in the nonprofit field. It was mentioned earlier that a growing number of investors are utilizing established investment firms to engage in socially responsible investing, but there has been a growth of nonprofit investment firms which utilize standard investment practices to attract funds from private donors who wish to know that their donations are used effectively and in socially responsible ways. Solomon (2015) reports that one of the first of these is the Acumen Fund, which was founded in New York in 2001. It has successfully mobilized investments from donors primarily in Western countries to fund projects and programmes in Asia and sub-Saharan Africa that have a measurable, positive impact. Although donors do not expect a dividend, they receive regular reports on how their funds are being used. They also expect that their funds will generate returns. These and similar funds differ from foundations in that they mobilize resources from sizeable numbers of individual donors rather than drawing on established endowments.

A more recent development, which builds on the experience of socially responsible investment, is the payment of dividends to donors. This has been fostered by the emergence of what are sometimes known as venture philanthropy or social venture funds. Some of these funds are managed by well-established commercial investment firms which have created specialized portfolios that provide loans to nonprofits which, together with interest, fees and capital repayments, generate returns for investors. Other are specialized funds that exclusively manage investments of this kind. Although loan repayments place an obvious burden on nonprofits, some have determined that the income they generate from services, contracts and the sale of products can cover their debt obligations, and it appears that more are securing resources in this way. Microfinance has provided an especially lucrative opportunity for venture philanthropists to benefit from nonprofits, and Bateman (2010) observes that this process has accelerated as many microfinance organizations have commercialized their operations. The Internet has also facilitated investing of this kind, and some Internet-based non-profit organizations have successfully attracted donors who fund microenterprise projects in the Global South from which they receive returns, usually in the form of loan repayments.

Another example of the overlap between commercial and nonprofit social investing is the creation of social impact bonds which, as Nicholls (2014) explains, mobilize resources to fund social projects operated by nonprofits as well as commercial providers in the expectation that the government will repay the capital investment, with profit, on condition that the project meets contractually specified outcomes. Independent evaluators are employed to monitor progress and determine whether contractual obligations have been met. Impact bonds originated in Britain in the correctional field, but as the Organisation for Economic Co-operation and Development (OECD) (2015) reports, they have been established in other countries as well. Like venture philanthropy, impact bonds involve investment risk but also offer the prospect of reward.

Some will question whether the pursuit of financial returns through social investments by nonprofit organizations is in keeping with the sector's traditional philanthropic commitments. Although recent innovations in the nonprofit sector amount to what Salamon (2014) calls a 'revolution' in philanthropy, they blur the distinction between nonprofit and commercial provision, and are probably facilitating the marketization of the field. The relentless preoccupation with generating resources may well become the primary goal of agency staff, at the expense of providing services that meet the needs of those who have historically been served by voluntary organizations. Whether this will sully the use of the concept of social investment in the nonprofit sector remains to be seen.

Community Studies and Social Investment

Although community studies is an amorphous field, it is well established at colleges and universities around the world, being largely but not exclusively concerned with training practitioners to promote social well-being at the community level. In some continental European countries, community studies is linked to social pedagogy which provides community-based educational and recreational services primarily for children and young people. In Britain, it encompasses youth and community work, community organizing and community economic development. In the United States, community economic development projects that create local jobs, improve infrastructure and provide affordable housing coexist with activities that promote political awareness and activism. In addition, coordinating the services of social agencies has been a prominent concern of the field. Also, as mentioned earlier, community development is well established in the developing world.

Various professional and paraprofessional groups including youth workers, social pedagogues, community organizers and community development workers are engaged in the field and a number of professional associations that represent their interests have been created. In many countries, community practice forms an integral part of social work, while in other countries it takes place in separate fields. Neverthe-less, social workers, youth workers, social pedagogues and community development paraprofessionals share a common commitment to promote social well-being at the community level.

These different forms of community engagement have a social invest-ment function even though the term is not widely employed in the field. By promoting non-traditional forms of social learning at the community level, social pedagogues help to mobilize human capital; and in the Global South, community development workers play a similar role by establishing literacy projects, child care centres and health care and nutritional programmes. Because community development programmes are explicitly committed to establishing economically productive pro-jects, creating employment, and raising incomes and standards of living, they actively promote social investments. In addition, as noted earlier, they uniquely integrate economic and social objectives. Local co-operatives are a good example of how economic and social activities are closely integrated, but many other projects including smallholding agriculture, the installation of village water supplies, the construction of village clinics and the creation of microenterprises also have a dual economic and social function, ensuring that productive economic activ-ities result in tangible improvements in people's well-being.

In recent times, the investment functions of community practice have been recognized and more systematically examined. In a discussion of community social work practice, Midgley (2010) argued that the invest-ment function of community interventions needs to be strengthened and repackaged within a wider developmental approach that emphasizes the role of programmes that promote human and social capital as well as employment opportunities. A particularly important contribution comes from Kretzmann and McKnight (1993), who criticize the tendency among many community practitioners to view low-income communities as beset with social problems. Instead, they contend, community strengths should be emphasized and community workers should build on existing assets to establish projects that have a positive long-term effect on community well-being. Their ideas have exerted a powerful influence on community practice in the United States and other Western countries and have also been adopted by the World Bank and incorporated into its lending policies. Moser and Dani (2008) reveal that asset building has been actively promoted by the Bank and is now an important feature of community development in the Global South.

Augmenting community development in the Global South, the asset approach is evolving to give greater priority to community social investments in Western countries as well. As is discussed in more length in Chapter 7 of this book, this approach now features prominently in community practice in the United States where social investment and local economic projects now form an integral part of the field. It is also shown that social capital theory has exerted considerable influence on the country's community development programmes. In addition, there is a greater emphasis on business investment in deprived communities. Inspired by Porter's (1995) writings, many community economic development programmes in American cities now actively seek to attract business investments. These developments have relevance for community practice in other parts of the world as well.

TOWARD A SYNTHESIS

This chapter has shown that the concept of social investment is not confined to the academic subject of social policy, but has been used in other academic and professional fields as well. Nor, as is commonly believed, is the discourse on social investment a recent innovation in social welfare thinking. Contrary to the view that social investment emerged as a new social welfare paradigm in the 1990s as a response to disquiet about the consumption-based welfare state, it has older roots. Similarly, the widely accepted belief that social investment is a European invention is belied by the widespread use of social investment policies and programmes in developing countries at both the national and local levels. The chapter has also shown that the use of the term in fields such as development studies, nonprofit management and community studies reveals its pluralistic character. This scholarship demonstrates that social investment is not the prerogative of the state but of a variety of agents and institutions operating at multiple levels.

The ways in which the concept has been used in diverse academic and professional fields suggest that a more nuanced appreciation of social investment is needed if the complex issues arising from the use of the term are to be understood, and if proposals for forging effective practical interventions are to be formulated. Although the typological categories employed by welfare state scholars give the field structure and coherence, they oversimplify complex processes. As noted earlier, their approach contrasts sharply with the more fluid use of the term in development studies, nonprofit management and community development, where social investments are viewed as discrete interventions rather than as a new and distinctive paradigm. In addition, social development writers blur the distinction between investment and consumption. Drawing on Keynesian ideas, they contend that allocations that foster consumption, such as cash transfers, may simultaneously function as investments. Also, particular policies and programmes are not usually classified in strictly consumption or investment terms, but as falling along a spectrum ranging from consumption to investment. The term is also used loosely in nonprofit management, where it refers both to the efficient allocation of resources and the impact of these resources on the future well-being of clients. The way in which scholars in the field now frequently associate social investment with market-based interventions further complicates matters.

To appreciate and accommodate these complexities, scholars in different academic fields should collaborate, share knowledge and learn from each other. The artificial boundaries that currently separate these fields need to be breached so that mutually beneficial learning can take place. Although writers such as Hall and Midgley (2004), Mkandawire (2004) and Surender and Walker (2013) have sought to link scholarship in social policy and development studies, there has been little information transfer and mutual learning between these fields. Scholars in development studies have little understanding of the conceptual approaches used in social policy, and at the same time, innovations in development studies are seldom referenced in social policy. Although these fields deal with different realities and may require different approaches, a synthesis of diverse academic perspectives is urgently needed if a unitary conception of social investment that has universal policy relevance is to emerge.

Collaborative research into the different academic and professional discourses on social investment could also clarify issues. For example, archival research into the history of social investment could be helpful in understanding the complex ways in which social investment ideas have been formulated and implemented at different times. This research could also help to analyse the differences between consumption and investment. It has been mentioned already that social policy discourse on the subject draws a clear distinction between the two, but this is not the case in development studies or community development. More incisive enquiry in this field would help to test the contention that the shift to social investment in Western countries has come at the expense of cash transfers and social services. Since attempts to assess whether this has actually taken place have not produced definite answers, more systematic research into this issue is required. In particular, the extent to which cash transfers promote consumption or investments should be subjected to rigorous analysis. Midgley (2008) contends that cash transfers can have an investment function if configured to achieve this objective. This is obviously the case with conditional cash transfers which are not only designed to alleviate poverty but to invest in human capital by increasing school enrolments and improving the health of mothers and children (Hall, 2012; Soares, 2013). Similar policy goals have been adopted in South Africa, where the Child Support Grant until recently has not imposed conditionalities (Patel, 2015).

An important issue is whether social investment is a revisionist form of neoliberalism, a social democratic project or a combination of the two. Although Bonoli (2013) points out that different views on this issue have been expressed, a more incisive analysis is needed to excavate the ideological roots of the social investment approach. Again, it is important that the complexities of the issue be appreciated, since it is clear that policy-makers with different ideological proclivities will use social investment in different ways. Midgley (2003) makes this point with reference to asset savings accounts in the United States, observing that the asset approach has supporters on both the political right and left. This suggests that asset programmes, like other social investments, can be configured within broader normative frameworks to pursue very different ideological agendas.

Finally, a unitary conception of social investment which has universal policy relevance is needed in view of the pressing social problems facing the global community. Although the adoption of the Millennium Development Goals and the more recent Sustainable Development Goals has made a significant contribution, concerted effort is needed if the challenges of world poverty, ill-health, poor nutrition, violence, gender oppression and a host of other problems are to be addressed. Academics need to collaborate much more closely to forge what Midgley (2017) calls a One World perspective that unites their disparate interpretations and policy agendas and has global relevance. Through closer collaboration, a conception of social investment may emerge that improves policy interventions and enhances people's well-being around the world.

REFERENCES

Abel-Smith, B. (1976). *Value for Money in Health Services*. London: Heinemann.

Bateman, M. (2010). *Why Doesn't Microfinance Work? The Destructive Rise of Local Neoliberalism*. New York: Zed Books.

Becker, G.S. (1964). *Human Capital: A Theoretical and Empirical Analysis with Special Reference to Education*. New York: Columbia University Press.

Bonoli, G. (2013). *The Origins of Active Social Policy: Labour Market and Childcare Policies in Comparative Perspective*. New York: Oxford University Press.

Cantillon, B. (2014). Beyond Social Investment: Which Concepts and Values for Social Policy-making in Europe?. In B. Cantillon and F. Vandenbroucke (eds), *Reconciling Work and Poverty Reduction: How Successful European Welfare States?*. New York: Oxford University Press, pp. 286–318.

Cantillon, B. and Van Lancker, W. (2013). Three Shortcomings of the Social Investment Perspective. *Social Policy and Society*, 23 (5), 459–468.

Chen, M. (2008). A Spreading Banyan Tree: The Self-Employed Women's Association, India. In A. Mathie and G. Cunningham (eds), *From Clients to Citizens: Communities Changing the Course of their Own Development*. Rugby, UK: Intermediate Technology Publications, pp. 181–206.

De Deken, J. (2014). Identifying the Skeleton of the Social Investment State: Defining and Measuring Patterns of Social Policy Change on the Basis of Expenditure Data. In B. Cantillon and F. Vandenbroucke (eds), *Reconciling Work and Poverty Reduction: How Successful European Welfare States?*. New York: Oxford University Press, pp. 260–285.

Domini, A. (2001). *Socially Responsible Investing: Making a Difference in Making Money*. Chicago, IL: Dearborn Trade.

Draibe, S.M. and Riesco, M. (2007). Introduction. In M. Riesco (ed.), *Latin America: A New Developmental Welfare State Model in the Making?*. New York: Palgrave Macmillan, pp. 1–17.

Esping-Andersen, G., Gallie, D., Hemerijck, A. and Myles, J. (2002). *Why We Need a New Welfare State*. New York: Oxford University Press.

Giddens, A. (1998). *The Third Way: The Renewal of Social Democracy*. Cambridge: Polity Press.

Giddens, A. (2000). *The Third Way and its Critics*. Cambridge: Polity Press.

Gilbert, N. and Gilbert, B. (1989). *The Enabling State: Modern Welfare Capitalism in America*. New York: Oxford University Press.

Grant, P. (2012). *The Business of Giving: The Theory and Practice of Philanthropy, grant making, and Social Investment*. New York: Palgrave Macmillan.

Hall, A. (2012). The Last Shall be First: Political Dimensions of Conditional Cash Transfers in Brazil. *Journal of Policy Practice*, 11 (1–2), 25–41.

Hall, A. and Midgley, J. (2004). *Social Policy for Development*. London: Sage Publications.

Helmore, K. and Singh, N. (2001). *Sustainable Livelihoods: Building on the Wealth of the Poor*. Bloomfield, CT: Kumarian Press.

Hemerijck, A. (2012). Two or Three Waves of Welfare State Transformation?. In N. Morel, B. Pallier and J. Palme (eds), *Towards a Social Investment Welfare State? Ideas, Policies and Challenges*. Bristol: Policy Press, pp. 33–60.

Hemerijck, A. (2013). *Changing Welfare States*. New York: Oxford University Press.

Holliday, I. (2000). Productivist Welfare Capitalism: Social Policy in East Asia. *Political Studies*, 48 (4), 706–723.

Hudson, J. and Kühner, S. (2009). Towards Productive Welfare: A Comparative Analysis of 23 Countries. *Journal of European Social Policy*, 19 (1), 34–46.

Hudson, J. and Kühner, S. (2012). Analyzing the Productive and Protective Dimensions of Welfare: Looking Beyond the OECD. *Social Policy and Administration*, 46 (1), 35–60.

Huo, J. (2009). *Third Way Reforms: Social Democracy after the Golden Age.* Cambridge: Cambridge University Press.

Jenson, J. (2010). Diffusing Ideas for After Neoliberalism: The Social Investment Perspective in Europe and Latin America. *Global Social Policy*, 10 (1), 59–84.

Jenson, J. (2012). Redesigning Citizenship Regimes: After Neoliberalism: Moving Towards Social Investment. In N. Morel, B. Pallier and J. Palme (eds), *Towards a Social Investment Welfare State? Ideas, Policies and Challenges.* Bristol: Policy Press, pp. 61–87.

Johnson, C.A. (1982). *MTTI and the Japanese Miracle: The Growth of Industrial Policy 1925–1975.* Stanford, CA: Stanford University Press.

Kerlin, J.A. (2014). *Social Enterprise: A Global Comparison.* Hanover, NH: Tufts University Press.

Kretzmann, J. and McKnight, J.L. (1993). *Building Communities from the Inside Out: A Path Toward Finding and Mobilizing Community's Assets.* Evanston, IL: Institute for Policy Research, Northwest and University.

Kwon, H-J. (2005). An Overview of the Study: The Developmental Welfare State and Policy Reforms in East Asia. In H-J. Kwon (ed.), *Transforming the Developmental Welfare State in East Asia.* New York: Palgrave Macmillan, pp. 1–26.

Landler, L. and Nair, V.B. (2008). *Investing for Change: Profit from Responsible Investment.* New York: Oxford University Press.

Levy, S. (2006). *Progress against Poverty: Sustaining Mexico's Progresa-Oportunidades Program.* Washington, DC: Brookings Institution Press.

Lewis, D. and Kanji, N. (2009). *Non-Governmental Organizations and Development.* New York: Routledge.

Livingstone, A. (1969). *Social Policy in Developing Countries.* London: Routledge & Kegan Paul.

Midgley, J. (1995). *Social Development: The Developmental Perspective in Social Welfare.* London: Sage Publications.

Midgley, J. (2003). Assets in the Context of Welfare Theory: A Developmentalist Interpretation. *Social Development Issues*, 25 (1–2), 12–28.

Midgley, J. (2008). Social Security and the Economy: Key Perspectives. In J. Midgley and K.L. Tang (eds), *Social Security, the Economy and Development.* New York: Palgrave Macmillan, pp. 51–84.

Midgley, J. (2010). Community Practice and Development Social Work. In J. Midgley and A. Conley (eds), *Social Work and Social Development: Theories and Skills for Developmental Social Work.* New York: Oxford University Press, pp. 167–189.

Midgley, J. (2013). Social Development and Social Welfare: Implications for Comparative Social Policy. In P. Kennett (ed.), *A Handbook of Comparative Social Policy.* Cheltenham, UK and Northampton, MA, USA: Edward Elgar Publishing, pp. 182–204.

Midgley, J. (2014). *Social Development: Theory and Practice.* London: Sage Publications.

Midgley, J. (2015). Social Investment, Inclusive Growth and the State. In R. Hasmath (ed.), *Inclusive Growth, Development and Welfare Policy: A Critical Assessment.* New York: Routledge, pp. 91–107.

Midgley, J. (2017). *Social Welfare for a Global Era: International Perspectives on Policy and Practice*. Los Angeles, CA: Sage Publications.

Midgley, J. and Tang, K.L. (2001). Social Policy, Economic Growth and Developmental Welfare. *International Journal of Social Welfare*, 10 (4), 242–250.

Mkandawire, T. (ed.) (2004). *Social Policy in a Development Context*. New York: Palgrave.

Morel, N., Palier, B. and Palme, J. (2012). Beyond the Welfare State as We Knew it?. In N. Morel, B. Palier and J. Palme (eds), *Towards a Social Investment Welfare State? Ideas, Policies and Challenges*. Bristol: Policy Press, pp. 1–32.

Moser, C. and Dani, A.A. (eds) (2008). *Assets, Livelihoods, and Social Policy*. Washington, DC: World Bank.

Myrdal, G. (1957). *Rich Lands and Poor: The Road to World Prosperity*. New York: Harper.

Myrdal, G. (1970). *The Challenge of World Poverty*. Harmondsworth: Penguin Books.

Nicholls, A. (2014). Filling the Capital Gap: Institutionalizing Social Finance. In S. Denny and F. Seddon (eds), *Social Enterprise: Accountability and Evaluation Around the World*. New York: Routledge, pp. 161–195.

Nyssens, M., Adams, S. and Johnson, T. (2006). *Social Enterprise: At the Crossroads of Market, Public Policies and Civil Society*. New York: Routledge.

Organisation for Economic Co-operation and Development (OECD) (2015). *Social Impact Investment: Building the Evidence Base*. Paris: OECD.

Patel, L. (2015). *Social Welfare and Social Development in South Africa*. Johannesburg: Oxford University Press.

Polak, P. (2008). *Out of Poverty: What Works when Traditional Approaches Fail*. San Francisco, CA: Berret-Koehler.

Porter, M.E. (1995). The Competitive Advantage of the Inner City. *Harvard Business Review*, 73 (3), 55–71.

Psacharopoulos, G. (1973). *Returns to Education: An International Comparison*. Amsterdam: Elsevier.

Psacharopoulos, G. (1992). *Returns to Investment in Education: A Global Update*. Washington, DC: World Bank.

Sachs, J. (2005). *The End of Poverty: Economic Possibilities for Our Time*. New York: Penguin Books.

Salamon, L.M. (2014). The Revolution on the Frontiers of Philanthropy: An Introduction. In L.M. Salamon (ed.), *New Frontiers of Philanthropy: A Guide to the New Tools and Actors Reshaping Global Philanthropy and Social Investment*. New York: Oxford University Press, pp. 3–88.

Schultz, T.W. (1959). Investment in Man: An Economist's View. *Social Service Review*, 33 (2), 109–117.

Schultz, T.W. (1962). Reflections on Investments in Man. *Journal of Political Economy*, 70 (5), 1–8.

Schultz, T.W. (1981). *Investing in People*. Berkeley, CA: University of California Press.

Sen, A. (1985). *Commodities and Capabilities*. Amsterdam: North-Holland.

Sen, A. (1999). *Development as Freedom*. New York: Knopf.

Sherraden, M. (1991). *Assets and the Poor: A New American Welfare Policy.* Armonk, NY: M.E. Sharpe.

Smillie, I. (2009). *Freedom from Want: The Remarkable Success Story of BRAC, the Global Grassroots Organization that's Winning the Fight against Poverty.* Sterling, VA: Kumarian Press.

Soares, S. (2013). The Efficiency and Effectiveness of Social Protection against Poverty and Inequality in Brazil. In J. Midgley and D. Piachaud (eds), *Social Protection, Economic Growth and Social Change: Goals, Issues and Trajectories in China, India, Brazil and Africa.* Cheltenham, UK and Northampton, MA, USA: Edward Elgar Publishing, pp. 153–165.

Solomon, L.D. (2015). *Alleviating Global Poverty: The Role of Private Enterprise.* San Bernadino, CA: Xlibris.

Surender, R. (2004). Modern Challenges to the Welfare State and the Antecedents of the Third Way. In J. Lewis and R. Surender (eds), *Welfare State Change: Towards a Third Way?.* New York: Oxford University Press, pp. 3–24.

Surender, R. and Walker, R. (eds) (2013). *Social Policy in a Developing World.* Cheltenham, UK and Northampton, MA, USA: Edward Elgar Publishing.

Taylor-Gooby, P., Gumy, J.M. and Otto, A. (2014). Can 'New Welfare' Address Poverty through More and Better Jobs?. *Journal of Social Policy*, 44 (1), 83–105.

United Nations (1971). Social Policy and Planning in National Development. *International Social Development Review*, 3, 4–15.

United Nations (2000). *The United Nations Millennium Declaration.* (Resolution 55/2). New York.

Waldfogel, J. (2010). *Britain's War on Poverty.* New York: Russell Sage.

World Bank (1975). *The Assault on World Poverty: Problems of Rural Development, Education and Health.* Baltimore, MD: Johns Hopkins University Press.

Yunus, M. and Weber, K. (2010). *Building Social Business: The New Kind of Capitalism that Serves Humanity's most Pressing Needs.* New York: Public Affairs Press.

2. Social investment in early childhood in Australia

Amy Conley Wright

The roots of lifelong health and development are established in early childhood, in the prenatal period to age five, when children's brains and bodies are being formed. Social investment through public policy is critical for partially offsetting inequality in financial and human capital by ensuring that children get basic provisions to meet their essential needs. This process is mediated by parents, by enabling them to receive more resources and time to care for their children and experience fewer barriers to access needed services. Social investment strategies include ensuring a minimum household income to meet material needs and provide basic nutrition, health care and protected time for bonding after birth, followed by safe alternative care when parents return to work. Policies that make a social investment in early childhood can produce a rate of return to society as well as individuals. In the short term, policies such as child care and income support enable parents to work while their children receive safe care and provide extra income to households to protect against poverty and economic shocks. In the long term, these social investments ensure that citizens have the health, social and cognitive skills that enable them to participate in the economy. This chapter examines social investment in early childhood in Australia, examining policies in the areas of social transfers, parental leave and early childhood education and care services, and making comparisons with the Organisation for Economic Co-operation and Development (OECD) averages to identify strengths, gaps and challenges.

WHY INVEST IN YOUNG CHILDREN?

The concept of social investment is a type of rhetorical framing of social policy, suggesting that societies do best when they provide opportunities to develop the potential of their taxpayers, citizens and workers (Gormley, 2012). The social investment approach is enacted through policies that foster the development of human capital and that help make efficient use of human capital (Morel et al., 2012). A balanced approach to social investment couples prevention of negative outcomes with social protection to compensate for risks already present in people's lives (Vandenbroucke and Vleminckx, 2011).

The 'social investment state' is positioned as an alternative welfare state that invests in human capital over economic maintenance (Giddens, 1998). For the social investment state, young children are the key to a prosperous future (Lister, 2003). The primary methods are investment in human and social capital, which build children's capabilities and strengthen their relationships with others (Midgley and Sherraden, 2000). Investing in young children is particularly powerful because there are multiple beneficiaries: the family, the young child and the society. For each of these beneficiaries, social investment can realize important social goals, including supporting workforce participation, building a foundation for later skill development and reducing social inequality. Looking to the future, investing in children now is essential to economic planning, since the social and cognitive capacities to participate in a knowledge-based, globalized economy are established in early childhood (Esping-Andersen, 2002). This is equally if not more important for developing countries, which can augment or replace remedial interventions with ones that invest in building stronger families and communities (Midgley, 1999; Conley, 2010).

One major type of social investment is social transfers that ensure basic minimum income. Social transfers such as child benefits can provide families with protection against economic shocks or hedge against persistent poverty (UNICEF, 2012). Single parents face greater structural demands of meeting children's caregiving needs while working, as well as greater vulnerability to job loss, and social transfers may be most effective in reducing poverty among this group of families (Maldonado and Nieuwenhuis, 2015). Social transfers may be unconditional and provided on the basis of child age, family income and/or family formation (such as special payments to single parents) or conditional, with receipt of funds predicated on behaviours such as ensuring school attendance or health services usage. While traditional social assistance is provided in the absence of employment, social transfers are most effective as an anti-child poverty tool when they are combined with the strategy of supporting parental employment (Esping-Andersen, 2002).

Social investments directed at supporting employment can enable parents to balance caregiving responsibilities with paid work. Policy approaches that can achieve this benefit include subsidized child care, paid parental leave and the right to a flexible work schedule. When parents, particularly mothers, withdraw from the labour force to care for young children, they can sustain short- and long-term economic consequences. Interrupted labour force participation has long-term consequences on women's lifetime earnings, directly through lost wages during periods of caregiving and indirectly through deprecation of human capital due to loss of skills and experience (Esping-Andersen, 2005). Paid parental leave has been demonstrated to support women's retention in the workforce (Houser and Vartanian, 2012) and attachment to their positions prior to leave (Laughlin, 2011), providing cost savings to employers as well as benefits to families. Because child care costs can be a barrier to workforce participation for mothers (Kimmel, 1998), subsidies for child care are an essential policy strategy to 'make work pay' by ensuring that the costs of child care do not create employment disincentives (Immervoll and Barber, 2006).

Early childhood care and education is another investment in human capital of children that also frees up the human capital of their parents so that their time is available for employment. For children to benefit from early childhood education and care, it is essential that they receive high-quality care. The case of subsidized child care in Quebec, Canada is instructive: a policy shift to highly subsidized child care for young children without sufficient attention to quality resulted in a significant increase in women's labour participation and children's participation in child care, and a number of negative outcomes for children, parents and parenting, including more child behavioural issues and poorer quality parent–child interaction (Baker et al., 2005). Participation in high-quality child care, on the other hand, is associated with positive outcomes in the areas of intellectual development, improved independence, concentration and sociability. Moreover, there are enduring impacts on academic achievement that persist into the high school years, and are especially notable for children from disadvantaged backgrounds with less stimulating home learning environments. The 'welfare model' of child care has a mixed set of goals to minimize the impact of early childhood disadvantage, including access to social services and behavioural management in addition to caregiving and education (Conley, 2010). Yet while child care is an important social context for children, parenting and home factors have the greatest impact in shaping long-term outcomes (Taggart et al., 2015).

For society, investments in children can be justified by the direct return on investment and the impact on future generations. As noted in Chapter 1 of this volume, returns on investment are those future resources generated by social investments. Investing in young children and their families realizes a present goal of enabling the workforce participation of parents and a future goal of producing a high-quality adult citizen, with both outcomes yielding economic resources. Economist James Heckman (2012) argues that for societies, an investment in early childhood is a more efficient use of public resources than investments at later ages. This argument is most succinctly made in his contention: "Make greater investments in young children to see greater returns in education, health and productivity." Improving 'child quality' in one generation translates into improved parent, worker and citizen quality for an adult generational cohort. Social investment can also reduce intergenerational transmission of social inequality. Research on publicly funded preschool in Latin America and Europe demonstrate benefits for disadvantaged children, by raising school readiness and promoting overall academic achievement, thereby reducing inequality of achievement (Waldfogel, 2015).

Criticisms of the social investment rhetorical framing as applied to young children and families question whether children are valued in the here and now as children, or only for their future contributions as adults (see Chapter 10 in this volume). Lister (2003) identifies the 'future worker-citizen' as the prime asset that is being developed in the social investment state. This view of children can emphasize the utilitarian outcomes of children's developmental or academic outcomes, rather than the quality of their experiences. The value of play, for example, can be minimized. A related criticism questions whether as future citizens, workers and taxpayers all children are viewed as having equal value. Children whose future productivity could be questioned may not be the target of social investments, such as children with disabilities or children who are refugees. This framing of children as future workers is emphasized over the 'child-citizen' rights-based rhetorical framing emphasized by the United Nations Convention on the Rights of the Child (Lister, 2003). The rights-based framing of children's issues is moralistic, identifying social expenditure on children as a social responsibility rather than an investment with an economic pay-off (Gormley, 2012).

INVESTING IN THE EARLY YEARS: AUSTRALIA'S APPROACH TO SOCIAL INVESTMENT

Ensuring that children get the best chance in life fits well with the Australian value of the 'fair go'. The 'fair go' can be understood as an endorsement of equality of opportunity, ensuring that all people have a chance to do well in life (McClelland and Smyth, 2014). This value is supported by a broad acceptance of social solidarity, which historians often trace to the challenges faced by early settlers and the need for cooperation to survive in harsh times. This value, expressed in 'mateship', did not historically extend to non-whites, including Indigenous Aboriginals and Torres Strait Islanders (Knightley, 2000). Indeed, Indigenous Australians were not recognized as citizens in the constitution until 1967 (McClelland and Smyth, 2014).

Australia has a long history of integrating social protection into a broader policy strategy of social investment (McClelland and Smyth, 2014). Smyth (2010) characterizes the Australian way of social policy as having strong productivist values, harmonizing the state and market to enable citizens to participate effectively, and making good wages the basis of social welfare. Evidence of this approach can be observed at the beginning of the twentieth century, at the time of federation of the Commonwealth of Australia, when the strategy of full employment was supported by expenditure on education and high primary school enrolment rates. Following economic hardships of the Great Depression and World War II, policy-makers embraced a Keynesian mixed economy, supporting the goal of full employment with mass immigration and public works expenditures, necessitating new federal taxation. At this time, the Commonwealth also introduced new social protections in the form of family allowances, maternity allowances, unemployment payments, health and dental services, and other supports that were means-tested and categorical. Social problems emerging in the 1950s and 1960s, related to immigration, women's entry into the workforce and poverty among the elderly, spurred development of more comprehensive welfare state policies. During the administration of Prime Minister Gough Whitlam in the early to mid-1970s, significant new social protection legislation was introduced, including the precursor (Medibank) of today's universal health care system, which was rolled back after his administration and then reintroduced in the early 1980s as Medicare (McClelland and Smyth, 2014).

This history has resulted in an approach to social welfare that is relatively unique, where employment through the market is central, enabled by social investments that build capabilities, and tempered through social protections for children, the elderly and other vulnerable populations. Esping-Andersen (1990) categorized Australia as a 'liberal' welfare state, with means-tested assistance, modest universal transfers, benefits for low-income and working-class people and little social reform. Yet Australia performs close to the social democratic states in terms of human development outcomes (Castles, 1994b). The designation of the 'wage earner's welfare state' (Castles, 1994a) appears more apt, with social protection in support of employment rather than as a right of citizenship. In their history of the social security system, Herscovitch and Stanton (2008) note that "maximising economic and social participation is and always has been a cornerstone of Australia's system" (p. 2), though this has primarily been true for a male breadwinner and has cast women at best in a secondary earner role (Mitchell, 1997).

Investment in young children has become a recent major focus of government (AIHW, 2015), driven by the Council of Australian Governments (COAG), an organization that exists to foster conversation and coordination between federal, state and local governments. Early childhood is included in the human capital stream of the Council's National Reform Agenda. This agenda seeks to secure Australia's future prosperity in an era when an ageing population and fewer working-age Australians will necessitate productivity gains, greater workforce participation and skilled workers who will be competitive in a global economic environment (Silver, 2008). Plans for developing the human capital of young children are set forth in *Investing in the Early Years: A National Early Childhood Development Strategy*. The vision of this strategy is: "By 2020 all children have the best start in life to create a better future for themselves and for the nation" (COAG, 2009, p. 13). This document outlines a strategy of strengthening protective factors and mitigating risk factors that have been demonstrated by research to have an impact on adult outcomes, thus it advocates for social investment as promotive of positive outcomes and preventive against negative ones. Throughout the document, statements are made that social investment in children has economic benefits, by being cost-effective and reducing future costs associated with negative outcomes (COAG, 2009): a 'pay now or pay later' argument.

The National Early Childhood Development Strategy presents an ambitious set of targets and an outcomes framework to measure progress. Two primary elements of social investments are established to meet these outcomes: support for children, parents, carers and communities, and responsive early childhood development services. The National Early Childhood Development Strategy stresses that families need the capacity to care for children, meaning that parents have time and resources, including finances, their own health and mental health, and social connections to others. This capacity is supported through social investments including taxation and income support policies (social transfers), paid parental leave and family-friendly policies. Responsive early childhood services include health care, education and care, and social services.

The following sections will examine three social investments in early childhood, highlighting Australian Commonwealth policies and programmes in the following areas: social transfers to families, paid parental leave and early childhood education and care. This is not an exhaustive list of social investment and notably leaves out important policies and services in areas such as maternal and child health.

Social Transfers

Family allowance payments were first introduced by the Commonwealth government in 1941, and historically have had an aim of providing protection against poverty, rather than a base level of income as in European social welfare systems (Whiteford and Angenent, 2002). A New Tax System (Family Assistance) Act 1999 and its amendments sets out a sliding level of financial support available to families, based on their income, through refundable tax benefits made as fortnightly cash payments. Under current policy, Family Tax Benefit is composed of two parts. Part A is an income-tested benefit paid per eligible child to meet the objective of helping families with the cost of raising children. Part B is an additional supplement for single-parent households and families with one primary income. Because the income thresholds are quite high, benefits can be combined with part-time employment for one parent in a two-parent household, or even full-time employment for a lone parent under the income cap (Whiteford and Angenent, 2002). Low-income sole parents with a child under age eight or partnered parents with a child under age six can also qualify for additional financial support through the Parenting Payment, depending on income and assets.

The 'No Jab No Pay' immunization requirement was introduced in January 2016 (Department of Social Services, 2016). This requirement put restrictions on a portion of the Family Tax Benefit (and the Child Care Rebate discussed later in the chapter), changing these payments from unconditional categorical cash transfers, available to all who met the income and household thresholds, to conditional cash transfers requiring compliance with the early childhood vaccination schedule. Conditional cash transfers provide payments to households on the condition that they make prescribed investments in human capital (Fiszbein and Schady, 2009). The introduction of this requirement has in effect added an additional policy goal to family assistance, to meet the national target of a 95 per cent or greater vaccination rate (Immunise Australia Program, 2016). Requiring compliance with vaccination schedules is common for cash transfer programmes in Latin America, where this is a condition for Mexico, Nicaragua, Brazil, Paraguay, Colombia and Honduras (Fiszbein and Schady, 2009), and conditional cash transfers have been used to meet the policy goal of boosting vaccination rates above 80 per cent (Brenzel et al., 2007*)*. However, vaccination as a condition is uncommon among OECD countries. Some states in the United States have used sanctioning welfare payments for vaccination compliance, withholding a significant portion (25–50 per cent) of payment (Medgyesi and Temesváry, 2013). This policy change has been questioned in terms of whether it violates Australia's commitment to the United Nations Convention on the Rights of the Child, which declares that children should not be punished for their parents' beliefs or action and governments should ensure children fully benefit from social security (Grant, 2016).

There is a trend towards "policing compliance" (Castles, 2001, p. 13) for beneficiaries of social transfers; that is, changing welfare payments from a right into charity. Targeting benefits through narrowing and policing eligibility is hardly new in Australia, reflecting the residual nature of the welfare state model (Castles, 1994a). The Northern Territory Intervention National Emergency Response made changes affecting Aboriginal families in certain communities, included placing restrictions on 50 per cent of all government income support payments to pay for essential items only, such as groceries, predicated on a government report finding rampant child sexual abuse (Buckmaster and Ey, 2012). While the benefit has been provided in fortnightly cash payments, the government is trialling delivering payments in pilot towns through a debit card, restricting its use to pay for essentials and to prevent the purchase of alcohol and tobacco products (National Welfare Rights Network, n.d.). The 'cashless welfare card' is stirring up controversy for the current Turnbull administration, with Australian Greens party senator Rachel Siewert introducing a motion to note on record "that the Healthy Welfare Card is a paternalistic approach to social security" (Langton, 2015). Others counter that this measure will encourage workforce participation by limiting cash for alcohol and gambling.

Paid Parental Leave and Family-Friendly Employment Policies

The norm of a male breadwinner able to support a family on his wages has been powerful both culturally and politically. Large numbers of women entered the workforce during World War II, but in the post-war period, men returned to work and women retreated to the home, as Australia experienced a baby boom. Women who worked outside the home in the 1950s typically left their jobs when they married, and for those working in public and some private agencies, the 'marriage bar' forbade the employment of married women until 1966 (Strachan, 2010). Unwed mothers who fell pregnant were forced to relinquish their children for adoption until the early 1970s, when the prevalence of adoption dropped and social assistance was extended to single mothers through the Supporting Mothers benefit (Higgens, 2011), changed to the Supporting Parents benefit in 1977 to include sole fathers. Australia lacked an infrastructure to support working mothers until provisions were made for child care and after-school care under the leadership of social worker Marie Coleman, director of the Office of Child Care, in the Fraser government of the late 1970s (Fitzherbert, 2009). The proportion of women in the workforce has risen steadily since the 1970s, though it remains below that of men, with 65 per cent of women and 78 per cent of men in the 20–74 age bracket employed in 2014–2015 (ABS, 2016).

Promoting welfare through wage protection rather than social security is the reason for Castles's (2001) widely adopted labelling of Australia as the wage earner's welfare state. The Australian Industrial Relations Commission (initially established as the Commonwealth Conciliation and Arbitration Court in 1904) established labour standards, including hours of work and leave requirements (Whiteford and Angenent, 2002). While the board primarily addressed the needs of individuals, 'test cases' set precedence and could be used by labour unions to seek contract changes. Such rulings established that an unskilled male worker should make a 'family wage', while a female worker received a lower minimum wage, until equal minimum wages were established in 1974. Test cases also set guidelines for maternity, and later parental, paid and unpaid leave (Brennan, 2009). The Industrial Relations Commission was replaced by the Fair Work Commission under the 2009 Fair Work Act. This legislation also established the right for employees who had been in their job for at least one year to receive 12 months unpaid parental leave, and the right to request an extension of an additional 12 months (Fair Work Ombudsman, n.d.).

Paid parental leave had a 'difficult birth' (Brennan, 2009) and was resisted by the Howard government in power in the 1990s on the grounds that it privileged working mothers over stay-at-home mothers. The social assistance system, particularly Family Tax Benefit Part B that is targeted to families with one primary wage earner, subsidizes families with a stay-at-home parent and was designed to do as much by the Howard government (Brennan, 2009). As an alternative to paid leave, Howard introduced the 'Baby Bonus', a AU$5000 payment made in instalments and intended to defray costs associated with the birth or adoption of a child. This payment was phased out in 2013 and replaced by the (less generous) Newborn Upfront Payment and Newborn Supplement.

Australia's Paid Parental Leave Pay was introduced in January 2011. Current policy allows for the primary carer of a newborn or recently adopted child to receive 18 weeks of Paid Parental Leave Pay at the federal minimum wage. A minimum of six weeks of paid leave is reserved for the mother (OECD, 2011). To qualify, the primary carer must meet a work and income test. The primary carer can transfer all or some unused leave to the child's other parent, and an additional two weeks of Dad and Partner Pay at the national minimum wage is also available. Alternatively, parents can access the Newborn Upfront Payment and Newborn Supplement, to assist with upfront costs associated with the birth or adoption of a newborn, but cannot receive this funding in addition to Paid Parental Leave Pay (Australian Government, 2014). The generosity of benefits is currently a politically contested issue. Former Prime Minister Tony Abbott's 'signature' legislation was to be a six-month parental leave at replacement wage, but this policy proposal was unsuccessful and new government investments are likely to focus instead on child care.

Work–life balance and family-friendly policies can also make a difference in enabling families of young children to combine employment with care. Under the Fair Work Act 2009, employees who are the parents and primary carers of children of school age or younger have the right to make a written request for flexible work. The request can be refused on 'reasonable business grounds' including if the request would be too costly or result in a significant reduction in productivity for the employer. This is in line with many other OECD countries (OECD, 2011). There is a high uptake of this benefit: in 2008, 64 per cent of working families with children under 12 reported that a parent had made use of flexible work hours to care for a child (ABS, 2010). An important caveat around supporting parental employment for the benefit of young children is that work is a net benefit for children if it is rewarding to parents, and a net negative if it is stressful and fatiguing (Brooks-Gunn and Duncan, 1997). Work pressures associated with intensification of work hours and insecure work are reported to have significant negative impacts on home life, with less time and less energy to spend with family members (Gallie, 2002). Yet Australians appear to be doing fairly well, with three in five Australians in 2007 reporting that they felt their work and family responsibilities were always or often in balance (ABS, 2016).

Early Childhood Education and Care Programmes

Australia began major investment in early childhood education and care (ECEC) services through the Child Care Act 1972. This policy was intended to support labour participation for mothers of young children through subsidies to nonprofit (subsequently amended to allow for-profit), centre-based long-day care that employed a minimum number of trained staff (Brennan and Adamson, 2012). From that time and to the current period, funding for early childhood education and care has been strongly associated with workforce participation for parents. Early childhood care and education in Australia is delivered through a market-based system, with a mix of for-profit, nonprofit and government-run services. The federal government subsidizes access to child care so that parents may work, while states have responsibility for early childhood education preschool services (Press and Hayes, 2000). While quality requirements have been featured since this initial Act, the focus on access and affordability to enable parental workforce participation has tensions with the competing policy goal of improving the quality of early education and care. To improve quality means reducing the ratios of children to educators and hiring more highly qualified educators, which causes the cost of the service to rise (Press and Hayes, 2000).

The primary Commonwealth funding for early childhood education and care programmes has been on the demand side, providing subsidies to parents, rather than supply-side funding for the operation of early childhood education and care programmes (Brennan and Fenech, 2014). This policy choice of focusing on the demand side has emphasized creating efficiency in Australia's market-based system through competition and choice (OECD, 2007). Under the Family Assistance Act, the Childcare Benefit (CCB) provides subsidies for approved child care services, for lower- and middle-income parents and carers who meet eligibility requirements, including confirmation that they are engaged in work, training or study, to receive the full 50 hours a week of subsidies (24 hours is available for families who do not meet this work test). Child Care Rebate is another payment that is not means-tested and covers child care costs after the Childcare Benefit is deducted, for up to 50 per cent of child care costs to a yearly ceiling of AU$7500 (Productivity Commission, 2014). Payments can be made directly to the service and provided to parents as a fee reduction, or paid as a lump sum to families at the end of the tax year (Whiteford and Angenent, 2002).

In addition to these general subsidies based on parents' work activity and income, there are targeted subsidies that provide additional support. Families who qualify for the maximum rate of Childcare Benefit, with a parent who is studying, working or in training, can qualify for Jobs, Education and Training Child Care Fee Assistance to cover most remaining out-of-pocket fees (Productivity Commission, 2014). Children considered at risk of 'serious abuse and neglect' are given priority access to available child care slots and Childcare Benefit can be paid at higher rates, covering more of the total costs, or for more than 50 hours (Australian Law Reform Commission, 2012), enabling child care to serve as a protective factor for children at risk. Grandparents who are full-time carers for their grandchildren can also qualify for additional child care funding under the Grandparent Child Care Benefit (Department of Education and Training, 2016). The Australian government covers about two-thirds of total early childhood care and education costs, for a yearly expenditure of approximately AU$7 billion (Productivity Commission, 2014).

Investing in the Early Years: A National Early Childhood Development Strategy, and other early childhood reforms emphasize the contributions of early childhood care and education to children's development and academic readiness. To qualify for child care benefits, services must meet minimum quality thresholds (OECD, 2007). Providers must receive accreditation, through a process involving self-study, developing a continuing improvement plan, and receiving an accreditation decision based on visits and moderation of assessments. From January 2012, all early childhood services through Australia are subject to site visits and ratings in the National Quality Standards to assess the quality of the environment. This is accompanied by the Early Years Learning Framework, which sets out parameters on broad learning outcomes and encourages educators to develop curricula tailored to the children, families and communities that they serve. These reforms mark an expansion of the Australian government's role in early childhood care and education going beyond subsidies towards measures that promote quality and recognize contributions of early childhood education to children's development (Productivity Commission, 2014). This change in focus is also signalled by the shift in responsibility for overseeing early childhood learning in the Commonwealth government portfolio. The Child Care Act had been administered under the Social Services portfolio, emphasizing ties to employment and family support (Press and Hayes, 2000), but under the Turnbull government has been shifted to the Education portfolio, a move recognized by the early childhood sector as acknowledging the educational as well as welfare goals of early childhood services (Learning Press, 2015). Yet the focus on demand-side subsidies provides limited policy levers in terms of promoting quality. Research in Europe suggests that a publically financed system can provide more equitable access to high-quality care (Baker et al., 2005).

In addition to policy goals of improving quality, the Council of Australian Governments has set new targets to provide universal access to 15 hours of preschool education from a university-qualified teacher for all children in the year prior to formal schooling, including all Indigenous four-year-olds in remote communities. Broadening access and meeting quality standards will require recruiting and retaining university-qualified teachers, difficult in a field where educators are paid significantly less than K-12 (kindergarten to year 12) teachers. Indeed, reviews of implementation of the new standards have found that services are having difficulty hiring university-trained teachers (Blair, 2014). In the current budget cycle, the federal government is providing direct subsidies to long daycares to offset remuneration costs for highly qualified teachers through an Early Years Quality Fund, but the long-term strategy to cover increased costs of ECEC is unclear (Harrington, n.d.).

AUSTRALIA IN INTERNATIONAL CONTEXT: STRENGTHS AND CHALLENGES

Given this mix of social investments in early childhood, how does Australia compare to other high-income OECD nations? With regard to early childhood outcomes, Australia is "middle of the road" (ARACY, 2013, p. 1), with areas of strengths and challenges. Australia is among the OECD countries with highest per capita spending on early childhood (OECD, 2015). It stands out for a high level of social expenditure on families through the Family Tax Benefit (OECD, 2007), and providing payments in cash rather than as tax concessions (Whiteford and Angenent, 2002), with 40 per cent of overall social expenditure payments going to the lowest quintile of households (OECD, 2014).

Australia lags other OECD countries in terms of generosity and duration of parental leave benefits. Payment at the national minimum wage is equivalent to 42 per cent of the national average wage, which is among the lowest payment rates in the OECD. The OECD average length of paid parental leave is more than one year, which Australia falls far short of at 18 weeks (OECD, 2016). About one-third of OECD countries provide parental leave payments at income replacement rates (OECD, 2011), but paid parental leave at replacement wage has been resisted by business interests and government in Australia due to stated concerns about the costs for businesses (Brennan, 2009). However, the Australian social assistance system does well at protecting sole-parent families from poverty during parental leave (OECD, 2011).

Australia is in the bottom third of OECD countries for participation in early childhood education and care (ARACY, 2013). Fewer than half of children under age six are enrolled in early childhood care and education, suggesting unmet need in this area (OECD, 2011). Australia ranked 30th out of 34 nations for percentage of children attending preschool before starting school (ARACY, 2013). The funding and enrolment targets associated with the *Investing in the Early Years* strategy is likely to impact upon outcomes in this area.

For children experiencing disadvantage, Australia performs fairly well compared to other OECD nations, with children less likely to experience income poverty than the general population (OECD, 2015), and it is in the one-third of OECD countries with lowest social inequality as measured by how far the poorest children are being left behind (UNICEF Office of Research, 2016). However, the percentage of young children in jobless families stands out as a problem, with Australia ranking 22nd out of 25 nations on this indicator (ARACY, 2013). Workforce participation by single parents is among the lowest in OECD countries, with just over 50 per cent of single parents participating in the workforce in 2009 (OECD, 2011). Means-tested family benefits may act as a disincentive for workforce participation, with high effective tax rates making low-paying work unattractive in terms of financial gain (Cox, 2008).

Indigenous children are the most vulnerable group in Australia, with poorer developmental outcomes than non-Indigenous children (ARACY, 2013). These gaps in outcomes between Indigenous and non-Indigenous children are greater in Australia than among general and Indigenous populations in the United States, Canada and New Zealand (Burns et al., 2012). Aboriginal families face complex, multiple disadvantages accumulated intergenerationally that create a vicious cycle that is difficult to break. The government has set 'Closing the Gaps' targets, with the goal of halving the gap in mortality rates for Indigenous children under five and ensuring all Indigenous four-year-olds have access to quality early childhood education and care within five years, including in remote areas which have less access to early childhood and health services (Hunter, 2009). A primary strategy to achieve these goals is integrated early childhood services, providing access to child and material health services, parenting and family support services, and early learning and child care. However, while 38 centres have been established, there is no ongoing federal funding for the centres and only some are receiving short-term state or territory funding (Power, 2014).

Australia is stronger on social protection for early childhood, as delivered through social assistance payments, than in social investment through parental leave and early childhood education and care. This fits a traditional Anglo-Saxon remedial welfare state model. A new social contract is emerging in Australian social policy, based on the concepts of social investment and social inclusion. The *Investing in the Early Years* early childhood development strategy is indicative of this shift to the 'social investment' state. Investment in early childhood is the "flagship" of the Council of Australian Government's human capital agenda (Smyth, 2010, p. 16). Supporting families to care for young children, and providing high-quality early childhood education and care in an equitable manner that reaches all young Australians, will be essential for the economic strategy of building human capital for future prosperity.

REFERENCES

Australian Bureau of Statistics (ABS) (2010). Child Care. *Australian Social Trends*, Vol. 4102.0, June. Retrieved from http://www.ausstats.abs.gov.au/ausstats/subscriber.nsf/LookupAttach/4102.0Publication30.06.106/$File/41020_ChildCare.pdf.

Australian Bureau of Statistics (ABS) (2016). 4125.0 – Gender Indicators, Work and Family Balance. Retrieved from http://www.abs.gov.au/ausstats/abs@.nsf/Lookup/by%20Subject/4125.0~Feb%202016~Main%20Features~Work%20and%20Family%20Balance~3411.

Australian Government (2014). Family Assistance Guide. Retrieved from http://guides.dss.gov.au/family-assistance-guide/1/2/18

Australian Institute of Health and Welfare (AIHW) (2015). *Australia's Welfare 2015*. Australia's welfare series no. 12. Cat. no. AUS 189. Canberra: AIHW.

Australian Law Reform Commission (2012). *Family Violence and Commonwealth Laws – Improving Legal Frameworks* (ALRC Report 117). Retrieved from http://www.alrc.gov.au/publications/family-violence-and-commonwealth-laws-improving-legal-frameworks-alrc-report-117.

Australian Research Alliance for Children and Youth (ARACY) (2013). *Report Card: The Wellbeing of Young Australians*. Retrieved from https://www.aracy.org.au/projects/report-card-the-wellbeing-of-young-australians.

Baker, M., Gruber, J. and Milligan, K. (2005). Universal Childcare, Maternal Labor Supply, and Family Well-being. NBER Working Paper No. 11832, December, Cambridge, MA: National Bureau of Economic Research.

Blair, T. (2014). *Early Childhood Education and Care Report*. Portfolio Reports, Federal Congress. Retrieved from http://www.icpa.com.au/documents/download/882/federal-icpa-portfolios/federal-early-childhood-portfolio/early-childhood-education-and-care-report-2014.pdf.

Brennan, D. (2009). The Difficult Birth of Paid Maternity Leave in Australia. In S. Kamerman and P. Moss (eds), *The Politics of Parental Leave*. Cambridge: Policy Press, pp. 15–32.

Brennan, D. and Adamson, E. (2012). Early Childhood Education and Care Policy. In J. Bowes, R. Grace and K. Hodge (eds), *Children, Families and Communities: Contexts and Consequences*. South Melbourne: Oxford University Press, pp. 255–268.

Brennan, D. and Fenech, M. (2014). Early Education and Care in Australia: Equity in a Mixed Market-based System? In L. Gambaro, K. Stewart and

J. Waldfogel (eds), *An Equal Start?: Providing Quality Early Education and Care for Disadvantaged Children*. Chicago, IL: Policy Press, pp. 171–192.

Brenzel, L.E., Barham, T. and Maluccio, J.A. (2007). Beyond 80%: Are there New Ways of Increasing Vaccination Coverage? Evaluation of CCT Programs in Mexico and Nicaragua. In *Evaluation of CCT Programs in Mexico and Nicaragua*. iHEA 2007 6th World Congress: Explorations in Health Economics Paper. Washington, DC: World Bank.

Brooks-Gunn, J. and Duncan, G.J. (1997). The Effects of Poverty on Children. *The Future of Children*, 7 (2), 55–71.

Buckmaster, L. and Ey, C. (2012). Is Income Management Working?. Canberra: Parliament of Australia. Retrieved from http://www.aph.gov.au/About_ Parliament/Parliamentary_Departments/Parliamentary_Library/pubs/BN/2011-2012/IncomeManagement#_Toc326674754.

Burns, A., Burns, K., Menzies, K. and Grace, R. (2012). The Stolen Generations. In J. Bowes, R. Grace and K. Hodge (eds), *Children, Families and Communities: Contexts and Consequences*. South Melbourne: Oxford University Press, pp. 239–252.

Castles, F.G. (1994a). Comparing the Australian and Scandinavian welfare states. *Scandinavian Political Studies*, 17 (1), 31–46.

Castles, F.G. (1994b). The Wage Earners' Welfare State Revisited: Refurbishing the Established Model of Australian Social Protection, 1983–1993. *Australian Journal of Social Issues*, 29 (2), 120–145.

Castles, F.G. (2001). A Farewell to Australia's Welfare State. *International Journal of Health Services*, 31 (3), 537–544.

Conley, A. (2010). Child Care: Welfare or Investment?. *International Journal of Social Welfare*, 19 (2), 173–181.

Council of Australian Governments (COAG) (2009). *Investing in the Early Years: A National Early Childhood Development Strategy*. Retrieved from https://www.coag.gov.au/sites/default/files/national_ECD_strategy.pdf.

Cox, E. (2008). *Mean Tests: Middle Class Welfare or Redistributive Fairness?* Sydney: Centre for Policy Development. Retrieved from http://cpd.org.au/2008/05/mean-tests-middle-class-welfare-or-redistributive-fairness/.

Department of Education and Training (2016). Grandparent Child Care Benefit. January. Retrieved from https://www.education.gov.au/grandparent-child-care-benefit.

Department of Social Services (2016). No Jab No Pay – Immunisation Requirements. Retrieved from https://www.dss.gov.au/our-responsibilities/families-and-children/benefits-payments/strengthening-immunisation-for-young-children.

Esping-Andersen, G. (1990). *The Three Worlds of Welfare Capitalism*. Cambridge: Polity.

Esping-Andersen, G. (2002). A Child-centred Social Investment Strategy. In G. Esping-Andersen (ed.), *Why We Need a New Welfare State*. New York: Oxford University Press, pp. 26–67.

Esping-Andersen, G. (2005). Children in the Welfare State: A Social Investment Approach. DemoSoc Working Paper, No. 2005–10. Retrieved from http://www.upf.edu/demosoc/_pdf/DEMOSOC10.pdf.

Fair Work Ombudsman (n.d.). Best Practice Guide Work and Family. Retrieved from https://www.fairwork.gov.au/how-we-will-help/templates-and-guides/best-practice-guides/work-and-family.

Fiszbein, A. and Schady, N.R. (2009). *Conditional Cash Transfers: Reducing Present and Future Poverty.* Washington, DC: World Bank Publications.

Fitzherbert, M. (2009). *So Many Firsts: Liberal Women from Menzies to Turnbull era.* Leichhardt, NSW: Federation Press.

Gallie, D. (2002). The Quality of Working Life in Welfare Strategy. In G. Esping-Andersen (ed.), *Why We Need a New Welfare State.* New York: Oxford University Press, pp. 96–129.

Giddens, A. (1998). *The Third Way: The Renewal of Social Democracy.* Polity: Cambridge.

Gormley, W.T. (2012). *Voices for Children: Rhetoric and Public Policy.* Washington, DC: Brookings Institution Press.

Grant, S. (2016). Silence Greets Rights Breaches. *Herald Online.* January. Retrieved from https://heraldonlinejournal.com/2016/01/15/silence-greets-rights-breaches/.

Harrington, M. (n.d.). Early Childhood Education, Budget Review 2013–2014. Retrieved from http://www.aph.gov.au/About_Parliament/Parliamentary_Departments/Parliamentary_Library/pubs/rp/BudgetReview201314/EarlyChildhood.

Heckman, J.J. (2012). Invest in Early Childhood Development: Reduce Deficits, Strengthen the Economy. Heckman Equation, 7. Retrieved from http://heckmanequation.org/heckman-equation.

Herscovitch, A. and Stanton, D. (2008). History of Social Security in Australia. *Family Matters,* 80. Retrieved from https://aifs.gov.au/publications/family-matters/issue-80/history-social-security-australia.

Higgens, D. (2011). Unfit Mothers … Unjust Practices? Key Issues from Australian Research on the Impact of Past Adoption Practices. *Family Matters,* 87. Retrieved from https://aifs.gov.au/sites/default/files/fm87g.pdf.

Houser, L. and Vartanian, T. (2012). *Pay Matters: The Positive Economic Impact of Paid Family Leave for Families, Businesses and the Public.* January. Center for Women and Work at Rutgers, the State University of New Jersey Publication. Retrieved 5 March 2015 from http://www.nationalpartnership.org/site/DocServer/Pay_Matters_Positive_Economic_Impacts_of_Paid_Family_L.pdf?docID=9681.

Hunter, B. (2009). Indigenous Social Exclusion: Insights and Challenges for the Concept of Social Inclusion. *Family Matters,* 82. Retrieved from https://aifs.gov.au/publications/family-matters/issue-82/indigenous-social-exclusion.

Immervoll, H. and Barber, D. (2006). Can Parents Afford to Work? Childcare Costs, Tax-benefit Policies and Work Incentives. Bonn: Institute for the Study of Labor (IZA). Retrieved from http://ftp.iza.org/dp1932.pdf.

Immunise Australia Program (2016). Vaccination Data. April. Retrieved from http://www.immunise.health.gov.au/internet/immunise/publishing.nsf/Content/vaccination-data.

Kimmel, J. (1998). Child Care Costs as a Barrier to Employment for Single and Married Mothers. *Review of Economics and Statistics,* 80 (2), 287–299.

Knightley, P. (2000). *Australia: Biography of a Nation.* London: Jonathan Cape.

Langton, M. (2015). Health and Welfare. *Monthly*, May. Retrieved from https://www.themonthly.com.au/issue/2015/may/1430402400/marcia-langton/health-and-welfare.

Laughlin, L. (2011). *Maternity Leave and Employment: Patterns of First-Time Mothers 1961–2008*. US Census Bureau Publication, October. Retrieved 5 March 2015, from http://www.census.gov/prod/2011pubs/p70-128.pdf.

Learning Press (2015). Childcare Moves from Social Services to Education in Turnbull Reshuffle. Retrieved from http://www.thelearningpress.com/parents-and-educators-welcome-childcare-move.html.

Lister, R. (2003). Investing in the Citizen-workers of the Future: Transformations in Citizenship and the State under New Labour. *Social Policy and Administration*, 37 (5), 427–443.

Maldonado, L.C. and Nieuwenhuis, R. (2015). Family Policies and Single Parent Poverty in 18 OECD countries, 1978–2008. *Community, Work and Family*, 18(4), 395–415.

McClelland, A. and Smyth, P. (2014). *Social Policy in Australia: Understanding for Action*, 3rd edn. South Melbourne: Oxford University Press.

Medgyesi, M. and Temesváry, Z. (2013). Conditional Cash Transfers in High-income OECD Countries and their Effects on Human Capital Accumulation. AIAS, GINI Discussion Paper, 84.

Midgley, J. (1999). Growth, Redistribution, and Welfare: Toward Social Investment. *Social Service Review*, 73 (1), 3–21.

Midgley, J. and Sherraden, M. (2000). The Social Development Perspective in Social Policy. In J. Midgley and T. Livermore (eds), *The Handbook of Social Policy*. Thousand Oaks, CA: Sage Publications, pp. 435–446.

Mitchell, D. (1997). Reshaping Australian Social Policy: Alternatives to the Breadwinner Welfare State. Discussion Paper no. 55. Canberra: Public Policy Program, Australian National University.

Morel, N., Palier, B. and Palme, J. (2012). *Towards a Social Investment Welfare State?: Ideas, Policies and Challenges*. Chicago, IL: Policy Press.

National Welfare Rights Network (n.d.). Healthy Welfare Trial on the Cards. *Welfare Rights Review*, 1 (3). Retrieved from http://www.welfarerights.org.au/welfare-rights-review/welfare-rights-review-vol-1-no-3/healthy-welfare-trial-cards.

OECD (2007). Babies and Bosses: Reconciling Work and Family Life, a Synthesis of Findings for OECD Countries. Retrieved from http://www.oecd.org/els/family/babiesandbosses-reconcilingworkandfamilylifeasynthesisoffindingsforoecdcountries.htm.

OECD (2011). Doing Better for Families. Retrieved from http://www.oecd.org/social/soc/doingbetterforfamilies.htm.

OECD (2014). Social Expenditure Update. Retrieved from http://www.oecd.org/els/soc/OECD2014-Social-Expenditure-Update-Nov2014-8pages.pdf.

OECD (2015). CO2.2: Child Poverty. Retrieved from http://www.oecd.org/els/family/CO_2_2_Child_Poverty.pdf.

OECD (2016). PF2.1: Key Characteristics of Parental Leave Systems. Retrieved from http://www.oecd.org/els/soc/PF2_1_Parental_leave_systems.pdf.

Power, J. (2014). Aboriginal Family and Children's Centres in Limbo. *Sydney Morning Herald*, 15 September. Retrieved from http://www.smh.com.au/nsw/aboriginal-family-and-childrens-centres-in-limbo-20140914-10fvqb.html.

Press, F. and Hayes, A. (2000). OECD Thematic Review of Early Childhood Education and Care Policy. Australian Background Report, Canberra, Commonwealth Government of Australia.

Productivity Commission (2014). Childcare and Early Childhood Learning: Overview. Inquiry Report No. 73, Canberra.

Silver, H. (2008). The National Reform Agenda: Origins and Objectives. In Peter Carroll, Rex Deighton-Smith, Helen Silver and Chris Walker (eds), *Minding the Gap: Appraising the Promise and Performance of Regulatory Reform in Australia*. Canberra: ANU E Press, pp. 63–72. Retrieved from http://press.anu.edu.au/anzsog/minding_gap/pdf/ch05.pdf.

Smyth, P. (2010). In or Out?: Building an Inclusive Nation. Australian Collaboration and Brotherhood of St Laurence. Albert Park, Victoria: Australian Collaboration. Retrieved from http://library.bsl.org.au/jspui/bitstream/1/1566/1/In_or_Out_PSmyth_2010.pdf.

Strachan, G. (2010). Still Working for the Man? Women's Employment Experiences in Australia Since 1950. *Australian Journal of Social Issues*, 45 (1), 117.

Taggart, B., Sylva, K., Melhuish, E., Sammons, P. and Siraj, I. (2015). How Pre-school Influences Children and Young People's Attainment and Developmental Outcomes over Time. June. Retrieved from https://www.gov.uk/government/uploads/system/uploads/attachment_data/file/455670/RB455_Effective_pre-school_primary_and_secondary_education_project.pdf.pdf.

United Nations Children's Fund (UNICEF) (2012). Integrated Social Protection Systems: Enhancing Equity for Children. New York: UNICEF Social and Economic Policy Analysis Unit. Retrieved from: http://www.unicef.org/socialprotection/framework/files/Full_Social_Protection_Strategic_Framework_low_res(1).pdf.

United Nations Children's Fund (UNICEF) Office of Research (2016). Fairness for Children: A League Table of Inequality in Child Well-being in Rich Countries. Innocenti Report Card 13. UNICEF Office of Research – Innocenti, Florence. Retrieved from https://www.unicef-irc.org/publications/pdf/RC13_eng.pdf.

Vandenbroucke, F. and Vleminckx, K. (2011). Disappointing Poverty Trends: Is the Social Investment state to blame?. *Journal of European Social Policy*, 21 (5), 450–471.

Waldfogel, J. (2015). The Role of Preschool in Reducing Inequality. *IZA World of Labor*, 219. Retrieved from http://wol.iza.org/articles/role-of-preschool-in-reducing-inequality/long.

Whiteford, P. and Angenent, G. (2002). The Australian System of Social Protection: An Overview, 2nd edition, June. Department of Family and Community Services, Occasional Paper No. 6. Retrieved from https://www.dss.gov.au/sites/default/files/documents/05_2012/no.6.pdf.

3. Housing and social investment: lessons from Hong Kong and Singapore

James Lee

In an environment of rapid economic growth with a high concentration of urban population, the demand for housing in East Asia has always been keen in the last four decades. However, economic development often seems to pair with spiralling house prices and problems of affordability for the working-class and, increasingly, middle-class households. At the same time, as a result of sustained periods of house price inflation, a large number of homeowners do benefit from rising asset values and hence increased wealth. While the wealth effect for individual households is highly varied, its impact on wealth distribution has been significant. Cities with a high percentage of home ownership tend to find a larger share of wealth amongst their propertied households, irrespective of whether it is supported by the government or bought through the market. Invariably, home ownership is connected with wealth accumulation and is a prime source of income inequalities for societies (Picketty and Zucman, 2014). At the policy level, studies have likewise demonstrated that East Asian states tend to use housing policy as a tool in economic policy to foster growth (Chua, 1997).

As a key dimension of social policy, housing is increasingly considered a major tool of social investment. While it provides a lifelong stream of residential services, housing is an important form of asset building and capital accumulation (Sherraden, 1991). How housing market perform-ance impacts upon national economies and vice versa is a topic widely studied by economists (Papadimitriou et al., 2007; Belsky, 2010). How-ever, how housing policy is connected with social investment has received much less attention. This chapter examines the role of housing policy as social investment in two contrasting high-growth urban econ-omies in East Asia: Singapore and Hong Kong. The chapter first explains the complex nature of housing policy and its social investment characteristics. Then it describes the particular role of housing policy in East Asian governance in the context of development. Finally, through the case studies of Hong Kong and Singapore, the chapter zooms in on the important relationship between housing policy, asset building and social security. The central purpose is to look beyond the residential dimension of traditional housing policy and to establish a logic of housing policy based on asset building, within the context of high-growth and densely populated urban economies in East Asia. Given the enormous potential of housing policy in social investment, its impact on wealth distribution and social justice, a thorough understanding of its role is vital to understanding the future trend of social policy and development in East Asia.

SOCIAL POLICY, SOCIAL INVESTMENT AND HOUSING POLICY

In his seminal analysis: 'What is Social Policy?', Richard Titmuss (1974) suggested the importance of seeing social policy as a right order of social relationship which enables the poor, the sick and the elderly to be able to maintain a socially just set of life opportunities. This should constitute the foundation of modern social policy, although we are far from achieving the ideal of a socially just set of social policies. The concept of social division of welfare further separates welfare into conventional social welfare provisions provided by the state and non-state sectors, occupational welfare provided by industries, and fiscal welfare, to better comprehend the scale and impact of social policy on social life. While this social organization looks comprehensive, what is lacking, however, is a perspective that could ascertain the long-term impact of social policy on life opportunities. This takes on two meanings. First, the combined effects of a certain configuration of social policies could have differential social benefits at a given level of implementation efficiency. Second, the returns on welfare over time could be different given various social investment effects of social policies. Thus, a static comparison of welfare indicators is only useful to the extent that it provides a snapshot on the current situation. This is something that is apparently difficult to measure, although it is well known that social welfare does carry long-term social investment benefits, but it is important to know the full impact of a certain configuration of social policies, particularly when some carry more tangible investment returns over time while others do not. As suggested in the Introduction of this book, the distinction between social policies that promote investment or consumption is not clear-cut.

Given these considerations, social policies can best be classified as running between the spectrum of consumption and investment. While some are more consumption-oriented, others are more investment-oriented. The very nature of social policy itself defines the level of investment returns and where it sits on the consumption–investment spectrum. For example, on the surface, residential home care for low-income elderly people is more consumption-oriented in terms of enhancing the quality of life for elderly people. However, if these residential care services could contribute towards relieving the burden of younger family members' carer-role, to the extent that they can better concentrate on work and productivity, such policy then carries an indirect social investment impact. Another example comes from the social protection field. As Midgley (2008) observes, income transfers are usually believed to promote consumption at the expense of economic development, but if properly configured they can also serve a strong investment function. In this regard, no social policy has a more direct impact on social investment than housing policy, as it is the only social policy that generates tangible investment returns over time. It is both consumption- and investment-oriented and aptly sits in the middle of the spectrum.

Even though the European Union (EU) has adopted seemingly social investment-oriented social policies since the 2000s, their usefulness is seriously questioned. Some studies (Cantillon, 2011; Morel et al., 2011; Vandenbroucke and Vleminckx, 2011) have demonstrated that the transition from the old distributive welfare state to a new social investment state is more difficult than expected. Poverty and unemployment still persist despite a highly targeted policy in the last 15 years aiming at increasing social expenditures on social investment. The attainment of the 2020 EU target of lifting 20 million people out of poverty now seems more distant than ever. Research findings have further suggested that the social investment paradigm may have shifted resources away from programmes that are more distributive to programmes that are less so, and that social investment might have contributed to a "re-commodification and retrenchment of unemployment benefits" (Vandenbroucke and Vleminckx, 2011, p. 451). These studies of the results of large-scale national social investment efforts, at least in Europe, do suggest that, other than difference in national social policy configurations, the nature of different social policies also counts. In other words, there is the possibility that certain social policies might be more effective in the long run to bring about desirable effects of social investment – for example, housing policy – than others.

The Particularity of Housing Policy in East Asia

Agus et al. (2002) suggest two major characteristics that characterize East Asian housing policies. First, housing has always been considered a major pillar of economic growth and is often treated by many governments as an integral part of overall economic policy. For example, in an effort to stimulate Hong Kong's failing economy and to consolidate Hong Kong's housing policy, the Secretary for Housing, Planning and Land made the following statement in 2002:

> the property sector, closely interwoven with every single aspect of our daily life, has been a major pillar of our economy. Together with the construction industry, it accounted for 14 per cent of the GDP [gross domestic product] over the past five years. To many people, buying property has been a principal channel to garner their wealth ... the plunging net asset values in private residential market has inhibited economic recovery ... To pump prime the deflation-battered economy, the Chief Secretary has asked the Housing Bureau to undertake a root and branch review of government's housing policy with a view to restoring the public's confidence. (Hong Kong Housing Authority, 2002, p. 1)

It is apparent that the Hong Kong government places great importance on the economic performance of the housing sector, particularly during an economic downturn, and saw it as a way to pump-prime the economy. This stands in stark contrast to Western industrial economies where two extreme positions normally take place: either the market is used as the main distributor of housing resources and the government refrains from intervention in any form, or social housing is part of a national welfare system where affordable housing is seen primarily as a social responsibility. The former position is more often associated with the North American housing system, while the latter is more European or Nordic. East Asian governments, however, do not fall into either extreme. Instead, many governments take an active role in devising various institutional structures to facilitate the housing function to tie in with development goals (Forrest and Lee, 2003). Agus et al. (2002) further suggest that governments in high-growth East Asian countries are more inclined to adopt a model of housing policy that combines a high degree of intervention by the state and yet allows market criteria to reign. In other words, the demarcation between state and market is much more fluid. In particular, the state does not simply apply market criteria in housing provision, but also plays a major role in the market, and in some cases monopolizes the market.

In this connection, one dimension of housing policy that has not been discussed thoroughly thus far concerns the nature of housing assets. For many homeowners, owning one's home represents the gradual build-up of a lifelong asset that can be realized in old age. Since the late 1970s, an extended period of buoyancy in housing markets lasting more than four decades in East Asia has successfully encouraged the development of an outlook where households generally believed in home-buying as their best investment for the future (Lee, 1999). It has also been suggested that capital gains derived from home ownership were considered an important source of income additional to wages and salaries in situations of labour market uncertainty (Smart and Lee, 2003). As a result, many East Asian governments encourage home ownership under the notion of stakehold-ership (Forrest and Lee, 2003; Chua, 1997). It is a position widely held by all social classes that home ownership is the best way to accumulate family wealth. Among policy-makers, it is held that housing policy, if properly managed, is not only able to satisfy housing needs for low- to middle-income households, but is also a useful way of providing long-term financial security for households and hence ultimately reducing the state burden of elderly care (Doling and Ronald, 2010). In addition, a policy on home ownership would provide a strong impetus to capital formation and hence contribute to GDP growth. Such a complex and dynamic relationship between the housing sector (both public and private), the social security system and the macroeconomy thus creates a labyrinth that provides the basis of a unique form of political economy that Haila (2000, 2015) coined 'the property states' in East Asia. She suggests that while real estate and housing is always a significant part of any economy, the unique structure of land ownership in places like Hong Kong and Singapore has enabled the economic significance of the housing sector to go beyond the normal realm of how housing operates in Western industrial economies, and thus strongly affects East Asian policy structure and outcome.

THE SINGAPORE CASE

As the one nation-state in East Asia that aspires to a social democratic philosophy, Singapore is the only government that has chosen an asset building policy through 100 per cent home ownership (Sherraden et al., 1995; Lee, 2000). How this happened is an intriguing story involving strong political ideals, careful social planning and a government that is prepared to monopolize the production of social goods to prevent market anomaly. As a social investment project in housing that originated in the 1960s, its social effectiveness is not only time-proven but also financially sustainable. It helps most families in Singapore to build assets through institutionalized savings. As a result of a high degree of home ownership (nearly 90 per cent) and a wide dispersion of assets, Singapore is able to achieve a Gini coefficient of 0.37 (2014), as well as being one of the most equal societies in East Asia (Singapore Ministry of Finance, 2015). Home ownership has not simply realized the goals of social investment, but has also achieved a degree of fairness in social policy unsurpassed by any other East Asian economies.

In the mid-twentieth century, Singapore was nothing more than a small tropical city with unpleasantly high humidity, abundant marshland, and a 1 million population mostly of Chinese descent. But by 1980, Singapore had already emerged to become one of the most recognized new economic powers in East Asia, with a per capita GDP of US$428, and a population of 1.6 million. In 2005, Singapore had increased its per capita GDP to US$29 866, with a population of 3.54 million; in 2014 it was US$56 284 with a population of 5.4 million. All this is the result of a careful configuration of social policies that foster growth on the one hand, and maintain a high standard of living on the other. Since the 1960s, public housing has been developed systematically to advance socio-economic integration.

It is a deliberate policy of the People's Action Party to achieve political legitimization through both sound economics and good social policies. To attract international capital, Singapore needs to build a multiracial workforce that is productivity-enhancing, well-supported by families who find their lives secure physically and financially. This brings forth a very different orientation of social policy. It concerns the systematic building-up of household assets, primarily through state-supported home ownership. The idea behind it was that only through securing home ownership as a long-term asset could individuals and families become secure over their life cycle. And to carry out such an important task, only the state has the power, resources and legitimacy to provide an umbrella institution that covers the entire population. As the welfare of the entire population hinges on such an institution, it could not possibly be purely a market institution, since it would be exposed to risks and instabilities that could be easily absorbed by private firms with profit motives. In the case of global financial turmoil such as the subprime crisis, the institution should be potentially shielded by built-in mechanisms giving the capacity to weather such risks. Singapore managed to do just that during the Asian Financial Crisis in the 1990s. The question is: how?

The Central Provident Fund and the Idea of Lifelong Asset Management

For Singapore, the beginning of one such institutional arrangement was accidental and intimately linked to a set-up established by the British colonial government in the 1950s. The Central Provident Fund began as a self-funded savings scheme to assist local government servants to save. It was similar to what the British set up for other colonies in Africa and Malaysia to ensure that colonial governments were not unduly burdened by social security expenditures (Kaseke et al., 2011). However, as it developed, the Singapore Provident Fund turned out to be an extremely valuable institutional legacy. From the outset, the emphasis of the scheme was focused on ensuring income security for old age. Despite pressure from workers calling for changes to enable them to withdraw their savings earlier, the government stood firm on the rule that savings could only be withdrawn at age 58. It was not until the late 1960s that the rules were liberalized, when the Home Ownership Scheme was introduced to allow people to finance the purchase of government-built flats with Provident Fund savings. Since then, it has been slowly adapting to the changing needs of an increasingly affluent population. Singaporeans can now use their savings for various purposes: other than retirement provision, Provident Fund money goes to investment, health care, insurance and higher education costs for children of aspiring middle-class people. In 2014, the total contribution rate for the Provident Fund was 37 per cent, with 17 per cent from the employer and 20 per cent from the employee. Provident Fund savings and interest go into three accounts: (1) the Ordinary Account is for retirement, home ownership, insurance, investment and education; (2) the Medisave Account pays hospital bills and approved medical insurance schemes; and (3) the Special Account is reserved for old age protection. Self-employed people also contribute 6 per cent of their annual net income to their Medisave Accounts on a monthly basis. A macro advantage of the Central Provident Fund is that money accumulated through the system has been vital to capital formation necessary for housing development by the Housing Development Board (HDB). In other words, Singapore has successfully solved a development capital issue faced by many developing countries in housing development: that is, how to build an adequate financial base for capital development.

While the Hong Kong government has continued to flag warnings about the lack of adequate capital for housing development from general revenues, Singapore has solved its housing finance problem on the basis of capital formation in the Central Provident Fund. Total savings amount to between 16 per cent to 30 per cent of gross national saving, and nearly half of GDP. In theory, balances have not been used to provide loans to government to build housing; the government financed all current and capital expenditures in housing from operating revenues. However, since Central Provident Fund savings must be invested in government bonds as well as in advanced deposits with the Monetary Authority, these monies eventually come in the form of operating revenues provided for the Housing Development Board.

The Central Provident Fund and Housing Development Board configuration is by far the most intriguing institutional arrangement in East Asia. The key purpose is to create an effective institution to integrate social and economic policies. Provident Fund savings help to generate funds that can stimulate the economy by providing a pool of long-term capital for investment (Asher, 1995). In addition, as a defined-contribution plan, it does not generate the distortions and welfare losses associated with systems that pay benefits to one generation by imposing taxes on another. Singapore housing, therefore, fits perfectly well into the social investment approach that emphasizes inclusion, stakeholdership and long-term returns.

THE HONG KONG CASE

Hong Kong presents a radically different mode of housing policy to Singapore, despite the two cities sharing similarities in size, culture and ethnic composition. While home ownership is keenly sought after by all, the government has taken a neoliberal stand, emphasizing the market nature of housing as well as the welfare role of public housing. Primarily, housing is considered a private domain decision and hence it should be produced and supplied mainly through the market. Low-income housing is considered a part of the residual welfare system, helping only low-income households when the market fails to provide sufficient affordable housing. The state has little role to play except to ensure a healthy supply of land for sale.

Unfortunately, the housing market has been through periods of rampant price increases since the 1970s, with prices increasing tenfold since the 1980s. Recurring market failures accounted for a gradual expansion of public sector housing, and yet the housing affordability issue has never gone away. Since the late 1980s, the government has been cautious not to expand the public sector for fear that it might interfere with the 'normal' development of the housing market. The prevalence of residual welfare

thinking by public officials has successfully fostered a culture of con-
servatism; one that sees housing policy only as a temporary measure to
ease housing needs until such time as the market corrects itself. However,
the housing market has seldom succeeded in correcting itself over the last
four decades. In 2015, 45 per cent of the population remained in the
public housing sector, with 30 per cent living in heavily subsidized rental
housing and 15 per cent in government-assisted Home Ownership
Scheme (HOS) housing, produced in small numbers annually and allocated with strict income criteria. It was the most popular housing policy
since 1976 and was perennially oversubscribed by eligible households,
far outnumbering its meagre supply. Nevertheless, the HOS officially
ended in 2003 under strong opposition from a political alliance made up
of large real estate developers.

Given these initial housing numbers, most governments would be
tempted to boast of their success in housing policy. However, according
to the 2016 International Housing Affordability Study, Hong Kong stands
as the world's most expensive city and hence the least affordable
globally, ahead of such places as Sydney, Vancouver and San Francisco
(Demographia, 2016). In the last two decades, the housing issue has
become a highly contentious political issue, so powerful as to result in
the removal of Hong Kong's first Chief Executive (Mr Tung Chee-hwa)
from office in 2005 (Cheung, 2005). Why, despite having a high degree
of state intervention in housing and a vibrant economy, had the government repeatedly failed to thwart house price inflation and to build
sufficient affordable housing? The answer lies in the existence of a
unique structure of urban political economy where real estate interests
have successfully dominated the economy over the last 40 years (Haila,
2000). In Hong Kong, 11 large developers constitute 75 per cent of the
entire housing market (Consumer Council, 1996). They dominate both
vertically and horizontally in the housing businesses, to the extent that
medium-sized and small construction firms almost do not exist. It is a
classic case of oligopolistic competition with low transaction costs and
high economic rent. It is the world's least regulated – or the freest –
housing market. Monopolistic competition has successfully enabled real
estate developers to influence public policies through playing key roles in
statutory bodies and government committees, such as the Executive
Council and the Legislative Council. The current Chief Executive of the
Hong Kong Special Administrative Region, Mr C.Y. Leung, was a former
owner of DTZ Holdings, a global real estate company originating from
Europe.

When the first Special Administrative Region Government assumed
office in 1997, it sought to tackle house price inflation by setting a new

housing production target. Developers and homeowners who feared that increased supply would undermine house prices were strongly opposed to it. This has been infamously coined the '85 000 Policy', where the government proposed to increase annual housing production to 85 000 units and to ultimately achieve 70 per cent home ownership. Unfortunately, the Asian Financial Crisis set in motion a series of market downturns that eventually led to the bursting of Hong Kong's biggest post-war housing bubble in 1998, and a market downturn lasting until 2004 when house prices collapsed more than 70 per cent from their 1997 peak. The 70 per cent home ownership target never got off the ground as Hong Kong suffered from its worst post-war recession. In 2001, the total number of households in negative equity was 65 000, or 15 per cent of all mortgages; while in 2003, the government decided to terminate the Home Ownership Scheme (Hong Kong Housing Authority, 2002). The key change was to roll back the state in assisted home ownership and to confine it to only the production of public rental housing for low-income households.

The Property State and its Dependence on Land Revenue

One key incentive for government to adopt a neoliberal housing policy stems from its dependence on land revenues (Tse, 1998). Historically, land sales provided a unique source of public revenues amounting to one-third of public revenues, thus providing an important financial basis for much social expenditure (Jones, 1990; Wilding and Mok, 1997). However, land sales are not risk-free. With a robust economy, the government could balance the trade-off between land sales and the provision of public housing for the masses. But the method became ineffective when the housing market ran out of control (Lee, 1999). The strong political lobby in recent years for the reinstatement of the government-run Home Ownership Scheme provides an example that illustrates the incompetence of government policies to effectively regulate cycles of rampant housing price inflation. It is now widely accepted that for a small open economy like Hong Kong, with strong institutional control and restrictions on land use, no government can effectively regulate price inflation given the monopolistic nature of the housing market and its inherent speculative tendency (Peng and Wheaton, 1994). To what extent can a government, so dependent on land revenues for public services, maximize financial returns on land without affecting its role as a protector of the public interest? Chris Patten, the last British Governor of Hong Kong, described this dilemma succinctly:

> A great deal of politics had been channelled into housing activities, and since elected politicians were responsible for so little, from left to right they tended to articulate tenant grievances rather than apply themselves to the fundamental causes of these problems. The construction of public housing has been regarded as a substitute for, or as an alternative to, the introduction of democratic politics. (Patten, 1998, p. 52)

I have also argued elsewhere that the degree of financialization of the real estate sector in a post-Fordist regime like Hong Kong might produce a positive income-stabilizing effect; nevertheless, such causality still demands greater empirical proof to be conclusive (Smart and Lee, 2003).

Home Ownership, Asset Building and Economic Crisis

Home ownership among Hong Kong households enjoys unquestioned popularity. While the overall number of public rental housing units has been increasing over the years, in relative terms and as a percentage of the tenure structure it has been slowly decreasing since the 2000s, from a high of 45 per cent in the 1980s to 30 per cent in 2015 (Housing Authority, Hong Kong, 2015). This could not have been achieved without deliberate effort on the part of the government, with the purpose of controlling expansion as well as to stimulate the growth of home ownership (Lee, 2003). The government recognized the policy potential of asset building as well as the necessity to cater for aspiring young families who wanted to move up the housing ladder when their income and family life cycle positions had shifted. At the same time, the government also began to consider public sector reform for the housing sector in the early 1980s, when the issue of efficiency in public rental housing production became a major problem of the then Housing Authority (Lee, 1999). The ethos in the entire 1980s and early 1990s was that government needed to roll back its involvement in housing and leave things to the market (Cheung, 2005). From 1976 to 2000, the government-backed HOS had steadily expanded to reach 13 per cent of the total housing stock. At the turn of the new century, the home ownership policy was seen as providing a ray of hope for aspiring young families who could not otherwise afford to buy from the market. However, although government policy had a vision to increase home ownership and had found asset building a desirable policy to pursue since the 1990s, market extremities and monopolistic competition again demonstrated the ineffectiveness of public policy to regulate the housing market. In fact, it had already been demonstrated by a Berkeley study of the relationship between real estate and economic crisis that a free market approach to housing contributed significantly to the onset of the 1997 Asian Financial Crisis (Quigley, 2001).

The Politics of Housing Policy

Housing market performance in Hong Kong has always been regarded as the main pivot of the economy. Stock market performances have always been closely related to house price movement, as major blue-chip stocks in the Hang Seng Index are linked to the real estate companies (Newell and Chau, 1996). Despite strong efforts to increase public housing production during the last decade of colonial rule (1987–1997), the government admitted that it had failed to stabilize the housing market. The political economy of housing was structured in such a way that there was only a limited role the government could play. In his memoir, former colonial Governor Patten admitted that the government's greatest failing rested in housing policy:

> our ability to apply the radical free market solutions that were required was limited by proximity to the transition. Any convincing attack on the monopoly effectively enjoyed by a few extremely rich property developers in Hong Kong, making grotesquely large profits, could have had a serious effect on market confidence at a sensitive time. (Patten, 1998, p. 51)

House prices fluctuate tremendously as developers seek to manipulate the market and housing consumption. Extreme price movements also reflect periods of socio-political instability. From 1996 to 2010, at least three historical periods could be cited. The first is the period during the political transition from early 1996 to October 1997, when home buyers and speculators anticipated rapid economic growth after the change of sovereignty. The second period spanned from the 2001 global technology stock market crash to the 2003 severe acute respiratory syndrome (SARS) epidemic, which culminated in the famous 1 July March for Democracy when 0.5 million citizens took to the street to protest against the first SAR Administration (Sing, 2003). It is interesting to note that in subsequent large-scale social protests in 2004 and 2005, the focus was all about house price inflation. Moreover, popular public accusations pointed to possible collusion of interests between the government and the major real estate developers (Zhao and Kao, 2016). Political pressures were escalating, as most political parties demanded that the government reinstate the Home Ownership Scheme that was terminated in 2003. The key political question is: should the government assist citizens to attain home ownership if the housing market continues to fail?

ASSET BUILDING WITH SOCIAL JUSTICE

To avoid the pitfall that Hong Kong faces, Singapore has taken a long-term social planning approach on housing since the 1960s. Realizing the vulnerability of any small open economy to speculative activities in the real estate sector, Singapore chose a drastically different policy direction from Hong Kong since independence. In order to forestall the gradual concentration of capital in the housing market, the state decided to monopolize housing production, and sees it as a primary social good with the state having exclusive responsibility. This does not mean the adoption of a central planning approach: housing is still considered primarily a commodity, but with the exchange process controlled by the state. The consequence is to thwart the inevitable advancement of neoliberal urbanism and its eventual domination in the accumulation process. Indeed, Singapore has achieved a comparatively lower level of social inequalities. In 2014, Singapore's Gini coefficient was 0.46. However, incorporating a high level of social policy transfers, the Ministry of Finance's estimate in 2015 suggested a lower rate of 0.37, evidence to demonstrate that asset building has a real effect in reducing social inequalities (Singapore Ministry of Finance, 2015). Lee Kuan Yew (2000, p. 94) said in his memoir:

> We believe in socialism, in fair shares for all ... because people are unequal in their abilities, if performance and rewards are determined by the market, there will be a few big winners, many medium winners, and a considerable number of losers ... A competitive, winner-takes-all society, like (colonial) Hong Kong in the 1960s, would not be acceptable in Singapore.

It is important to note, in the design of Singapore's social system, that Lee's vision of social justice has been carefully built in. It is a form of visionary social engineering. The decision to take a monopolizing role in housing provision at the beginning reflects a design to steer the market in such a way that it will not compromise social justice with growth, even if it means constraining capitalist initiatives in real estate development. The marginal revenue of investment in housing is thus amassed through a socially organized institution, making sure that capital gains go to individual households rather than into the pockets of developers. In this way, Singapore has adopted a cardinal principle of social welfare raised by Sherraden (1991, p. 53) in *Assets and the Poor*: "there is a pervasive assumption ... that level of household income and consumption constitutes an adequate definition of welfare. This assumption overlooks household welfare as a long term dynamic process rather than simply an amount of goods and services consumed".

This chapter has attempted to explain one successful and one failed case of East Asian welfare developmentalism (Midgley and Tang, 2009). The central argument is to demonstrate that the social investment potential of housing policy through home ownership has been very much understudied. For Singapore, fair housing policy is realized through two levels of capital circulation operating under conditions of dynamic equilibrium, with policy adaptations monitored over a sufficiently long time span. The integration of economic and social policy is made first through the linking of housing and the Central Provident Fund within the social security system, and then through capital formation and the monopolization of mortgages by the housing authority. This impacts on the construction sector, the development sector (monopolized by the Housing Development Board) and the wider economy. This institutional arrangement has successfully broken down the traditional market–state dichotomy, and justifies why the state should have a unique role in some jurisdictions such as Singapore. State capacity is enhanced when the government produces what it promised: affordable housing, stable housing prices and secured future property value for old age. The uncertainty is of course how far this is sustainable, both in the wake of globalized risks in the real estate sector, and given the susceptibility of any housing market to shifting housing demand over time. To what extent could the Singapore housing system be immune from exogenous factors beyond state control? This is an empirical question that needs more probing. However, since the establishment of the housing institution in the 1960s, the Singapore system has survived five decades. Singapore housing is still affordable and forms a core wealth component of the entire population. To satisfy rising aspirations, however, public flats are now more stratified, to allow families to upgrade at least once as family size and aspiration increases. For Hong Kong, despite an equal emphasis on asset building, a free market housing policy has led to the creation of a fluctuating housing market with extreme housing affordability problems. In a social development context, while housing policy is integrated with economic development, the result is disastrous compared to Singapore.

For Singapore, one could of course easily challenge this housing and Central Provident Fund social investment configuration, and argue that it is merely operating one big savings bank with rules and restrictions on withdrawal and consumption that is nothing near to a conventional social security system. In neo-classical economics, one might even argue that such arrangements could be detrimental to the general level of social welfare as consumption is orchestrated by the state, thus thwarting individual choice and freedom in the creative use of income. However, two important theoretical implications could arise. The first concerns adopting an asset-based approach in social policy. Housing is primarily geared towards the building up of lifelong assets, almost to the extent of sidelining its residential use. The second concerns the adoption of a lifelong wealth management approach. The Central Provident Fund is a state-directed wealth management institution where every Singaporean abides by the law to trade off present consumption for future consumption. Two issues are raised. One is about whether guided consumption in the form of the provident fund could lead to inefficiency. The other is an ethical issue concerning whether the state has the right to assume a paternal role in advising how people consume over their lifetime. These are both salient points that students of East Asian social welfare should further explore. However, the Singapore housing system does achieve a much wider dispersal of property ownership, with a resultant fairer distribution of assets. This could never be achieved in Hong Kong where housing is left almost entirely to the free market, with consequential ineffectiveness in governance and severe income inequalities. By upholding Lee Kuan Yew's (2000) social democratic values – 'a fair but not welfare society' – Singapore is modelling herself on Nordic welfare states, but with a clever twist of orientalism: substituting social security with the Central Provident Fund, where individual risk rather than pooled risk is emphasized.

In conclusion, perhaps Singapore has solved a problem posed by John Rawls in a 2001 restatement of his original *A Theory of Justice*. Rawls questions the usefulness of contemporary welfare state capitalism to be able to satisfy the requirements of the Difference Principle, where a very unequal concentration of assets are permitted to be left in only a few hands under very restrictive conditions. Although welfare provisions may be generous and guarantee a decent social minimum in contemporary welfare state capitalism, a principle of reciprocity to regulate economic and social inequalities is not present or recognized. Since societies and economies continue to be troubled by the absence of fairness, social division and unrest deepen and slowly destabilize both local and global systems. The case of Hong Kong aptly reflects Rawls's concern. However, the comfort one finds in Singapore's success in housing policy does raise some hope for governments aiming at reaping the real benefits of social investment.

REFERENCES

Agus, R., Doling, J. and Lee, D. (eds) (2002). *Housing Systems in South and East Asia*. Basingstoke: Palgrave Macmillan.

Asher, M.G. (1995). Compulsory Savings in Singapore: An Alternative to the Welfare State. NCPA Policy Report No. 198, September.

Belsky, E. (2010). Housing Wealth Effects and Course of the US Economy: Theory, Evidence, and Policy Implications. In S. Smith (ed.), *Blackwell Companion to the Economics of Housing*. London: Wiley, pp. 82–95.

Cantillon, B. (2011). The Paradox of the Social Investment State: Growth, Unemployment and Poverty in the Lisbon Era. *Journal of European Social Policy*, 21 (5), 432–449.

Cheung, A. (2005). Hong Kong's Post 1997 Institutional Crisis: Problems of Governance and Institutional Stability. *Journal of East Asian Studies*, 5 (1), 135–167.

Chua, B. (1997). *Political Legitimacy and Housing: Stakeholding in Singapore*. London: Routledge.

Consumer Council (1996). *How Competitive is Hong Kong's Residential Housing Market?*. Hong Kong: Consumer Council.

Demographia (2016). International Housing Affordability Survey 2016. Retrieved from www.demographia.com.

Doling, J.Y. and Ronald, R. (2010). Home Ownership and Asset-based Welfare. *Journal of Housing and the Built Environment*, 25 (2), 165–173.

Forrest, R. and Lee, J. (2003). *Housing and Social Change: East West Perspectives*. London: Routledge.

Haila, A. (2000). Real Estate in Global Cities: Singapore and Hong Kong as Property States. *Urban Studies*, 23 (6), 2241–2256.

Haila, A. (2015). *Urban Land Rent: Singapore as a Property State*. Chichester: Blackwell.

Hong Kong Housing Authority (2002). A Statement on Housing Policy by Hon. M. Suen, Secretary for Housing, Planning and Lands. Retrieved from http://www.cityu.edu.hk/hkhousing/pdoc/press20021113e.pdf.

Hong Kong Housing Authority (2015). *Housing in Figures 2015*. Retrieved from www.housingauthority.gov.hk.

Jones, C. (1990). Hong Kong, Singapore, South Korea, and Taiwan: Oikonomic Welfare State, *Government and Opposition*, 25 (4), 446–462.

Kaseke, E., Midgley, J. and Piachaud, D. (2011). The British Influence on Social Security Policy: Provident Funds in Asia and Africa. In J. Midgley and D. Piachaud (eds), *Colonialism and Welfare: Social Policy and the British Imperial Legacy*. Cheltenham, UK and Northampton, MA, USA: Edward Elgar Publishing, pp. 144–159.

Lee, J. (1999). *Home Ownership and Social Change in Hong Kong*. Aldershot: Ashgate.

Lee, J. (2003). Home Ownership Scheme and its Continuing Needs. In Y.M. Yeung and K.Y. Wong (eds), *Fifty Years of Public Housing in Hong Kong: A Golden Jubilee Review and Appraisal*. Hong Kong: Chinese University of Hong Kong Press, pp. 259–282.

Lee, K.Y. (2000). *From Third World to First: The Singapore Story: 1965–2000*. New York: Harper Collins.

Midgley, J. (2008). Social Security and the Economy: Key Perspectives. In J. Midgley and K.L. Tang (eds), *Social Security, the Economy and Development*. New York: Palgrave Macmillan, pp. 51–84.

Midgley, J. and Tang, K. (2009). *Social Policy and Poverty in East Asia: The Role of Social Security*. London: Routledge.

Morel, N., Palier, B. and Palme, J. (eds) (2011). *Towards a Social Investment Welfare State*. Bristol: Policy Press.

Newell, G. and Chau, K. (1996). Linkages between direct and indirect property performance in Hong Kong. *Journal of Property Finance*, 7 (4), 9–29.

Papadimitriou, D., Hannsgen, G. and Zezza, G. (2007). The Effect of a Declining Housing Market on the US Economy. Levy Economic Institute Working Paper 506, 11 July.

Patten, C. (1998). *East and West: The Colonial Governor of Hong Kong on Power, Freedom, and the Future*. London: Macmillan.

Peng, R. and Wheaton, W. (1994). Effects of Restrictive Land Supply on Housing in Hong Kong: An Econometric Analysis. *Journal of Housing Research*, 5 (2), 263–278.

Picketty, T. and Zucman, G. (2014). Capital is Back: Wealth Income Ratios in Rich Countries 1700–2010. *Quarterly Journal of Economics*, 129 (3), 1255–1311.

Quigley, J. (2001). Real Estate and the Asian Crisis. *Journal of Housing Economics*, 10 (2), 129–161.

Rawls, J. (2001). *Justice as Fairness: A Restatement*. Cambridge, MA: Harvard University Press.

Sherraden, M. (1991). *Assets and the Poor: A New America Welfare Policy*. Armonk, NY: ME Sharpe.

Sherraden, M., Nair, S., Vasoo, S., Liang, N.T. and Sherraden, M.S. (1995). Social Policy Based on Assets: The Impact of Singapore's CPF. *Asian Journal of Political Science*, 3 (2), 112–33.

Sing, M. (ed.) (2003). *Politics and Government in Hong Kong: Crisis under Chinese Sovereignty*. London: Routledge.

Singapore Ministry of Finance (2015). Income Growth, Inequality and Mobility Trends in Singapore. MOF Occasional Paper, August.

Smart, A. and Lee, J. (2003). Financialization and the Role of Real Estate in Hong Kong's Regime of Accumulation. *Economic Geography*, 79 (2), 153–171.

Titmuss, R. (1974). *Social Policy: An Introduction*. London: Allen & Unwin.

Tse, R. (1998). Housing Price, Land Supply and Revenue from Land Sales. *Urban Studies*, 35 (8), 1377–1392.

Vandenbroucke, F. and Vleminckx, K. (2011). Disappointing Poverty Trends: Is the Social Investment State to Blame?. *Journal of European Social Policy*, 21 (5), 450–471.

Wilding, P. and Mok, K. (1997). Hong Kong Social Policy Under Conditions of Full Employment. In P. Wilding, A. Huque and J. Tao (eds), *Social Policy in Hong Kong*. Cheltenham, UK and Northampton, MA, USA: Edward Elgar Publishing, pp. 145–166.

Zhao, S. and Kao, E. (16 September 2016). Hong Kong Government Will Look into Reviewing Private Consultations on Housing Projects, *South China Morning Post*.

4. Social investments and poor families in India: the role of early childhood and employment programmes

Sony Pellissery

In the literature on social policy in developing countries, a distinction is sometimes made between 'productivist' and 'protective' welfare states (Rudra, 2007; Haggard and Kaufman, 2008). This distinction indicates the orientation of policies in a dual economy. Apart from a small section of the labour force, the majority of the population (around 92 per cent in the case of India) gain their livelihood from the informal economy. In the formal sector, social policy interventions are similar to those in many Organisation for Economic Co-operation and Development (OECD) countries. On the other hand, a unique set of social policy instruments unheard of in OECD countries exist for the people in the informal economy (Pellissery, 2013). In protective welfare regimes, the focus is to limit commodification, while productivist regimes encourage commodification. This line of inquiry, and the lens which is used to view the Global South, is influenced by the developments in OECD countries, where commodification was central to the process of welfare state creation (Polanyi, 1944; Esping-Andersen, 1990). The aim of this chapter is to develop a framework to understand the origin of social investment through indigenous approaches and models as a response to socio-economic problems that existed in the Global South, particularly with reference to India.

The discipline of development economics has had considerable influence on policies in the Global South. In developing countries, social investment has been given increasing attention in recent years (Midgley, 2014). However, interventions in the form of social investment policies have existed since the 1960s in the countries of the Global South such as India. This chapter aims to illustrate the context within which social investment approaches were adopted in India. It first gives a historical context for the origin of social investment expenditures in India by locating different development models in the country since independence. The next section provides a brief overview on social investment expenditures and the types of intervention. The chapter then deals with early childhood programme and employment programme, to argue the exact nature of social investment policies. The chapter concludes with a discussion of development and social investment in India.

THE ORIGINS OF DEVELOPMENTAL MODELS IN INDIA

Three distinct development models and interventions existed in early independent India. Their origins can be traced to the ideological leanings of three social reformers and policy-makers of the nascent nation in the late 1940s. First, Mahatma Gandhi, icon of the Indian independence struggle, who emphasized the illness of markets and, therefore, the need to have development based on local resources. His concept of *swaraj* (literally meaning 'self-rule') was an ideal combination of political freedom by giving power to the people, and economic freedom through individual emancipation, particularly the poorest of the poor. Second, Jawaharlal Nehru, first Prime Minister of the country, was hugely influenced by the Soviet planning models as well as capitalist advancements in Western Europe. He emphasized a developmental model that could combine both these approaches. His ideas of national development through industrialization and the public sector came into direct conflict with Gandhi's ideas of development based on local resources. A third development model was propounded by B.R. Ambedkar, chairman of the drafting committee of the Indian Constitution, who emphasized a social justice model for development. Coming from the historically excluded community of lower castes, he emphasized how social democracy may not be feasible without participation of the masses through 'annihilation of the caste'. In the 'transformative constitution' of India (Baxi, 2013), Ambedkar emphasized the realization of social rights prior to economic rights. Positive action from the state was required to achieve this, and the Indian Constitution came to be known for positive liberty (the capacity for acting according to one's will) rather than negative liberty (protection from obstacles and restraints on action) (Nussbaum, 2006).

These development models were not compatible with each other, although there were important overlaps. Therefore, when national planning was taking place to achieve welfare objectives, this ideological chasm prevented the reaching of consensus. In this context, an ideology-neutral Planning Commission was set up (Guha, 2008) to reconcile these extremely diverging development models. The Planning Commission (primarily comprised of economists) was mandated to come up with a blueprint for development through five-year plans. The plans were to be discussed and vetted in the National Development Council, comprised of chief ministers and elected representatives. Thus, a middle way to strike a balance between technocrats and politicians was found.

Among development economists, some scholars have given serious consideration to the fundamental differences between economies in the Global South and North. These theorists agree on the fact that stagnation is caused by the poverty trap: limited capital availability, unskilled labour which is underutilized, primitive technology for production, and low per capita income are the main obstacles to progress. Different theorists differ on the solutions to this situation (Rao, 1952; Nurkse, 1953; Mirrlees, 1975). Michal Kalecki (1976) is the most noted scholar among these theorists, for a definitive answer to the question of differences between the Global South and North. His view is summarized below:

> The crucial problem facing the underdeveloped countries is thus to increase investment considerably, not for the sake of generating effective demand, as was the case in an underemployed developed economy, but for the sake of accelerating the expansion of productive capacity indispensable for the rapid growth of national income. (Kalecki, 1976, p. 23)

"Unlike the Western countries, the issue of low productivity was related to the social structure and the attitudes supported by that structure, the widespread existence of absentee land ownership and tenancy being of particular importance" (Myrdal, 1968, p. 1546). This meant that investment in technology or education alone would not increase productivity without institutional reforms. To substantiate this, elsewhere I have elaborated how land ownership defined poverty in South Asia (Pellissery, 2016), and how caste functions as a social structure of discrimination (Pellissery, 2015).

Development as a concept and practice influenced policies and interventions to achieve the welfare objectives in many post-colonial nation-states, including India. Developmental praxis aims to reorganize the economic and social system to enhance the quality of life and to expand the choices for individuals and households (Sen, 1999). The history of developmental thought informs us that at different epochs different focuses gained momentum. In the early period, development was purely seen as modernization. Later, it was assumed to be economic growth, to be attained through stages of growth and balanced growth. Eventually, the basic needs approach shifted from being commodity-oriented to being human development-oriented. In more recent times, intergenerational approaches through sustainability have gained momentum (see Thorbecke, 2006 for a summary of this history). Despite these different focuses in orientation, the unity of the social, economic and political to achieve development was recognized throughout.

It is in light of this developmental approach that programmes and interventions need to be assessed. Immediately after the independence of India in 1947, the inadequacy of savings for the growth of investment was realized. As a newly independent state, the investable income had to be generated by increasing the consumption level (which was abysmally low) by raising the standard of living of the vast majority of poor people. Agricultural development and substantial increase of food production was the key strategy for this (Mozoomdar, 1996). The approach adopted to achieve it was community development. Under this approach, village government (typically with a population size of 2500) was the key unit of reference. Community development was the arena where social, economic and political met: policy was not separated into 'social policy' and 'economic policy'. This trend of focusing on the people's institutions through community development manoeuvred the growth of the strong institution, and subsequently defined the priorities for growth and progress. This culminated in the Constitutional amendment in 1992 whereby the village republics (*Panchayat Raj*) were bestowed with financial and political autonomy. Most often, village republics have focused on productivist investments such as facilitating business entrepreneurship for the poorest groups (the *Kudumbashree* model in the state of Kerala is an excellent example of self-help groups of women working with the village government to produce and market commodities by drawing capital from banks), ensuring accountability by monitoring the programmes of education and employment. For instance, in the case of education, the school monitoring committee could check teacher absenteeism. Similarly in public works programmes, social accountability evaluations are conducted by village governments.

In the next section, where the different social development and social investment programmes are examined, it is observed how community institutions are involved in each of them. This development of the capacity of the human resources to define and operationalize development programmes is a key method to make social change.

DEVELOPMENT PROGRAMMES AS SOCIAL INVESTMENT

India's development programmes were defined primarily through five-year plans. So far, 12 such plans have been rolled out in the country. Space limitations do not allow me to systematically look at the details of these plans here. I examine some flagship programmes of the Government of India in this section to examine how social investment received attention in these programmes. Towards the end of this section, I examine how community involvement, an aspect which was discussed in the previous section, was integral to each of these social investment programmes.

At the outset, it is important to recognize that the concept of 'social' has no universal understanding across nation-states. Kaufmann (2012) has pointed out how the German understanding of 'social' is distinct from the Anglo-Saxon tradition. In the Indian context, in different local languages of India, 'social' stands for community identities. However, in the context of this book when I refer to 'social investment' across different nation-states, there is very little space to emphasize this India-specific understanding of 'social'.

As an independent nation, one of the key concerns was to feed its citizens and avoid hunger. This is an important measure to avoid revolution and to stabilize a country. Yet, India has not achieved this objective even now. According to the International Food Policy Research Institute (2015), India currently ranks 55th among the 117 countries surveyed for the Global Hunger Index; 190 million people go hungry every day in India. Among the poor sections of society, 70 per cent of income is spent on food alone. These alarming figures are despite the fact that India produces sufficient grain for all of its people, and it is the biggest producer of milk in the world.

Food-importing policies of the 1950s gave way to what is known as the Green Revolution in the 1960s, based on bio-technological inventions. Three interlinked policies were introduced in the mid-1960s, consisting of: (1) output price policies, including minimum support prices for farmers when grain is procured; (2) input price subsidies; and (3) a public distribution system (PDS) to provide relatively low-cost food grains without harming the interests of the producers. This new agricultural strategy was largely successful in increasing production, which more than doubled from 63 million tons in 1965 to 154 million tons in 1991, and drastically reduced the need for food grain imports (Suryanarayana, 1995). What is important to note here is the integrated approach of food production and food distribution. Very often, social policy researchers looking for social sector expenditure have separated the public distribution system from the other two policies (the public distribution system consists of a network of more than 40 000 Fair Price Shops, and claims to distribute annually commodities worth more than INR15 000 crore to about 16 crore families, making it the largest distribution network of its type in the world). However, development economics viewed all three as being inseparable. From the social investment perspective, a much more integrated approach to food policies is required. By increasing investment in roads and irrigation, food production and the supply chain would have been integrated. This would have made pulses and micronutrients (through vegetables) available for the masses, for the malnutrition crisis that India is facing. Note that the Government of India passed the National Food Security Act in 2013; however, an integrated approach of food production and distribution is missing from this new Act.

A second development intervention that deserves attention from the point of view of social investment is *Sarva Shiksha Abhiyan*. This is a programme aimed at the universalization of elementary education, in which the government guarantees free education up to the age of 14. This was later enacted as the Right to Education Act in 2006. It is a comprehensive programme in the sense that apart from providing quality education to the children, the principles of child care are also practiced, through the midday meal scheme. Children from poor families are often forced to skip schooling since their families force the children to undertake work to earn money. To avoid this problem, children are provided with a cooked meal in the school, so that when children attend school their nutritional needs are taken care of as well. Approximately 120 million children in more than 1 265 000 schools are served food every day. As part of the Right to Education Act, a range of social investment measures are undertaken, such as ensuring the quality of education through standard infrastructure such as toilets, playgrounds, uniforms, school books, and so on. Local communities form school committees to monitor various quality aspects of the programme.

A third important development intervention worth mentioning is the National Rural Health Mission (NRHM). The NRHM, which was launched in 2005, adopts a synergistic approach covering vital determinants of health such as nutrition, sanitation, hygiene and safe drinking water. Its major goals are to reduce infant and maternal mortality rates, and the prevention of communicable and non-communicable diseases. An innovative cash transfer programme that is being implemented as part of the rural health scheme is providing cash incentives (for the first two live births) to women who undergo institutional delivery. This has significantly reduced maternal and neonatal mortality.

All three of these investments – for ensuring food security, for education and for health care – are important and huge investments in human capital. Different states in India performed differently in this regard. States such as Kerala, which made substantial investments, have been rated as comparable to those of European welfare states, and as surpassing the achievements in China (Dreze and Sen, 1995). In a country like India, where the mean age of the population is 28 years, interventions to improve human capital are critical to reap the benefits of demographic dividends.

Apart from these, a number of development programmes are also designed and implemented at the level of both central government and state governments. Some of the examples are dry land development programmes, providing access to electricity in rural areas, watershed development programmes, and financial assistance to construct houses, among many others. What is important to note is that most of these programmes are being administered by the Rural Development Ministry, and thus the development focus brings a strong social investment perspective.

Having given an overview of various development interventions, the rest of the chapter focuses on two programmes which demonstrate how the social investment approach was at the heart of the development interventions in India. These two programmes are the early childhood programme and an employment guarantee programme.

THE CASE OF THE EARLY CHILDHOOD PROGRAMME

In the most populated Indian state of Uttar Pradesh, infants dying before reaching their first birthday, in rural areas, are 74 per 1000 births compared to 54 in urban areas (AHS, 2011). For India as a whole, infant morality was reduced from 57 deaths in the first year in 2006 to 50 per 1000 live births in 2009. What is important to recognize is that with adequate care and protection, the scenario can be changed. Logit regression models (see Radhakrishna and Ravi, 2004) have noted that apart from the attributes of the mother such as education and nutritional status, antenatal visits significantly reduce the chances of child mortality. In rural India, 28 per cent of women received no antenatal care, compared to urban areas where this was 9 per cent (International Institute for Population Sciences, 2005–2006).

It is in this context that the importance of the Integrated Child Development Scheme (ICDS) can be understood, which is the subject matter of this section. The scheme was inaugurated in 1975 as a nodal department under the Ministry of Women and Child Development, tasked with the promotion of the well-being of pregnant women, nursing mothers, adolescent girls and children below the age of six (MWCD, 2013). Locally, this is known as the *Anganwadi* programme. The word '*Anganwadi*' is derived from the Hindi word '*angan*', which means courtyard or play centre, and represents a child care centre located within the village, which acts as a focal point for the delivery of services at the community level, as well as a meeting place for women's groups and other frontline workers to promote awareness and joint action for child development and women's empowerment. One female *Anganwadi* worker is allocated for a population of 1000 beneficiaries, and acts as a bridge between the community and the organized health care and educational sector.

Currently, approximately 1 299 000 *Anganwadi* workers are working in about 1 342 000 *Anganwadi* centres spread across the country. The Integrated Child Development Scheme covers about 89.3 million children and pregnant and lactating mothers. Until the year 2008–2009, the entire administrative cost under the scheme was met by the central government, but as per revised guidelines, the share is now 75 per cent for the Government of India and 25 per cent for the regional state governments. The scheme was instituted in order to take a holistic view of the child's development. The Ministry of Women and Child Development (2009) outlined the following as objectives of the scheme: to improve the nutritional and health status of children in the age group 0–6 years; to lay the foundations for proper psychological, physical and social development of the child; to reduce the incidence of mortality, malnutrition and school dropout; to achieve coordinated policy and its implementation amongst the various departments to promote child development; and to enhance the capability of the mother to look after the normal health and nutritional needs of the child through proper nutrition and health education. This integrated vision is a hallmark of the social investment approach.

Children under the age of six years in India number more than 110 million. This huge absolute number means that India holds the largest population of malnourished children in the world, leading to high mortality and a myriad of other problems such as lack of hygiene, disease and lack of education. In India, 43 per cent of children below five years of age are underweight and malnourished, thus their risk of dying is increased. It is in this context that the Indian government's early childhood programme has to be appreciated. The scheme is one of the largest child care programmes in the world, offering a package of six services, namely: supplementary nutrition, nutrition and health education, preschool non-formal education, immunization, health check-ups, and referral services (MWCD, 2013). This therefore helps to break the cycle of child mortality, morbidity, malnutrition, reduced learning capacity, school dropout and other related issues. The philosophy and approach behind the scheme was based on the consideration that the overall impact would be greater if different services were delivered in an integrated manner, since the efficacy of a particular service depends on the support that it receives from related services.

The Integrated Child Development Scheme espouses the principles of early childhood care and development, a cardinal element in the holistic development of children. As argued by Dreze (2006), the first six years of childhood have a decisive and lasting influence on a child's health, well-being, aptitude and opportunities. This is what the World Bank (2004) refers to as the 'Barker Hypothesis', the theory that conditions in utero have a long-term impact on a child's life chances: "For, up to a point, consumption is investment in personal productive capacity. This is especially important in connection with children: to reduce unduly expenditure on their consumption may greatly lower their efficiency in after-life" (Pigou, 1928, p. 29). See a restatement of this idea in Morel et al. (2012), and in Chapter 2 of this book.

In Tanzania, for instance, children who were born to mothers who received the right amounts of iodine during pregnancy, due to a government intervention of supplying iodine capsules to pregnant women, stayed longer in school and their productivity increased later in life compared to their siblings whose mothers did not take the capsules when they were in utero (Banerjee and Duflo, 2011). In contexts where informal labour and social security measures are limited, there are greater chances for poor women to neglect their own health and that of their children to gain access to livelihood opportunities. Such decisions (foregoing long-run benefits for short-term gains) are made in households as poor coping strategies, in the context of uninsured risks and stark vulnerability limiting their choices. Therefore, care for pregnant women and young children serves as protective as well as productive support.

Banerjee and Duflo (2011) argue that although micronutrients are cheap, it is important to know exactly what to eat, but not everyone has that information. It is this information assymmetry, which is so chronic in professionalized services such as health and education, that compels state intervention in the provision of services (Batley and Mcloughlin, 2015). In such contexts, providing the services directly by the state could be extremely effective. The Integrated Child Development Scheme has three components, namely: the nutrition, health and early childhood care, and preschool education components.

The nutrition component comprises supplementary feeding, which is not meant to substitute but to promote timely and appropriate complementary feeding at home, and aims at benefiting pregnant women, lactating mothers (only up to six months, during which period there are increased food requirements as they are supposed to exclusively breast-feed their babies), children from six months to six years, and adolescent girls. It also comprises nutritional health education, growth monitoring and promotion where mothers are counselled on the importance of good nutrition during pregnancy, lactation and early childhood as well as proper child care and feeding practices; and prophylaxis against Vitamin A deficiency and control of nutritional anaemia, by directly administering Vitamin A to children aged nine months to five years, and iron tablets to pregnant women, adolescent girls and children with anaemia, respectively.

The health component encompasses health check-ups, immunization and referral services. Children have their weight taken and recorded and their health checked regularly by medical staff, who also diagnose minor ailments and treat them, as well as monitor the health of adolescent girls and pregnant women (both antenatal and postnatal). It also encompasses immunization of pregnant women and adolescent girls against tetanus, and children against six preventable diseases: poliomyelitis, tuberculosis, diphtheria, tetanus, pertussis and measles, which are major causes of child mortality, disability, morbidity and related malnutrition. Referral services are provided when, during health check-ups and growth monitoring, sick, malnourished or disabled children needing prompt medical attention are identified.

The early childhood care and preschool education component is seen as the backbone of the Integrated Child Development Scheme, as children aged 3–6 years converge at the *Anganwadi* centres for preschool non-formal education aimed at providing a learning environment for the promotion of social, emotional, cognitive and physical development of the child. This promotes universalization of primary education by providing children with necessary preparation for primary school, and offering substitute care for younger siblings, thus freeing the older ones, especially girls, as well as allowing mothers to go out and work without worrying about who should baby-sit their younger children.

The Integrated Child Development Scheme has an inbuilt convergence feature, which provides a platform for better governance and delivery of services in the *Anganwadi* centres. The *Anganwadi* worker and her assistant are the basic functionaries of the scheme, who run the centres all over the country in collaboration with the health, education, rural development and other departments. A typical centre provides primary health care and nutritional supplementation for poor and low-caste children and women in Indian villages. The Integrated Child Development Scheme depends on community intervention for its efficacy.

Anganwadi workers are recruited from the villages in which they serve, to garner local support, and one major component of local participation is that the space for the *Anganwadi* centre is provided by the community. Since the worker hails from the community where she works, it is assumed she is better placed to know and understand the problems being faced by her community, and is well versed in the ways of her village, knows most people by their names, and interacts with them on a regular basis. Hence, like a community health worker, she is a very useful link between the community and relevant government departments.

Child care services incorporate a pivotal part of social investment, stressing that investment in the education and health of young children yields returns and ensures that the needs of children are met not just in the present but also in the future. Early child development programmes help to combat the detrimental effects of poverty on development. This, according to Radhakrishna and Ravi (2004), means that by the time children reach primary school age, they will be more able to participate and succeed, and that they will reach adolescence with the intellectual, physical, social and emotional foundations necessary to become responsible citizens. Midgley and Tang (2001) argue that human capital investments are not only needed in children in general, but particularly among children of the poor who grow up with deficits that seriously impede their life chances. Needless to say, preschool programmes that raise nutritional standards, improve health conditions, inculcate beginning educational skills and foster positive social change among young children, should be actively promoted.

Boosting resources in one area, say better nutrition, can lead to improvements in another, for instance education. Interventions that help children and families to create a network of social connections and build human capital may result in a number of secondary benefits, including the promotion of positive parenting behaviours and increased participation in children's schooling (Conley, 2009). Due to poverty, some families may have limited resources to invest in improving their children's life chances (Sen, 1999), hence the welfare approach to child care needs to be reconceptualized as an investment strategy and expanded to serve more disadvantaged children (Conley, 2009). This is because children who are provided with high-quality care and education grow into adults with practical skills that enable economic participation, and emotional intelligence that allows for the development of relationships, trust and reciprocity.

THE CASE OF THE EMPLOYMENT GUARANTEE PROGRAMME

The Indian economy is a typical case of an underemployed labour market. It has a huge unskilled young population. By 2020, the median age of the Indian population will be 29 years. Demographic transition per se does not guarantee a demographic dividend. Currently, the supply of skilled manpower in India is approximately 3.4 million. According to the International Labour Organization (ILO), there will be a demand for 500 million skilled workers in India by 2022. This gap warns against the redundancy of a dogmatic pursuit of skill development without parallel creation of jobs. It is fiscally inefficient and morally disenfranchising. The vast majority of the unskilled labour force restrict themselves to the less-mechanized agrarian sector. Hence the paradox of 60 per cent of the labour force being 'employed' in agriculture, while agriculture contributes only 15 per cent of gross domestic product (GDP). These uniquely different issues in the labour market call for different approaches than are adopted in Western welfare states, such as unemployment benefit programmes or activation programmes. A brief background to the uniqueness of the Indian labour market is essential to appreciate the National Rural Employment Guarantee Act (NREGA) as a social investment policy.

Most theorists on Indian rural labour (Bardhan and Rudra, 1981, 1986; Binswanger and Rosenzweig, 1984; Dreze and Mukherjee, 1987; Bhaduri, 1983; Walker and Ryan, 1990; Datt, 1996) have found it difficult to fit the complexity of Indian rural labour markets into the oft-used theoretical frameworks of labour markets, such as subsistence theories, efficiency wages, interlinked markets, and equilibrium with perfect competition (see Dreze and Mukherjee, 1987 for an overview of some of these difficulties). The reasons suggested for these difficulties have been summarized by Radhakrishna and Sharma (1998, p. 3) as follows:

> In view of the close linkage between land, labour and credit markets, labour market conditions of supply and demand alone cannot explain the process of determination of wages and income of rural labour. The concept of livelihood

or survival strategies adopted by rural labour has been found to be crucial in understanding the outcomes of labour arrangements.

These interlinked processes operate through non-market forces and the informal nature of employment contracts (Harriss-White, 2003; Kannan, 2004). It is in this wider context of power dynamics that state intervention through enactment of laws such as the Minimum Wages Act, 1948 and the Bonded Labour System (Abolition) Act, 1975 has failed to make an impact. Besides, the privatized agricultural land possession allows the existence of an informal labour market in the agriculture sector. In other words, labour continues to be a decommodified element, and welfare state interventions designed for the commodification process are far from realistic in the Indian context.

Nurkse's (1953) theoretical proposal that rural labour, which is found in surplus in developing countries, could be put to effective use for national development, is at the heart of the rationale for employment guarantee programmes. However, historically, it is the relief component, aimed at the enhancement of the population affected by natural disasters (for example, drought) that has been the chief motivating factor behind employment guarantees (Hirway and Terhal, 1994). In India, prior to the employment guarantee concept, public works programmes came into existence. The first nationwide public works programme in India was the Rural Works Programme in 1960. Since then a significant number of programmes, funded both by state and central governments, have been implemented in rural India (Hirway and Terhal, 1994). All these programmes had the twin goals of poverty alleviation and economic development. The western Indian state of Maharashtra was, in 1972, the first state to guarantee employment under public works, in response to a severe drought. Policy-makers visualized that by providing gainful employment to poorer people, they would create durable assets in rural areas, such as water harvesting tanks, which could avert water crisis in drought years. The uniqueness of this policy approach drew international attention; ultimately, employment guarantee schemes came to be seen as a model for best practice in the implementation of public works programmes. Following the Maharashtrian model, the Government of India initiated the countrywide National Rural Employment Guarantee Programme in 2005.

The challenge of securing employment is very great for casual labourers during lean agricultural seasons. The National Rural Employment Guarantee Programme is a response to this situation. Under the programme, able-bodied persons willing to do unskilled work are guaranteed manual labour, including manual earth-moving, shifting soil and breaking rocks, through a self-selection method. Workers contribute to the creation of durable assets such as percolation tanks, wells, minor irrigation projects, reforestation, rural roads, soil conservation and horti-cultural programmes. The programme is administered on a project basis. The project coordinators (the district collector) are required to prepare technical details of the projects, keeping in mind the principle of a wage expenditure to material expenditure ratio of 60:40, and to approve those projects cleared by government engineers. They lie in reserve until a time when the demand for work under the employment guarantee is generated from the village level. The work is provided within a 5 kilometre radius of the residence of the job seeker. Each household registered for the programme is entitled to 100 days of employment per year. Should the government fail to provide jobs for the registered houses, there is a provision to receive unemployment allowance.

The National Rural Employment Guarantee Programme was the first piece of national legislation to operationalize the Indian Constitution's directive policy regarding the 'right for work for all' (Article 41). Its impressive design and international reputation provided a reason for this scheme to be adopted as a model when a national programme was being designed. In September 2005, the Indian government passed legislation which enshrined a guarantee of 100 days of employment to any rural head of household within the nation, who is the holder of a 'job card' and willing to engage in manual labour. In February 2006, the National Rural Employment Guarantee Act which established the programme com-menced its five-year implementation trial plan in selected districts, which was incrementally expanded. So far, 157.18 crore person days of jobs have been created under the programme. Though it is similar to other employment guarantee schemes in various respects, one key difference is the power given to local governments through a decentralized implemen-tation of the programme.

DEVELOPMENT AND SOCIAL INVESTMENT IN INDIA

This chapter has demonstrated how different development programmes in India have over the years defined social, economic and political activities as being closely integrated. This interconnectedness of sectors is a key characteristic of social investment. As Midgley and Tang (2001) argue, a key counterfactual to developmental welfare is the disaggregation of the social and economic. Creating intersectoral mechanisms through central-ized planning, bringing social service agencies closely together within a unified development framework, is increasingly given priority. In India, a succession of national development plans have promoted this idea in seeking to introduce social programmes that are closely linked to economic development objectives. Indeed, some of these programmes such as the two discussed in this chapter make a positive contribution to the country's overall development efforts and can therefore be described as social investments. As discussed at the beginning of this chapter, planners and political leaders in India were initially committed to rapid economic growth, with social welfare being regarded as a separate but desirable area of policy-making that would address pressing social needs. Since then, however, social programmes have been much more closely integrated with the country's development efforts, resulting more recently in high priority being given to anti-poverty measures, nutrition, preschool education and other human capital interventions. Unlike the welfare state in Europe, where the 'social' is pitted against the 'economic', and where efforts to address the negative effects of markets characterize social policy, social policy in India has evolved in ways that foster a close integration between the economic and social. By adopting a broader interpretation and recognizing the twin elements of the political economy approach, which recognizes the importance of both social and economic interventions, social investments facilitate the pursuit of human aspirations, rather than addressing only social problems.

REFERENCES

Annual Health Survey (AHS) (2011). Census of India: Annual Health Survey 2011–12 Report. New Delhi: Government of India.

Banerjee, A.V. and Duflo, E. (2011). *Poor Economics: A Radical Rethinking of the Way to Fight Global Poverty.* New York: Public Affairs.

Bardhan, P.K. and Rudra, A. (1981). Terms and Conditions of Share-cropping Contracts: An Analysis of Village Survey data in India, *Journal of Development Studies*, 16 (3), 287–302.

Bardhan, P.K. and Rudra, A. (1986). Labour mobility and the boundaries of the village moral economy, *Journal of Peasant Studies*, 13 (2), 93–115.

Batley, R. and Mcloughlin, C. (2015). The Politics of Public Services: A Service Characteristics Approach, *World Development*, 74, 275–285.

Baxi, U. (2013). Preliminary Notes on Transformative Constitutionalism. In O. Vilhena, U. Baxi and H. Viljoen (eds), *Transformative Constitutionalism*. Pretoria: Pretoria University Law Press, pp. 19–48.

Bhaduri, A. (1983). *The Economic Structure of Backward Agriculture*. London: Academic Press.

Binswanger, H. and Rosenzweig, M.R. (1984). Contractual Arrangements, Employment and Wages in Rural Labour Markets: A Critical Review. In H. Binswanger and M.R. Rosenzweig (eds), *Contractual Arrangement,*

Employment and Wages in Rural Labour Markets in Asia. New Haven, CT, USA and London, UK: Yale University Press, pp. 1–40.

Conley, A. (2009). Childcare: Welfare or Investment?. *International Journal of Social Welfare*, 19 (2), 173–181.

Datt, G. (1996). *Bargaining Power, Wages and Employment: An Analysis of Agricultural Labour Markets in India*. Delhi: Sage Publications.

Dreze, J. (2006). Universalization with Quality: ICDS in a Rights Perspective. *Economic and Political Weekly*, 41 (34), 3706–3715.

Dreze, J. and Mukherjee, A. (1987). Labour Contracts in Rural India: Theories and Evidence. Development Research Programme, London School of Economics, No. 7.

Dreze, J. and Sen, A. (1995). *India: Economic Development and Social Opportunity*. Oxford: Oxford University Press.

Esping-Andersen, G. (1990). *Three Worlds of Welfare Capitalism*. Cambridge: Polity Press.

Guha, R. (2008). Autonomy and Ideology. *Economic and Political Weekly*, 2 February.

Haggard, S. and Kaufman, R. (2008). *Democracy, Development and Welfare States: Latin American, East Asia and Eastern Europe*. Princeton, NJ: Princeton University Press.

Harriss-White, B. (2003). *India Working: Essays on Society and Economy*. Cambridge: Cambridge University Press.

Hirway, I. and Terhal, P. (1994). *Towards Employment Guarantee in India: Indian and International Experiences in Rural Public Works Programmes*. Delhi: Sage Publications.

International Food Policy Research Institute (2015). *Global Hunger Index*. New York: IFPRI.

International Institute for Population Sciences (2005–2006). National Family Health Survey, India [NFHS-3]. Retrieved 15 March 2017 from http://rchiips.org/nfhs/nfhs3.shtml.

Kalecki, M. (1976). *Essays on Developing Economies*. Hassocks, UK: Harvester Press.

Kannan, K.P. (2004). Social Security, Poverty Reduction and Development: Arguments for Enlarging the Concept and Coverage of Social Security in a Globalizing World. ESS Paper No. 21 of ILO, Geneva.

Kaufmann, F. (2012). *European Foundations of Welfare State*. London: Bergham Books.

Midgley, J. (2014). *Social Development: Theory and Practice*. Los Angeles, CA: Sage.

Midgley, J. and Tang, K. (2001). Social Policy, Economic Growth and Developmental Welfare. *International Journal of Social Welfare*, 10, 244–252.

Ministry of Women and Child Development (2009). *Report on Malnutrition*. New Delhi: Government of India.

Mirrlees, J.A. (1975). Pure Theory of Underdeveloped Economies. *Agriculture in Development Theory*, 4, 84–108.

Morel, N., Palier, B. and Palme, J. (eds) (2012). Beyond the Welfare State as We Knew it?. In N. Morel, B. Palier and J. Palme (eds), *Towards a Social*

Investment Welfare State? Ideas, Policies and Challenges. Bristol: Policy Press, pp. 1–32.

Mozoomdar, A. (1996). The Rise and Decline of Development Planning in India. In Kuldeep Mathur (ed.), *Development Policy and Administration.* New Delhi: Sage Publications, pp. 41–84.

MWCD (2013). *Ministry of Women and Child Development 2012–2013 Annual Report.* New Delhi: Government of India.

Myrdal, G. (1968). *Asian Drama.* New Delhi: Kalyani Publishers.

Nurkse, R. (1953). *Problems of Capital Formation in Underdeveloped Countries.* New York: Oxford University Press.

Nussbaum, M.C. (2006). Poverty and Human Functioning: Capabilities are Fundamental Entitlements. In D.B. Grusky and R. Kanbur (eds), *Poverty and Inequality.* Stanford, CA: Stanford University Press, pp. 47–75.

Pellissery, S. (2013). The Informal Economy: Dilemmas and Policy Responses. In R. Walker and R. Surender (eds), *Social Policy in a Developing World.* Cheltenham, UK and Northampton, MA, USA: Edward Elgar Publishing, pp. 81–100.

Pellissery, S. (2015). Caste and Distributive Justice: Can Social Policies Address Durable Inequalities?. *Social Policy and Administration*, 49 (6), 785–800.

Pellissery, S. (2016). Land-alienation infused poverty in India. In G. Wright, E. Braathen, J. May and M. Ulriksen (eds), *Poverty and Inequality in Middle Income Countries.* London: Zed Books, pp. 201–222.

Pigou, A.C. (1928). *A Study in Public Finance.* London: Macmillan.

Polanyi, K. (1944). *The Great Transformation.* New York: Farrar & Rinehart.

Radhakrishna, R. and Ravi, C. (2004). Measurement of Changes in Economic Welfare in India: 1970–2001. *Journal of Quantitative Economics*, 2 (2), 55–75.

Radhakrishna, R. and Sharma, A.N. (1998). Introduction: Towards Empowering Rural Labour. In R. Radhakrishna and A.N. Sharma (eds), *Empowering Rural Labour in India: Market, State and Mobilisation.* Delhi: Institute of Human Development, pp. 1–20.

Rao, V.K.R.V. (1952). Investment, Income and the Multiplier in an Under-developed Economy. *Indian Economic Review*, 1, 55–67.

Rudra, N. (2007). Welfare States in Developing Countries: Unique of Universal. *Journal of Politics*, 69 (2), 378–396.

Sen, A. (1999). *Development as Freedom.* New York: Oxford University Press.

Suryanarayana, M. (1995). PDS: Beyond Implicit Subsidy and Urban Bias – the Indian Experience. *Food Policy*, 20 (4), 259–278.

Thorbecke, E. (2006). The Evolution of Developmental Doctrine: 1950–2005. UNU-WIDER Research Paper No. 2006/155.

Walker, T.S. and Ryan, J.G. (1990). *Village and Household Economies in India's Semi-arid Tropics.* Baltimore, MD, USA and London, UK: Johns Hopkins University Press.

World Bank (2004). *Making Services Work for the Poor.* World Development Report, Washington, DC: World Bank.

5. Employment policy and social investment in Norway

Espen Dahl and Thomas Lorentzen

The Nordic countries, Denmark, Finland, Norway and Sweden, are considered social investment states *par excellence* (Hemerijck, 2012). Examples that testify to this view are a large volume of active labour market programmes, accessible and affordable child care and preschools, policies to reconcile work and family life, comprehensive educational systems and emphasis on life-long learning (Dølvik et al., 2015; Morel et al., 2012; Morel et al., 2009). Advocates of the social investment paradigm argue that a 'new welfare architecture' is necessary to meet new social risks and challenges such as tertiarization of the economy, precarization of labour, globalization, professionalization, more vulnerable family forms and weaker social security nets (Esping-Andersen et al., 2002; Harsløf and Ulmestig, 2013; Morel et al., 2012).

Previous and updated comparative analyses of social investment profiles in labour market and social policies broadly confirm this portrait of Norway as a social investment nation (Dahl and Lorentzen, 2008; Schøyen, 2016). Since the financial crisis hit in 2007 many countries have experienced austerity policies and retrenchment in their welfare provisions (Hemerijck, 2012). The Norwegian economy was only mildly and transiently affected by the financial crisis. However, later drops in oil prices and an accompanying rise in unemployment may fertilize the soil for more austere policies, policies that may deviate from a social investment paradigm.

Against this background, the ambition of this chapter is to give an updated institutional account and analysis of labour market and related social policies over recent years in a Social Democratic country, Norway. We ask whether the latest reforms in labour market policies are still characterized by a social investment profile. We direct attention to changes that have taken place over the past ten years, since the period up to the mid-2000s is rather well covered (Dahl and Drøpping, 2001; Dahl and Lorentzen, 2008; Huo, 2009). More specifically, our aim is to discuss the goals of the reforms, their structure and content, and where possible their consequences, in particular for disadvantaged groups, as revealed by research evaluations. We are primarily interested in reforms that are intended to expand the labour market attachment of disadvantaged and vulnerable groups, since a significant rationale for recent policy changes has been the ambition to integrate these groups into the labour market, a broadening of the target population that Norway shares with other countries (Bonoli and Natali, 2012). This interest is also prompted by the fact that an important criticism directed towards social investment policies is that they are ineffective in reducing social inequalities and poverty (Cantillon, 2011). We see social investment as characteristics of policies and public programmes rather than characteristics of welfare states or entire welfare regimes.

Given these delineations, we examine recent reforms in the following three policy areas: (1) the tripartite collaboration to form an inclusive working life; (2) new legislation regarding regulation and protection of labour; and (3) reforms in the welfare system, including a massive merger of work and welfare organizations, unification of benefits, and the introduction of a new programme targeted at the hard-to-serve.

WHAT DO WE MEAN BY SOCIAL INVESTMENT POLICIES?

Key features of the notion of social investment are discussed in Chapter 1 of this volume. Here, we will briefly define the elements in what is often dubbed a social democratic version of the social investment paradigm, since we are dealing with a welfare state of a social democratic type. More important is that the characterizing traits that we define seem to be necessary ingredients of successful social investment policies (Cantillon, 2011; Esping-Andersen et al., 2002; Morel et al., 2012; Vandenbroucke and Vleminckx, 2011). As mentioned a new trend in active labour market policies (ALMP), in particular in social democratic countries, is that increasingly they are designed to reach out also to disadvantaged groups such as immigrants, the unskilled, disabled and chronically ill, youth with behavioural problems, high school drop-outs, and the elderly with reduced work capacity (Huo, 2009). Participation in the labour market is seen as the key to better individual living conditions, health and well-being, and to economic growth and societal progress. Accordingly, the role of public policy is to furnish people with resources that enable them to cope with the challenges posed by brute market forces and to provide the incentives to encourage them to do so. Here, a diversity of active labour market programmes of a human capital development type play an important role (Huo, 2009). Social investments are oriented towards future individual and collective benefits rather than towards present consumption, for example, generous cash benefits. Yet, the idea is that well-designed cash benefits may be productive, and are a precondition for a successful social investment strategy (Esping-Andersen et al., 2002; Midgley, 1999; Morel et al., 2012). Equality of opportunity is as important for social democrats as it is for liberals, but it is not sufficient. One cannot ignore the existing and increasing inequalities in outcome, for example income, as the older generation's (in)equality of outcomes lays the ground for the younger generation's (in)equality of opportunity. The two are actually inseparable (Therborn, 2013). Furthermore, as Morel et al. (2012) argue, equality also applies to equality between the genders, ethnic groups, and in access to goods and services of high quality, and that in order to be successful, social investment must come as a policy package integrating investment and protection measures, adopting a life course approach and a universal scope. Since the 'Golden Age' of social democracy and the subsequent emergence of structural unemployment, social democrats have also been preoccupied with supply-side challenges in the labour market. However, in some accounts they also bring in demand-side issues such as the need for investing in decent working conditions (Esping-Andersen et al., 2002).

We will use these conceptual tools to appraise the reforms in labour market policy and relevant social policy over the past ten years. Our assessment will be based on central policy documents, scholarly policy analyses, research-based evaluations of reforms and programmes, and national and international statistics. First, we will give a short account of some essential traits of the Norwegian society to establish a context for the more detailed analysis that follows.

THE NORWEGIAN 'MODEL'

Norway is a member of the social democratic welfare regime type. Some key institutional features are an open and export-oriented economy, cooperation between the social partners, a collective and centralized wage bargaining system, comprehensive and rather generous social protection, and an emphasis on social services (Dølvik et al., 2015). Gross domestic product (GDP) per capita is very high in international comparisons (Statistics Norway, 2015). As judged by the United Nations Human Development Index, Norway has for several years been the best country in the world to live in (http://hdr.undp.org/en/content/human-development-index-hdi). Social capital in terms of trust and participation in voluntary organizations is high (Halvorsen, 2014). Employment rates are among the highest in the world, in particular among women, the elderly and people with chronic illness (van der Wel et al., 2012). Income inequalities, as measured by the Gini coefficient, are at a relatively low level, but have increased over the past decade, now reaching 0.24 (Dahl et al., 2014). Although Norway is renowned for a compressed wage structure, inequalities in earnings and wages have also grown over the past decades (Dahl et al., 2014). Nonetheless, in comparative terms the model has been able to combine strong economic growth with a relatively low level of inequality over the last decade. The Norwegian economy and labour market were mildly affected by the 2007 financial crisis and had a quick recovery. However, due to currently low oil prices and hence a sluggish economy in certain regions, unemployment has risen to almost 5 per cent. In an international perspective this is not alarming, but it is about twice the rate it was in 2007, just before the financial crisis hit (Statistics Norway, 2016). Norway has a distinctly knowledge-intensive labour market as only 5 per cent of the workforce positions require no formal education (OECD, 2010). It is predicted that demand for workers with high education will continue to increase, while the demand for workers with little or no formal qualifications will decrease even further (Gjefsen et al., 2012).

In the ten-year period we are covering, the country had a 'red/green' government from 2005 to 2013 consisting of the Social Democratic Party, the Socialist Party and the Agrarian Party. This government was replaced in the autumn of 2013 by a coalition consisting of the Conservative Party and the Right-Wing Party, called the 'blue/blue' government. This government is supported by the Liberal Party and the Christian Democratic Party. In 1992, an official report coined the term 'work approach'. Since then it has been a yardstick and a guideline for almost every social policy and labour market reform (Dahl and Lorentzen, 2008). The core idea is that ordinary work should be the first option for all able-bodied persons, and that all public benefits and services should be designed to support this goal. However, policies to pursue the work approach may differ in a number of ways, ranging from severe retrenchment in benefits to make work pay, to providing expensive programmes to build human capital among disadvantaged groups, and all combinations thereof. So the question is: what strategies has Norway launched, developed and refined over the past ten years to pursue the work approach? This is the subject of the next sections.

THE AGREEMENT ON A MORE INCLUSIVE WORKING LIFE

The Cooperation Agreement on a More Inclusive Working Life is signed by the three social partners: the government, the employers' organizations and the organizations of the employees. This tripartite Agreement was first signed in 2001 and has been renewed several times since. The basic goal structure has been the same all along. In the current Agreement, valid for the period 2014–2018, the overarching goal is to "improve the working environment, enhance presence at work, prevent and reduce sick leave and prevent exclusion and withdrawal from working life" (p. 2). Three secondary goals are quantified, first, to achieve a 20 per cent reduction in sick leave compared with the 2nd quarter 2001; second, to prevent withdrawal and increase employment of people with impaired functional ability; and third, to extend active employment after the age of 50 by 12 months (NAV, 2014).

The Agreement is accompanied by a number of different strategies and focuses on both the supply side and the demand side of the labour market. Supply-side measures include work ability assessments, individual plans, human capital development schemes such as training, and efforts to strengthen self-efficacy and work motivation. Demand-side measures include strategies such as legislation; wage subsidies; organizational innovations, among them the establishment of so-called Working Life Centers; communication and information campaigns to lower the barriers for employment among vulnerable groups; and initiatives to eradicate misconceptions and stereotypies among employers (Øverbye and Hammer, 2005, p. 22).

The Agreement is a true-born child of the Norwegian corporative tradition. It has been acclaimed by many, and few will disagree that the primary goal is worth pursuing. However, it has also provoked critique. Critics have pointed out that the main emphasis by far has been on reducing sick leave, and much less on the aim to raise employment rates among disabled people. Here, there is a contradiction in the goal structure: it is hard, perhaps impossible, to reduce sick leave significantly at the same time as one increases employment among disabled persons, since these people tend to need more sickness leave than others. Numbers obtained from population surveys reveal that workforce participation among disabled people has been fairly stable during most of the Agreement period. It is rational for the Agreement companies to avoid hiring disabled people in order to keep sickness rates as low as possible. In this way, at least in theory, the Agreement may reinforce employment obstacles for disabled people who are outside the labour market. In the worst-case scenario, the (unintended) result may be a deeper division between labour market insiders and outsiders.

The inclusive work arrangement has been rather thoroughly evaluated. The latest evaluation concludes that the Agreement is close to achieving the first goal, which is to reduce sickness absence rates significantly. The second goal, to increase work force participation among the disabled, is not achieved; and neither is the third goal, to prolong economic activity for workers above 50 years of age. It should be added that the evaluation indicates that the Agreement has led to a sharper focus on employee health, the working environment and safety at the workplace, and has led to a strengthening of prevention and enabling measures (Ose et al., 2013).

The Agreement on work inclusion is a complex, multilayered initiative and so are the effects and consequences. On the one hand, by focusing on the demand side – that is, the attempts to modify and adapt work demands, provide healthy working environments, and measures to increase the employers' willingness to hire vulnerable groups – the initiative appears to be a 'true' social investment strategy. Institutional innovations such as the introduction of the Working Life Centers support this assessment. Further, the emphasis on reducing sick leave is likely to benefit vulnerable groups such as the low-educated and people in poor and low-paid jobs. On the other hand, the downside of the Agreement is that the barriers to the labour market have not been lowered for disabled people without work. This is likely to be an unintended and undesired side-effect of the Agreement and a result of the dominant effort to reduce sickness absence rates. This reasoning resonates well with the conclusion drawn by the evaluation of the Agreement. It states that the efforts to reduce sickness absence have probably reduced employers' will to include disabled people in the workforce (Ose et al., 2013). The intention behind the Agreement and the institutions it has brought about bear the mark of a true social investment strategy. However, in effect the Agreement is less successful as a social investment strategy since it has not improved the employment prospects of one of its prime target groups: disabled people outside the labour market.

NEW LEGISLATION REGARDING REGULATION AND PROTECTION OF LABOUR

The most recent changes in Norway's Working Environment Act ('the Act') came into effect on 1 July 2015. The amendments affect temporary employment, working time, age limits, maximum penalties and the collective right to sue. The public discussion that preceded the passing of the bill was quite heated and culminated in a two-hour nationwide general strike in January 2015. The most controversial issue was the proposition to admit temporary employment (Røed Steen, 2015). Prior to 2015, the main rule in Norwegian working life was fixed labour contracts. The change in the Act implies a general admission to hire employees for up to 12 months on temporary contracts, and there is no requirement for justification. The work tasks can thus be limited in time, or permanent. Three constraints to this general admission apply, among them a quarantine of 12 months on the actual work tasks (that is, a ban on subsequently hiring another person to carry out work of the same type), and the imposition of an upper limit of 15 per cent of the staff that can be hired temporarily (Norwegian Government, 2015).

Advocates of the amendments in the Act argued that they would ensure greater flexibility in working life and give more people, in particular vulnerable groups like young people and the disabled, a better chance to enter working life and to reduce exclusion from the labour market. It was maintained that more flexible working times would benefit the workers, the employers and the society (Innst. 207 L, 2014–2015, p. 4). The critics stated that the Act was flexible enough as it was, and that the proposed changes would undermine the workers' rights. They underlined that the main purpose of the Act was to protect the workers and also to enable vulnerable workers to take part in the labour market. They further claimed that the changes would imply that power would be shifted from the employees to the employers, and that the employees would be exposed to more strain and experience less predictability. As a consequence, they argued, it would be likely that the changes in the legislation would lead to the opposite of what its proponents believed (Norwegian Parliament, 2015, p. 5). These are gloomy predictions, but not entirely taken out of thin air. Of course, it is far too early to tell the actual consequences of the new legislation in Norway, but research-based evidence from other countries may shed some light on the question. Research carried out by the Organisation for Economic Co-operation and Development (OECD), and referred to in the public debate, indicates that the introduction of temporary work does not lead to more jobs and recruitment of more vulnerable workers. Rather, the consequence is a larger proportion of temporary jobs in the labour market (Røed Steen, 2015). It remains to be seen how the Norwegian labour market will be affected. After all, there are restrictions that might put a cap on the number of temporary jobs. Yet, the direction of the reform and experience from elsewhere makes it unlikely that the reform will strengthen vulnerable workers' capabilities and opportunities. Hence, this initiative can hardly be characterized as a genuine and effective social investment strategy.

REFORMS IN THE WELFARE SYSTEM

In the late 1990s, several European countries took measures to improve cooperation between public employment services, social assistance providers and other agencies involved in the income maintenance and activation of the jobless. This development came forth together with the reorientation of welfare states towards activation (Champion and Bonoli, 2011). In Norway, a conspicuous new element in organizational reform was the emphasis placed on coordination of services and the expansion of target groups for labour market inclusion services.

The Norwegian labour and welfare reform merged employment and national insurance administrations and partnered this new structure with municipal benefits and social services (Askim et al., 2011). The setting up of the Norwegian Labour and Welfare administration between 2006 and 2010 constitutes one of the most radical coordination initiatives adopted in Europe (Champion and Bonoli, 2011). It represents a complete redesigning of the organizational landscape of the provision of benefits and employment services, and has involved all relevant agencies.

The expansion of target groups for activation policy led to a much more heterogeneous mass of recipients, such as social assistance beneficiaries, persons with reduced health, young unemployed without work experience, immigrants, as well as the ordinary unemployed. Activation of persons with differing needs and problems required the involvement of a wide range of public agencies. Often, the jobless had several caseworkers representing different branches and agencies where communication and cooperation were sparse. Soon the lack of coordination between the Norwegian Public Employment Services, social assistance providers and the national social security office was seen as a problem for the activation of the jobless. In the late 1990s, problems of coordination between the national Public Employment Services and social assistance offices with regard to activation programmes, and the inadequacy of the system dealing with multiple problems, led parliament to plead for a more coordinated social security system (Duell et al., 2009).

Through merging of units, restructuring and the implementation of new programmes, the reform was meant to revitalize the work approach and change the relation between citizens and the welfare state, giving the users a more comprehensive and efficient offer of services. The new labour and welfare offices were supposed to provide a seamless service for users by providing a single entry point into the welfare system (Askim et al., 2011). Revitalizing the work approach meant new activity requirements for those on sickness benefits, and close and early intervention to prevent permanent disability. Reduced health was no longer considered a sufficient criterion for benefits; thorough work assessment was thought to uncover the functional capabilities and any remaining capacity for work (Brage, 2007). Just like simultaneous reforms abroad, the reform emphasized user obligations, at the same time as the ideal of user involvement, user accountability and individual-adapted programmes were accentuated. The Norwegian reform was, together with the Job-centre Plus reform in the United Kingdom, considered the most encompassing and intense of the simultaneous reforms elsewhere in Europe (Champion and Bonoli, 2011).

Perhaps the most important aim of the labour and welfare reform was formulated as a slogan: 'More people in work, less on social benefits'. In particular it aimed to open the doors for vulnerable groups, and to give them access to a variety of work-oriented measures so that they could become self-sufficient and independent. So, the crucial question is whether the labour and welfare reform has improved the work opportunities for the users of the organization's services. An 'authoritative' quantitative evaluation of the reform, applying a quasi-experimental design and using register data, found that the establishment of labour and welfare offices led to longer time for the unemployed and the recipients of social assistance to (re-)enter work. However, the evaluation indicated that the negative effect on this crucial outcome was restricted to the first couple of years after the new offices were established. The authors interpret this finding as a consequence of the restructuring process as such, and not as evidence that the new organization performs worse than the old one (Fevang et al., 2014). Based on the evidence that we have now, it seems that a reform that carries the stamp of social investment has not so far lived up to its bold ambition. Perhaps one can say that the jury is still out on this question.

Unification of Social Security Benefits

The massive organizational restructuring of the labour and welfare reform led to several other changes in the ways benefits and services were provided for the jobless. One such innovation that came into being in 2010 was the Work Assessment Benefit, which was a merger of three separate benefits. Until 2010, there were three separate benefits available for persons with health problems but who were (still) not permanently excluded from the workforce. The rehabilitation benefit was for persons who had exceeded the time limits of the generous sickness benefit given to those in gainful employment. Thus, after a maximum of one year on sickness benefits, persons still undergoing treatment could apply for rehabilitation benefit, which was compensated at 66 per cent of the former income (Bragstad and Brage, 2011). Furthermore, in 2004, the disability benefit was divided into one temporary and one permanent benefit. This was done as a reaction to the increasing number of disabled towards the end of the 1990s (Bragstad, 2009). The temporary disability pension was meant to serve as an alternative for persons who still had prospects of returning to the workforce. With the introduction of the temporary disability benefits, the authorities wanted to bring forward a change of attitude in the population, signalling that health problems no longer guaranteed access to a permanent source of income (Bragstad, 2009). This latter benefit was included in the new Work Assessment Benefit. The third benefit, vocational rehabilitation, included a range of active labour market programmes such as training, work practice, wage subsidies and so on (Bragstad and Brage, 2011). In 2010, the rehabilitation benefit, temporary disability pension and vocational rehabilitation were transformed into the Work Assessment Benefit.

Echoing the overall intention of the labour and welfare reform, the Work Assessment Benefit was meant to offer a comprehensive and unitary offer for persons moving between several different health-related benefits (Kann et al., 2013). Until the introduction of the Work Assessment Benefit, persons with health problems had been wavering between several benefits, each requiring separate casework and documentation. Merging these benefits into one should free case worker resources, simplify regulations and provide the basis for close individual follow-up. Furthermore, the intention was to give more of the health-impaired jobless access to the activation programmes of the former Public Employment Services. Work Assessment Benefit requires that applicants have lost 50 per cent or more of their work capacity. Health is not in itself a direct criterion, but is indirectly through the way it affects the capacity to work (Kann et al., 2013). Work Assessment Benefit is granted while the recipient is undergoing active treatment, going through active labour market programmes or subjected to work assessment. With the introduction of Work Assessment Benefit, young health-impaired persons without job experience were given access to the full repertoire of the former Public Employment Services for rehabilitation and job training. This was a group that formerly only had access to the meagre municipal activation apparatus. Thus, the prospects of bringing this weak group into work were supposed to be better after the introduction of Work Assessment Benefit. Here we see an example of how changes in the benefit structure are accompanied by provision of work-related services, often targeted at disadvantaged groups.

The Work Assessment Benefit was meant to provide jobless persons not covered by traditional social security benefits with an alternative income alongside the necessary measures to bring them back into employment. Critics have dubbed the Work Assessment Benefit a waiting room for disability benefit (Kann and Kristoffersen, 2014). It is still too early to assess the long-term effects of this innovation whose first participants completed the four-year programme in 2014. Yet, the preliminary results are not so encouraging, as only 25 per cent of the participants are gainfully employed six months after they have left the programme (Kann and Kristoffersen, 2014). Thus, even if the programme answers to the several of the formal criteria of the social investment notion, few of the participants seem to make use of the possibilities created through the programme. This might indicate how difficult it is to reach and help those who have multiple barriers to entering the labour market.

Other Changes in Benefit Schemes

In general, other schemes in the Norwegian social security system have not been subject to nearly such profound changes as those we now have discussed. Øverbye and Stjernø (2012) have reviewed changes in the key institutional aspects of the benefit schemes. The authors conclude that entitlements to benefits are rather unchanged and remain broad, that is, are contingent universal. As regards admission and eligibility criteria, behavioural conditions have increased, including requirements of activity and participation, and of claimants' active involvement in making individual plans in collaboration with the street-level bureaucrat. Criteria for determining benefit levels are also, in general, left unchanged. Finally, there has been no general reduction in duration (Dahl and Lorentzen, 2008). This conclusion is largely in line with an analysis of the development from the 1960s up to the middle of the 2000s (Huo, 2009). There are, however, two notable and recent exceptions to this general picture.

In the summer of 2015 a tightening of the conditionality in the Social Service Act was enacted. Conditions for receipt have been in the legislation since 1992. The old formulation was that conditional activity 'can' be imposed. The tightening implies that conditions of activity 'shall' be imposed unless there are good reasons to do otherwise. The message is somewhat softened by formulations such as: the conditions must not be disproportionally burdensome for the recipient, or limit their freedom to choose in an unfair way. Failure to comply with a condition may lead to reduction of the social assistance benefit. Imposing conditions without accompanying capacity-building measures is hardly an initiative that deserves a social investment stamp.

The second exception is a cut in the child allowance to parents who receive disability benefit. This rule took effect in January 2016 and implies that the child allowance will be reduced if the sum of disability benefit and child allowance exceeds 95 per cent of pre-disability income (Rud, 2016). The idea is to stimulate disability beneficiaries to search for work, and that benefits should never exceed earnings. A likely consequence is that low-income earners with many children will lose substantial amounts of money. It has been calculated that under the new rule, a single disabled parent with four children and with US (US$)42 000 in previous income will lose nearly US (US$)5280 per year (Rud, 2016). Simple and one-sided benefit cuts like these are not a part of a social investment package.

The Qualification Programme

The Qualification Programme was launched early in the labour and welfare reform process in 2007. The programme was sold as the most important means to prevent poverty and social exclusion. The target group of the programme was persons with extensive and complex problems, and limited or no earned rights to social security. According to the authorities, persons belonging to this group were in need of support in order to avoid passivity and a situation of permanent exclusion from the workforce and poverty (Frøyland and Spjelkavik, 2014). The Qualification Programme was based on the experiences of several predecessors that had been subject to trials, and was meant to bring participants into work and activity by offering them systematic, tailored and comprehensive follow-up. The Qualification Programme answered to the purpose of the labour and welfare reform since it required cooperation between several institutions at both the municipal and the state level. Thus the programme includes work-related elements and job-seeking activities which require involvement from the municipality, the county level, work and welfare sector, and other agencies. Seen from a social investment point of view, the programme is interesting since it builds on the so-called 'betterment approach' which has been common in Norway (Frøyland and Spjelkavik, 2014). This methodology is meant to bring the participants' qualifications up to a certain level where they match the demands existing in the labour market. Qualification of the participants is mainly achieved through courses and training, but also on progressive chains of labour market programmes.

The Qualification Programme was by definition a social investment strategy, meant to boost human capital and prepare the weakest for work. Although the purpose of the programme answers to the notion of being a social investment strategy for the weakest, the programme has failed to include the weakest. Evaluations have shown that persons without drug problems and mental health problems are often the preferred participants in the programme (Schafft and Spjelkavik, 2011). The cream-skimming of participants seems to have become more common over the last years (Schafft and Spjelkavik, 2011). The most recent effect evaluation of the programme indicates a positive effect on work participation (Markussen and Røed, 2014). However, an outflow analysis shows that very few participants move to a job, and even fewer get a job that is more permanent: about 10 per cent of the participants (Lima and Ohrem Naper, 2013). In addition to cream-skimming, it is also a problem that few (between 5 and 10 per cent) of the annual total stock of social assistance recipients are enrolled into the programme. This raises serious concerns as to whether the programme is able to reduce poverty through the work avenue for the hardest-to-serve. Also, although benefits are not means-tested, the participants are far from affluent when they participate in the programme: 60 per cent of the recipients of qualification benefit may be defined as poor, that is, earning less than 60 per cent of median household income (Dahl et al., 2014).

The Qualification Programme is quite clearly a human capital development programme (Gubrium, 2009). As such, it is a typical social investment programme in terms of the resources it commands, how it is designed, and its target groups. However, a more detailed and comprehensive assessment of the programme, covering recruitment, selection patterns and outcome, suggests that although intentions are good, the programme does not deliver work nor sufficient income for many of the most vulnerable and hard-to-serve.

EMPLOYMENT POLICY: IS NORWAY STILL A SOCIAL INVESTMENT STATE?

In this chapter we have reviewed and appraised recent reforms in the labour market and related social policy reforms in Norway in light of a social investment perspective. We have asked whether these recent reforms still carry the stamp of social investment. Our yardsticks for identifying social investment reforms have been outlined. Where data have been available, we have also tried to evaluate the (short-term) effects of the reforms on important socio-economic outcomes such as work participation and earnings, in particular for disadvantaged groups, that are often targets of the reforms.

A rather mixed picture emerges. Some reforms and parts of larger reforms carry the stamp of true social investment, for example the comprehensive organizational merger (the labour and welfare reform), the formation of the Work Assessment Benefit and the Qualification Programme. Other reforms, such as changes in the Work Environment Act, cuts in benefits for disability beneficiaries with low pre-disability earnings, and stricter conditions for receiving social assistance benefit, clearly do not. These latter reforms have been launched by a conservative and right-wing coalition government. Yet, it should be added that these reforms mostly tend to be carefully designed, are rather moderate in nature and restricted in scope, for example amendments in the Work Environment Act.

Often ambitions and goals have the best of social investment intentions without, however, being able to show very convincing and successful results, for example in terms of transition to employment. Prominent examples are the Qualification Programme for social assistance recipients, and the comprehensive labour and welfare reform. Further, complex reforms may have different effects for different vulnerable groups. The implementation of inclusive working life may, for example, benefit working people with frequent sickness absence, but may not improve employment records for disabled people.

The overarching research question of this article was: is Norway still a social investment state? The answer is yes, but the most recent developments lead away from it, although in quite short and cautious steps. The yardsticks we have defined to identify and label policy reforms in our data material may be challenged: social investment may be defined somewhat differently, for example, with a stronger focus on equality of opportunity, a heavier emphasis on obligations and stricter conditions for benefit receipt, and a far more sceptical view on cash benefits. Our response to this is that our notion has been derived from lessons drawn from empirical research on social investment policies. To justify our definition and use of the concept we refer to the scholarly discussion and empirical research on socio-economic effects of social investment policies that have been conducted in Europe over the past 10–15 years. In our view, this evidence quite convincingly indicates that in order for social investment initiatives to be effective they need to have (at least) the characteristics that we have pointed out (Cantillon, 2011; Vandenbroucke and Vleminckx, 2011; Morel et al., 2012; Hemerijck, 2012).

This, however, may raise a problem for our analysis. If Norway, along with the other Nordic countries, is among the best students in the social investment class, and the outcomes of these policies are rather moderate, even disappointing, doesn't that imply that social investment policies fail to deliver? Not necessarily. One should keep in mind that many of the recent policy initiatives are targeted at population groups that are extremely hard-to-serve, for example long-term social assistance recipients. These people lack a variety of resources and suffer from multiple problems. This means that the public initiatives that target these groups are in fact very ambitious. Therefore, it is also easy to fail. Perhaps one might say that sometimes the goals of the reforms seem overambitious and overoptimistic. One could argue that as long as governments have these high ambitions, they should test even more radical measures. At the end of the day, the success of many reforms hinges ultimately on the employers', private and public, will and ability to hire and retain disadvantaged workers. Although some measures, for example the inclusive working life initiative, address the demand side, employers could be enabled and encouraged to be more responsible and to be held more accountable (Frøyland and Spjelkavik, 2014). Evidence is piling up suggesting that recovery and rehabilitation are more effective when taking place at the workplace, and that work at its best may have positive health effects (Frøyland and Spjelkavik, 2014). Here we may point out a shortcoming in the prevailing social investment paradigm that we have adopted in this chapter. In the usual accounts, it focuses on the labour supply side and has not much to say about the demand side, such as the employers. For the social investment approach to be more effective and better tailored to serve the needs of disadvantaged groups, we will argue that social investment strategies should also embrace measures that make employers more interested in, willing and able to hire and retain vulnerable workers.

REFERENCES

Askim, J., Fimreite, A.L., Moseley, A. and Holm Pedersen, L. (2011). One-Stop Shops for Social Welfare: The Adaptation of an Organizational Form in Three Countries. *Public Administration*, 89 (4), 1451–1468.
Bonoli, G. and Natali, D. (2012). *The Politics of the New Welfare State*. Oxford: Oxford University Press.
Brage, S. (2007). Trender i de skandinaviske sykefraværsordningene. *Arbeid og Velferd*, 2, 24–29.

Bragstad, T. (2009). Tidsbegrenset uførestønad – evaluering fire år etter inn-
føring. NAV-rapport 2009/3. Oslo: Arbeids og velferdsdirektoratet.

Bragstad, T. and Brage, S. (2011). Unge på arbeids- og helserelaterte ordninger.
Arbeid og Velferd, 2, 36–47.

Cantillon, B. (2011). The Paradox of the Social Investment State: Growth,
Employment and Poverty in the Lisbon Era. *Journal of European Social
Policy*, 21 (5), 432–449.

Champion, C. and Bonoli, G. (2011). Institutional Fragmentation and Coordination Initiatives in Western European Welfare States. *Journal of European
Social Policy*, 21 (4), 323–334. doi:10.1177/0958928711412220.

Dahl, E., Bergsli, H. and van der Wel, K.A. (2014). Sosial ulikhet i helse. En
norsk kunnskapsoversikt. Oslo: Oslo and Akershus University College of
Applied Sciences.

Dahl, E. and Drøpping, J.A. (2001). The Norwegian Work Approach in the
1990s: Rhetoric and Reform. In N. Gilbert and R.A. Van Voorhis (eds),
*Activating the Unemployed. A Comparative Appraisal of Work-Oriented Pol-
icies*. New Brunswick, NJ: Transaction Publishers, pp. 267–292.

Dahl, E. and Lorentzen, T. (2008). Norway: Social Security, Active Labour
Market Policies and Economic Progress. In J. Midgley and K.L. Tang (eds),
Social Security, the Economy and Development. Basingstoke: Palgrave,
pp. 210–237.

Dølvik, J.E., Fløtten, T., Hippe, J.M. and Jordfald, B. (2015). *The Nordic model
towards 2030. A new chapter?*. Oslo: Fafo.

Duell, N., Singh, S. and Tergeist, P. (2009). Activation Policies in Norway.
OECD Social, Employment and Migration Working Papers, No. 78. Paris:
OECD Publishing. DOI: http://dx.doi.org/10.1787/226388712174.

Esping-Andersen, G., Gallie, D., Hemerijck, A. and Meyers, J. (eds) (2002). *Why
We Need a New Welfare State*. New York: Oxford University Press.

Fevang, E., Markussen, S. and Røed, K. (2014). NAV-reformen: Støvet legger
seg etter en turbulent omstilling. *Søkelys på arbeidslivet*, 31 (1–2), 83–99.

Frøyland, K. and Spjelkavik, Ø. (eds) (2014). *Inkluderingskompetanse: Ordinært
arbeid som mål og middel*. Oslo: Gyldendal Akademisk.

Gjefsen, H.M., Gjelsvik, M.L., Roksvaag, K. and Stølen, N.M. (2012). Utdannes
det riktig kompetanse for fremtiden? Økonomiske analyser, 3/2012. Oslo:
Statistisk sentralbyrå.

Gubrium, E. (2009). The Qualification Program: A New Work Approach for
Norway's Social Assistance Recipients?. Master's thesis. Oslo: Oslo and
Akershus University College of Applied Sciences.

Halvorsen, K. (2014). *Velferd. Fra ide til politikk for et godt samfunn*. Oslo:
Cappelen Damm Akademisk.

Harsløf, I. and Ulmestig, R. (eds) (2013). *Changing Social Risks and Social
Policy Responses in the Nordic Welfare States*. Basingstoke: Palgrave
Macmillan.

Hemerijck, A. (2012). When Changing Welfare States and the Eurocrisis Meet.
Sociologica, 1. doi: 10.2383/36887.

Huo, J. (2009). *Third Way Reforms: Social Democracy after the Golden Age*.
New York: Cambridge University Press.

Kann, I.C. and Kristoffersen, P. (2014). Arbeidsavklaringspenger – et venterom for uførepensjon? *Arbeid og Velferd*, 2, 101–115.

Kann, I.C., Kristoffersen, P. and Thune, O. (2013). Arbeidsavklaringspenger – gjennomstrømming og avgang fra ordningen. *Arbeid og Velferd*, 1, 41–57.

Lima, I.A. and Ohrem Naper, S. (2013). Kommer deltakerne i kvalifiserings-programmet i jobb?. *Arbeid og Velferd*, 2, 43–59.

Markussen, S. and Røed, K. (2014). Leaving Poverty Behind? The Effects of Generous Income Support Paired with Activation. Discussion Paper No. 8245. Bonn: IZA.

Midgley, J. (1999). Growth, Redistribution and Welfare: Towards Social Investment. *Social Service Review*, 77 (1), 3–21.

Morel, N., Palier, B. and Palme, J. (2009). What Future for Social Investment?. Research Report. Stockholm: Institute for Future Studies.

Morel, N., Pallier, B. and Palme, J. (eds) (2012). *Towards a Social Investment Welfare State? Ideas, Policies and Challenges*. Bristol: Policy Press.

NAV (2014). Cooperation Agreement on a More Inclusive Working Life. https://www.google.no/search?q=Cooperation+Agreement+on+a+More+Inclusive+Working+Life.andie=utf-8andoe=utf-8andgws_rd=crandei=UPuNV8vHIMWS6QT3-IGwCw.

Norwegian Government (2015). Changes in the Work Environment Act. https://www.regjeringen.no/no/tema/arbeidsliv/arbeidsmiljo-og-sikkerhet/innsikt/arbeidsmiljoloven/lovendringeri-arbeidsmiljoloven-fra-1.-juli–2015/id2410600/.

Norwegian Parliament (2015). Innst. 207 L (2014–2015). Innstilling til Stortinget fra arbeids- og sosialkomiteen. https://www.stortinget.no/no/Saker-og-publikasjoner/Publikasjoner/Innstillinger/Stortinget/2014-2015/inns-201415-207/.

OECD (2010). *Off to a Good Start? Jobs for Youth*. Paris: OECD.

Ose, S.O., Dyrstad, K., Slettebak, R., Lippestad, J., Mandal, R., Brattlid, I. and Jensberg, H. (2013). Evaluering av IA-avtalen (2010–2013). Trondheim: Sintef.

Øverbye, E. and Hammer, T. (2005). Strategier for et inkluderende arbeidsliv. In T. Hammer and E. Øverbye (eds), *Inkluderende arbeidsliv? Erfaringer og strategier*. Oslo: Gyldendal Akademisk, pp. 11–31.

Øverbye, E. and Stjernø, S. (2012). Arbeidslinja, arbeidsmotivasjon og velferdsstat. In S. Stjernø and E. Øverbye (eds), *Arbeidslinja – arbeidsmotivasjonen og velferdsstaten*. Oslo: Universitetsforlaget, pp. 12–27.

Røed Steen, J. (2015). Norway: Reaction to New Working Environment Act. http://www.eurofound.europa.eu/observatories/eurwork/articles/law-and-regulation/norway-reaction-to-new-working-environment-act.

Rud, S. (2016). Lavtlønnede taper mest når barnetillegget for uføre endres. *Aftenposten*, 5 January.

Schafft, A. and Spjelkavik, Ø. (2011). Evaluering av Kvalifiseringsprogrammet: sluttrapport. AFI-rapport 4/2011. Oslo: Work Research Institute.

Schøyen, M. (2016). Den norske velferdsstaten: En sosial investeringsstat?. *Tidsskrift for velferdsforskning*, 19 (1), 4–23.

Statistics Norway (2015). Økonomiske analyser 1/2015. Oslo: Statistics Norway.

Statistics Norway (2016). Labour Force Survey figures. https://www.ssb.no/en/arbeid-og-lonn/statistikker/aku/kvartal/2016-04-28.

Therborn, G. (2013). *The Killing Fields of Inequality*. Cambridge: Polity Press.

Vandenbroucke, F. and Vleminckx, K. (2011). Disappointing Poverty Trends: Is the Social Investment State to Blame?. *Journal of European Social Policy*, 21 (5), 450–471.

van der Wel, K.A., Dahl, E. and Thielen, K. (2012). Social Inequalities in 'Sickness': Does Welfare State Regime Type Make a Difference? A Multilevel Analysis of Men and Women in 26 European Countries. *International Journal of Health Services*, 42 (2), 235–255.

6. The Child Support Grant in South Africa: gender, care and social investment

Leila Patel

Although many countries in the Global South do not explicitly frame their social policies around the notion of social investment as defined in Northern welfare states, it was shown in Chapter 1 of this book that social investment ideas are widely used in the developing world. This is particularly evident in the fields of education, child care and social protection where there has been a significant expansion of cash transfers. Social protection policies evolved in response to the need to find novel solutions to address high rates of poverty among women, children and families that could yield long-term social and economic benefits for them and for society at large (World Bank, 2015), and were linked to the United Nations Millennium Declaration which prioritized poverty reduction as a major goal of development effort.

Despite the growth of social protection policies in the Global South, the gender and care dimensions of social protection policies remain poorly understood. Few studies apply a gender lens to the analysis and assessment of social protection policies in the African context, and research into the relationship between social protection and social investment is still neglected. This chapter addresses this gap by reflecting critically on these issues with reference to South Africa's Child Support Grant (CSG), which is one of the country's most expansive poverty reduction social protection programmes, reaching 11.6 million or 60 per cent of the population of children in 2016. The grant has been fairly extensively evaluated, providing access to important data on its profiles, use and effects. Empirical evaluations suggest that it has positive effects in reducing poverty (Bhorat and Cassim, 2014), improved food security (Aguero et al., 2006) and high rates of school attendance and stable school performance (Case et al., 2005). The Child Support Grant may therefore be considered to be a positive social investment in human capital development of children as it is widely accepted that improved nutrition, health and education are associated with longer-term positive effects on future employment and income (Henshall Momsen, 2004; Patel, 2015). Longitudinal research, however, needs to be conducted to confirm some of these preliminary findings in larger national samples over time.

Although the country's welfare policies make cursory reference to social investment today, the programme forms a core element of the country's social development approach and its pioneering role in promoting developmental welfare in the Global South has been internationally recognized since the Mandela government adopted the White Paper for Social Welfare (Patel, 2015). The White Paper and its policy proposals formed a part of the government's wider commitment to embrace a social development perspective that would seek to meet basic social needs, promote participation, and link economic and social policies within an egalitarian development process that would rely extensively on social investment ideas. As Patel (2015) points out, social development was the guiding framework for the country's development efforts.

Notwithstanding the positive outcomes of cash transfers in South Africa and in other developing countries, limited attention has been paid to the gender and care dimensions of social protection as a social investment strategy. In this regard, Molyneux (2007) cautions against designing and implementing social protection policies and poverty reduction programmes in developing countries that could privilege the position of one disadvantaged group (children) over another (women). Likewise, with reference to South Africa, one may ask whether there is likely to be a trade-off between meeting the needs of children versus that of women. Although the Child Support Grant was not designed to empower women, what is known about its potential to do so, since the majority of beneficiaries are women? And what do men make of the grant? Is it likely to have gender-transformative effects in intra-household relations? Is cash sufficient to meet the complex care needs of disadvantaged families? And finally, what are the implications of the grant from a social investment perspective?

This chapter attempts to answer some of these questions by drawing on the available literature on the Child Support Grant, which includes macro- and micro-level data as well as findings from quantitative and qualitative studies. The chapter is structured as follows. First it provides an overview of the grant with reference to its unique design features. Then it reviews the literature and the issues pertaining to the gender dimensions of social protection strategies for children and families that are relevant to the South African context. Much of this literature focuses on the design features of conditional cash transfers in Latin American countries and their effects on women and children. While there are differences between these programmes and cash transfers in South Africa, it is nonetheless relevant to attempt to understand the particularities of the gender dynamics of social protection strategies for children and their families in the local context. Three themes, based on the questions posed above, are explored in greater depth later in this chapter. These relate, first, to the notion of 'maternalism', women's empowerment and child well-being. Maternalism refers to the positioning of women as conduits for the promotion of child well-being in keeping with heteronormative beliefs about women's roles in caregiving. A second theme examines the perspectives of men in relation to the Child Support Grant and what we know about their (non-)engagement in the care of children. A third theme returns to the nexus between cash, care services and social investment. Finally, some concluding observations are made about the salient gender and care dimensions of the grant and its implications for future welfare policies in South Africa.

ABOUT THE CHILD SUPPORT GRANT

South Africa's social welfare and social protection policies were overhauled when a democracy was established in 1994. Since then, social assistance for older persons, people with disabilities and children has expanded significantly, reaching more than 16 million people. The largest programme in terms of reach is the Child Support Grant, which was designed and rolled out in 1998. Briefly, the grant is a non-contributory monthly cash transfer paid to the primary caregiver of a child, subject to a fairly generous means test. A flat rate of ZAR330 per month is paid to the caregiver of a child to provide complementary material support to poor households, particularly in relation to enhancing food security. The programme was initially targeted at children under six years of age, and due to its positive impact it was scaled up to include children up to 18 years of age. In view of the beneficial outcomes referred to above, the programme is now widely regarded locally and internationally as part of a new wave of social protection interventions to address poverty within a social development approach in the Global South (Midgley, 2014; World Bank, 2015).

The Child Support Grant has unique design features which sets it apart from many other poverty reduction programmes in low- and middle-income countries, which is pertinent to a gender analysis. For the first decade of the programme it was an unconditional cash transfer, but this was changed in 2009 when the government introduced the condition that children should be enrolled in school. This condition requires that grant beneficiaries submit proof of school attendance every two years. This means that the primary caregiver presents herself at a local office of the South African Social Security Agency (SASSA). There is little evidence of how this works in practice, but it does involve some additional time pressures on female grant recipients. This differs from the Latin American conditional cash transfers where women grant beneficiaries are required to take children for regular health check-ups, ensure that children attend school, attend health education programmes and spend a certain amount of hours on unpaid community work. These conditions were found to increase the time burdens experienced by women, and failure to meet these requirements could result in them being excluded from the programme (Molyneux, 2007).

Further, eligibility to the Child Support Grant is gender-neutral, with the grant being paid to the primary caregiver responsible for the care of children, who may be their biological parent, a relative or a non-relative. Child and family social protection policies in the Global South are in the main targeted at the female primary caregiver of the child, and are fashioned on the male breadwinner model of post-World War II welfare state programmes in the North. In theory, the Child Support Grant design is not based on a maternalist model of care, fashioned on the gender division of care between men and women. However, in reality it has ended up being a maternalist model of care as very few men take up the grant. Some of the reasons are related largely to socio-cultural heteronormative beliefs about care being women's work. This is explored below by reflecting on the views of men about the grant.

These particular features of the Child Support Grant reflected an attempt to design social protection policies that could address the systemic disadvantage experienced by poor families due to *apartheid* and migrant labour policies that resulted in the disruption of family and community life (Budlender and Lund, 2011; Lund, 2008). Patterns of care arrangements were established early on, whereby large numbers of children were cared for apart from their parents by grandparents and kin in rural areas while their parents migrated to urban areas in search of employment. Further, large numbers of children continue to be cared for in female-headed households with the nuclear family structure not being the dominant family form (Patel and Mavungu, 2016). The design of the Child Support Grant was influenced by these factors including high rates of poverty in families and in anticipation of the impact of the HIV/AIDS epidemic on the care responsibilities of families and on women (Lund, 2008).

Despite the progressive design features of the Child Support Grant, the majority of beneficiaries are women, estimated to be 98 per cent in 2014 (Department of Social Development, 2014). This is an increase of 5 per cent since 2008 (Vorster and de Waal, 2008). Finally, a particular feature of the grant is that it is a fully publicly funded means-tested social assistance programme that is a social right guaranteed by the South African Constitution and the Bill of Rights. The grant forms part of an overall set of socio-economic rights that include the right to health care, basic education, housing and basic services such as water, electricity and sanitation. The Constitution also upholds the rights of children to parental and family care, nutrition and appropriate social services. Gender equality is guaranteed, along with the right to equality of all citizens. In keeping with the spirit of the Constitution, welfare and other public policies are designed to work synergistically to reduce poverty, improve human development and capabilities as well as enhance gender equality. As will be shown below, the nexus between cash and social care services is unevenly integrated and delivered due to state failures in service delivery, which undermines social justice and the dignity of caregivers (Hochfeld, 2015).

CONCEPTS AND APPROACH

The term 'social protection' is an umbrella term that is used for a wide variety of public and private strategies to promote income security and access to basic services. Its strategies range from cash transfers as part of social assistance, social insurance and private savings on the one hand, to employment, livelihoods support and access to basic services such as water, electricity, social and care services on the other hand (Patel, 2015). The focus however in this chapter is on social assistance as a cash transfer programme to reduce child and family poverty. The Child Support Grant may be considered to be a social protection innovation that tackles poverty reduction at its source, that is, at the household level where care responsibilities are unequally distributed (Molyneux, 2007). Internationally, analyses and classifications of welfare regimes have been censured for being gender-blind and for not recognizing the unpaid care work of women and how this contributes to the development of human capabilities of children, and to production and social reproduction. Care responsibilities for children, older persons and people with disabilities are disproportionately borne by women caregivers who are responsible for physical, emotional and social care (Razavi, 2014). In disadvantaged families, the cost of care may also increase financial pressures on families. Often, the primary caregiver is not able to be employed; she may experience social isolation, expend emotional resources and may forfeit opportunities for education and wider social participation, and compromise self-care. This care work is taken for granted, it remains invisible, is unpaid and is seldom calculated into gross domestic product.

It is these realities that prompted a shift away from a sole focus on gender discrimination by feminists towards a more equal distribution of care responsibilities in the family and for more state support for child care and for care services (Folbre, 2008). In the field of social protection, the need for policies and strategies has been identified to tackle not only the economic aspects that contribute to poverty, but also the non-economic ones such as gender and generational inequalities, stigma, discrimination and social oppression. Sabates-Wheeler and Devereux (2012) refer to this approach as transformative social protection. In addition, there is also a growing awareness of the way in which social protection programmes tend to marginalize men by focusing on women primary caregivers only. Some attention has been given to understanding whether and how social protection programmes contribute to women's empowerment in countries such as Mexico (Adato et al., 2000) and South Africa (Patel et al., 2012). Kabeer's (1999) empowerment framework is used across these two studies to assess how women use cash resources to achieve their own goals and exercise their agency. Adato et al.'s (2000) dimensions of empowerment is a useful way of assessing the impact of social protection programmes on women's empowerment, for example decision-making powers of women in their households to spend cash, knowledge of rights, gendered beliefs, personal empowerment (self-assertion), and care and domestic responsibilities. Cash transfers have often been justified on the basis that money given to women is likely to be spent on children and collective household consumption needs (UNICEF, 2006), while men were less likely to do so.

The transformative approach is relevant in the South African case as social protection policies and the Child Support Grant, in theory, were intended to be part of an integrated and comprehensive approach to poverty reduction and the promotion of gender equality. Also, as mentioned earlier, the grant and other social protection initiatives formed an integral part of the government's commitment to social development (Department of Welfare, 1997; Patel, 2015). However, in practice there are many challenges of an institutional, political, economic and socio-cultural nature that have worked against the comprehensive implementation of social development policies and programmes locally.

THE CHILD SUPPORT GRANT, GENDER AND SOCIAL TRANSFORMATION

The question of the potential of the Child Support Grant to promote social transformation using a gender lens requires further discussion. Three themes were highlighted at the outset that are pertinent to answering this question. The first examines the connection between maternalism, women's empowerment and child well-being. Theoretically speaking, these concepts are contradictory and might be irreconcilable. But, how does it work in practice in the case of the Child Support Grant? Molyneux (2007, p. 72) argues that social protection strategies in Latin America "depend on gender divisions for their functioning but in some ways actively reinforce them". Although male primary caregivers of children may access the grant, the majority do not. The second theme examines the views of men (recipients and non-recipients) about the grant, based on micro-level qualitative studies; while the third theme speaks to the wider question of whether and how the grant works with other social development investment strategies to reduce poverty, and specifically the gendered nature of poverty in the South African context.

Maternalism, Women's Empowerment and Child Well-Being

It was suggested previously that the Child Support Grant in practice leans towards a maternalist model of care, and that this has less to do with the design features of the programme than with gendered beliefs about the dominant role of women in caregiving in the family and the household. Study findings of women grant beneficiaries, most of whom were not employed, and who lived in an urban community in Soweto, Johannesburg, indicate that they spent 85 per cent of their time on care and domestic responsibilities, while 13 per cent cared for other children who were not beneficiaries of the grant (Patel et al., 2012). Women face additional care demands due in part to the HIV/AIDS epidemic. Using time use surveys, Budlender (2008) estimated that women spent 246 minutes per day (4 hours) of unpaid care work in the home compared to men who spent 89 minutes (1.5 hours). Focus groups with non-profit organizations engaged in community care programmes confirmed that beliefs about gender divisions in care are widely held and that men viewed themselves as the breadwinners and heads of households, and that care work was perceived to be women's work (Patel, 2010).

Does placing cash in the hands of women through the Child Support Grant reinforce the gender division of labour, or does it empower women? Research locally shows that women do spend the money wisely on the needs of children, and that the money is used to buy food and for general household expenses (Patel and Hochfeld, 2013). There is also evidence from the latter study that women beneficiaries are frequently the sole financial decision-makers in the home, with almost 50 per cent being the sole decision-makers. This may be considered to be a less significant form of empowerment (for example, decisions about household expenditure) as it reinforces the traditional gender division of responsibilities. Also, since single-parent families are over-represented among grant beneficiaries (45 per cent), these women may already enjoy considerable decision-making power over expenditure. The situations between women may differ depending on their circumstances, and for those who were previously constrained in this way, this may be a step forward.

Patel et al.'s (2015) quantitative analysis using structural equation modelling shows that the Child Support Grant increases women's financial independence and financial decision-making power, which improves child well-being most notably by increasing caregiver engagement in the care of children. Other positive effects were also found, such as improved child health, nutrition and schooling. The authors conclude that the grant has some transformative effects and that the design of the grant combines the best of both worlds by empowering women and improving the well-being of children. However, more research is needed on how the grant influences the gender and generational power relations in households.

Turning to the gendered nature of poverty, feminists have correctly pointed out that although both men and women are poor, they are affected in different ways, with women having the greatest responsibility for managing poverty (Molyneux, 2007). This is borne out in Posel and Rogan's (2012) analysis of gender trends in poverty in South Africa. Four sets of General Household Survey data were analysed between 1997 and 2006. The authors found that poverty rates declined for men and women, and for male- and female-headed households. Social grant income (that is, the Child Support Grant, old age pensions and disability grants) had a positive effect in reducing the depth of poverty for females and female-headed households. But the analysis points to the persistency of the gendered nature of poverty and the fact that the reduction in poverty favoured males and male-headed households. A subsequent analysis of the National Income Dynamics Survey 2008 data (Southern Africa Labour and Development Research Unit, 2016) confirms this trend and finds that women and people living in female-headed households are up to 30 per cent poorer than men on average, using income poverty as an indicator (Rogan, 2014). A similar poverty risk does not appear to exist when the same analysis is done using a multidimensional poverty measure beyond income. But a lack of nutrition, sanitation and clean water, including higher risk of child mortality, was more prevalent in female-headed households than male-headed households. This was thought to be due to larger numbers of female-headed households being located in rural areas, which continue to have high rates of poverty despite the payment of social grants (Rogan, 2014). This points to the importance of access to basic services and quality health care, which is considered further in the nexus between cash and care services. The Child Support Grant is most effective in reducing chronic poverty. Eighty-five per cent of beneficiaries now live with caregivers in households that were above the upper band of the poverty line of ZAR924 per month (US$63.26, or US$2.1 per day). This finding is derived from an analysis of grant beneficiaries and their households using the National Income Dynamics Survey (NIDS) Wave 1 data for 2008 (Patel and Mavungu, 2016). Without the grant, these children and their caregivers (who are mainly women), would be significantly poorer. The grant is therefore an important social investment in children as well as supporting women in their care responsibilities. Different studies have found that income from cash transfers is pooled and used for general household needs (Delany et al., 2008). The income from the grant, although small, also benefits the household as a whole (Neves et al., 2009).

Reducing chronic poverty has some benefits in supporting women in managing poverty and in improving their psychosocial well-being (Plagerson et al., 2011). But it does not seem to have an impact on changing gender relations even though it buys food (Patel and Hochfeld, 2013). This is examined further below with reference to the perspectives of men on the Child Support Grant.

Male Perspectives on the Child Support Grant

Limited research has been conducted on male beneficiaries of the Child Support Grant. This might be due to the fact that few men have applied for the grant. There is also the difficulty of identifying respondents who would be willing to participate in such studies, possibly because of the assumption that men are reluctant to speak about sensitive and personal matters. Qualitative research studies conducted at the Centre for Social Development in Africa since 2012 indicate the contrary: men were eager to participate in focus groups and interviews to share their views on a range of issues such as father absence and the meaning of fatherhood (Mavungu et al., 2013), and whether and how the grant might build their capabilities (Brils, 2012), among others. Brils (2012) identified three ways in which men are connected with the grant. First are the direct beneficiaries, who are primary caregivers. They are widowed, divorced or are caring for their own children or those of relatives. The second group of men are indirect beneficiaries, that is, the person who actually cares for the child such as a biological father, a grandfather or an uncle. In this scenario, he receives the money via a third party who is the registered primary caregiver of the child with the South African Social Security Agency, which administers the grant and other social protection pro-grammes. This may be due to the primary caregiver living in another city or town, who in turn sends the money each month to the actual caregiver. The reason for not changing the payment arrangement seemed to be due to bureaucratic and logistical complications. The last group is made up of non-beneficiaries of the Child Support Grant. In this arrangement, his partner is the primary caregiver who receives the grant. The non-beneficiary, however, lives in the household with the primary caregiver of the child. Of the three groups, Brils (2012) contends that the males who were direct beneficiaries of the grant had a very strong knowledge of the grant, and cited similar benefits articulated by female beneficiaries reported on above. The indirect beneficiaries had a weaker connection to the grant, although their experiences of the benefits of the grant were similar to the males receiving it directly. The third group (non-beneficiaries) had the weakest connection to the grant. For them, it was a grant to support the mother or the primary caregiver of the child.

Although not mentioned in Brils's study, there is a large group of men who are absent fathers, who have a limited engagement with their children and whose mothers or relatives receive the grant on their behalf. One out of four fathers are absent from their children's lives and do not live with them (Holborn and Eddy, 2011; Mavungu et al., 2013). This phenomenon appears to have increased since the end of *apartheid*. And it is in these instances that female beneficiaries were most aggrieved about the non-involvement of fathers, and particularly for not paying mainten-ance for their children (Beernink, 2012).

Male constructions of fatherhood across the qualitative studies men-tioned above centred on the provider role of the male. For those men who were direct and indirect beneficiaries, the material support provided by the Child Support Grant was highly valued. They used the money for food, clothes and school-related expenses, and for treats for the children (Brils, 2012). Notwithstanding these benefits, they were preoccupied with working, finding work or with pursuing additional livelihood activities. Unemployment and poverty were barriers that affected their self-concept and their masculine identity, and they felt that they had failed as providers. Absent fathers in Mavungu et al.'s (2013) study confirmed this perspective among poor fathers who were disengaged from their children's lives and where a lack of income and employment was cited as a major reason for their absence.

Although male beneficiaries of the Child Support Grant identified with the notion of 'social fathering' – that is, the social role of fathers beyond being material providers only, such as caring, nurturing children, and 'being there for them' – they subscribed to gendered norms and beliefs about the primacy of the mother in the lives of children (Van der Meer, 2016). Some male beneficiaries identified barriers such as a lack of skills to perform these roles, and resistance to performing what they perceived to be feminine tasks (Hoornstra, 2016). Some men felt that there was a perceived bias against them, as society stereotyped all men as being incompetent and disengaged. This was particularly painful for those men who embraced fatherhood and who expressed the desire to only be 'a good father'. While some men reported experiencing a level of social disapproval in their communities about doing care work, others felt supported by their peers, which served to strengthen their paternal identity. Disapproval was also encountered from street-level bureaucrats at the offices of the South African Social Security Agency, who were found to be unhelpful and discouraged them from applying for the grant. This made some of the men feel ashamed and self-conscious in what were perceived to be feminine spaces. Many men interviewed did not know that they could qualify for the grant (Van der Meer, 2016).

The preliminary evidence points to positive perspectives on their everyday lives by direct and indirect male beneficiaries of the grant. However, men experienced barriers in accessing the grant, such as a lack of information and knowledge of application processes, and bias from social security personnel when applying for the grant. Despite male beneficiaries taking responsibility for care of their own children and that of relatives, they still subscribed to dominant socio-cultural beliefs about the primacy of women's roles in caregiving, with men being the providers. Female beneficiaries who were not in relationships with the fathers of their children felt disadvantaged, as fathers refused to pay private maintenance since they commenced receipt of the grant (Patel et al., 2012). Researchers are only beginning to explore some of the complexities of the gendered nature of care with reference to the Child Support Grant. Further in-depth research is needed with male beneficiaries of the grant to draw inferences about whether the impacts are different when the primary caregiver is not a woman, and how men might be supported in their care roles.

The Nexus between Cash, Care and Social Investment

The view that "care matters for social and economic development" (UNRISD, 2010, p. 1) has already been expressed, and it is clear that the Child Support Grant makes an important contribution to this process. With respect to economic development, the grant makes a contribution to human capital development by investing in the human capabilities of children, which is in keeping with social investment theory as discussed in Chapter 1 of this book. The injection of cash into poor households is also considered to stimulate demand for consumption goods, with positive benefits for economic growth along the lines of Keynesian economic theory. Although there is a lack of conceptual clarity about the social investment approach, it was shown in Chapter 1 that there is some convergence around a set of key ideas. This is also revealed in the European literature on the subject (Morel et al., 2009) and in the social development literature focusing primarily on the Global South (Midgley, 2014). One of these key ideas is that social investment policies tend to favour investments in children and families as these are associated with long-term benefits for society in terms of educational attainment, employability and income. Although there is no longitudinal evidence yet to support such claims in South Africa, it would appear from the impact evaluations to date that the grant has the potential to achieve such outcomes.

But it is in the important area of social reproduction that the Child Support Grant has received less attention, particularly from a gender perspective. 'Social reproduction' refers to the social processes and human relations that sustain people, their families and/or households and communities, and upon which productive activity depends (Bakker, 2003). It was argued earlier that care and social support in the private domain, in the family and the household, also matters as women are unequally burdened with care responsibilities that remain unrecognized and invisible. Further, the point was also made that women bear a disproportionate burden for care which is a public good and is integral to the achievement of gender equality (Folbre, 2008).

While cash or material support has had significant benefits for children and their families, it is limited in meeting the complex social care needs of families. Hochfeld's (2015) research draws attention to the psycho-social needs of women recipients of the grant, who experienced various life stressors that have impacted on their personal well-being such as depression, childhood experiences of sexual abuse and domestic violence, substance abuse, and economic insecurity due to job losses and chronic illness. She argues that South Africa's welfare system has prioritized material support over the provision of enabling welfare services that would build the capabilities of women beneficiaries of the Child Support Grant. A lack of recognition of the psychosocial needs of caregivers, particularly women who are the main providers of care, is manifested in the inadequate allocation of public resources for these types of social welfare services.

Other types of services are also crucial to human development outcomes. Besides cash transfers, access to basic education for poor children is free and reaches 60 per cent of children living in communities that meet the poverty targeting thresholds. Significant gains have been made in expanding access to education of poor children: 92 per cent of Child Support Grant beneficiary children are attending school, based on an analysis of the data for 2008 (Patel and Mavungu, 2016). Moreover, close to 9 million children have access to a daily school meal through the National Primary School Nutrition Programme (Graham et al., 2015). But the quality of public education remains poor (Motala, 2014). A lack of education and skills is among the factors that have had a significant impact on the chances of young people obtaining jobs after they leave school and exit the grant system. Young women are more vulnerable to unemployment and make up the largest group who are not in employment, education or training (Statistics South Africa, 2014).

This points to the limits of cash transfers, as so much depends on the quality of schooling and on the delivery of other public services. The low labour market participation rates of women in a context of unusually high unemployment, of around a quarter of the general population, is another factor that limits the impact of the grant. *Apartheid* spatial planning resulted in black communities being far removed from employment opportunities, leading to very high transportation costs. These factors together with the lack of access to affordable child care may account for the low labour market participation rates of Child Support Grant primary caregivers. In 2008, approximately 58 per cent of children in families receiving the grant aged 3–5 years of age had no access to a child care facility, based on the analysis of the 2008 data by the Centre for Social Development in Africa. Although access to other basic services such as water, electricity, sanitation and housing has improved since the mid-1990s (Statistics South Africa, 2011), service delivery failures continue to fuel protests, often of a violent nature, in communities 20 years after the creation of a democratic society.

The lack of coordination and integration of services impacts on the potential of Child Support Grant families to flourish. From this perspective, Hochfeld (2015) argues that state failure in the delivery of public services is a form of misrecognition of the worth and dignity of claimants. It is therefore a form of social injustice for women carers, who are the main providers of social care services (Hochfeld, 2015).

GENDER, CARE AND SOCIAL INVESTMENT

The gender-transformative potential of South Africa's Child Support Grant was explored in this chapter with reference to a review of the local literature. In the absence of national longitudinal research on the social outcomes of the grant, the inferences are preliminary and much more research needs to be conducted. The analysis suggests, first, that the grant has reduced chronic poverty and the depth of poverty for females and female-headed households. But poverty remains a highly gendered phenomenon in South Africa. Grant receipt had some positive effects on the increased financial decision-making power of women, which was strongly associated with greater engagement in the care of their children. Second, despite these improvements and support for women's everyday lives and in easing the burden of care, in practice the grant has had limited impact on changing gender relations and maternalist notions of care. Both women and men subscribe to these views. Gendered beliefs and norms about care appear to be resistant to change, despite the gender-neutral design of the Child Support Grant. Third, the limited research on the impact of the grant on male primary caregivers does not enable us to draw conclusions because of the small size of the samples in the micro-level qualitative studies. What it does show is that where men do engage in care, they experience its benefits positively. Of concern is that fewer men are claiming the grant. Because male caregiving is unusual, it challenges dominant gender frameworks, leading to bias and stereotyping of men who care. The role of street-level bureaucrats in stigmatizing men who apply for the grant needs to be researched further. Information about grant applications targeted at potential male beneficiaries and the public at large is needed to change the feminization of the grant. This will not be an easy task. Socio-cultural beliefs about the gendered division of labour are widespread and can only be tackled when care work is detached from its association with gender (Shefer, 2014). When care work is not valued in itself as a social good, in both the private and the public spheres, the sexual division of labour is reinforced.

This review of the literature and research locally confirms the interconnection between cash and social care services as a crucial element in reducing poverty and, specifically, the gendered and multidimensional nature of poverty in South Africa. One may conclude that cash transfers for children and families are a necessary but not a sufficient mechanism for the achievement of long-term social development and gender transformation. The Child Support Grant is an important social investment in the lives of children and their carers but, by itself, it is limited and needs to work together with other public services, family support and community-level social interventions, coupled with greater access to livelihood opportunities to bring about sustained well-being. In addition, investments in skills development, employment creation and the provision of psychosocial support and child care services are other social investments that are needed to support children and families. Social investment policies in developing countries may need to be adapted to specific country conditions and imperatives. But a gender-neutral approach to social investment may have the unintended effect of deepening gender inequality.

These pointers are useful for other African and developing countries that are searching for more gender-sensitive social protection and welfare service policies. More inclusive, integrated and nuanced social policies are needed to respond to both poverty and gender inequality. As we continue to search for social development solutions, the complexity of the human condition and the lived realities of people's everyday lives should not be lost sight of, as well as how they exercise their agency to achieve their social goals.

REFERENCES

Adato, M., de la Brière, B., Mindek, D. and Quisumbing, A. (2000). *The Impact of PROGRESA on Women's Status and Intrahousehold Relations*. Washington, DC: International Food Policy Research Institute.

Aguero, J.M., Carter, M.R. and Woolard, I. (2006). The Impact of Unconditional Cash Transfers on Nutrition: The South African Child Support Grant. Brasilia: International Poverty Centre. Retrieved from http://www.ipc-undp.org/pub/IPCWorkingPaper39.pdf.

Bakker, I. (2003). Neoliberal governance and the reprivatisation of social reproduction: Social provisioning and shifting gender orders. In I. Bakker and S. Gill (eds), *Power, Production and Social Reproduction*. Basingstoke: Palgrave, pp. 66–82.

Beernink, M. (2012). It Takes Two to Tango, You Know: The Perception of Female Child Support Grant Recipients on the Effect of the Child Support Grant on Paternal Involvement. Master's Thesis, Department of Interdisciplinary Social Science, Utrecht University, Netherlands.

Bhorat, H. and Cassim, A. (2014). South Africa's Welfare Success Story II: Poverty-Reducing Social Grants. *Brookings Africa in Focus*, 28 January.

Retrieved from http://www.brookings.edu/blogs/africa-in-focus/posts/2014/01/27-south-africa-welfare-poverty-bhorat#.

Brils, F.A. (2012). Opportunities and Limitations of Poor South African Fathers: The Child Support Grant and the Capabilities of Fathers to Practice Fatherhood in South Africa. Master's Thesis, Faculty of Social and Behavioural Sciences, Utrecht University, Netherlands.

Budlender, D. (2008). The Statistical Evidence on Care and Non-Care Work across Six Countries. Gender and Development Programme Paper No. 4. Geneva: United Nations Research Institute for Social Development.

Budlender, D. and Lund, F. (2011). South Africa: A legacy of family disruption. *International Institute of Social Studies, Development and Change*, Special Issue: Seen, Heard and Counted: Rethinking Care in a Development Context, 42 (4), 925–946.

Case, A., Hosegood, V. and Lund, F. (2005). The Reach and Impact of Child Support Grants: Evidence from KwaZulu-Natal. *Development Southern Africa*, 22 (4), 467–482.

Delany, A., Ismail, Z., Graham, L. and Ramkisson, Y. (2008). *Review of the Child Support Grant: Uses, Implementation and Obstacle*s. Johannesburg: Department of Social Development, CASE, SASSA and UNICEF.

Department of Social Development (2014). *Analysis of the SOCPEN Database*. Pretoria: Republic of South Africa.

Department of Welfare (1997). *White Paper for Social Welfare*. Pretoria: Department of Welfare.

Folbre, N. (2008). Reforming care. *Politics and Society*, 36 (3), 373–387.

Graham, L., Hochfeld, T., Stuart, L. and Van Gent, M. (2015). Evaluation Study of the National School Nutrition Programme and the Tiger Brands Foundation In-School Breakfast Feeding Programme in the Lady Frere and Qumbu Districts of the Eastern Cape. University of Johannesburg: Centre for Social Development in Africa.

Henshall Momsen, J. (2004). *Gender and Development*. London: Routledge.

Hochfeld, T. (2015). Cash, Care and Social Justice: A Study of the Child Support Grant. Thesis submitted to the Faculty of Humanities, University of Witwatersrand, Johannesburg.

Holborn, L. and Eddy, G. (2011). *First Steps into Healing the South African Family*. Johannesburg: South African Institute of Race Relations.

Hoornstra, H. (2016). Who Cares? Father-Identity, Perceived Expectations and the Gendered Division of Care for Children in South Africa. Masters thesis, Utrecht University, Netherlands.

Kabeer, N. (1999). Resources, Agency, Achievements: Reflections on the Measurement of Women's Empowerment. *Development and Change*, 30 (3), 435–464.

Lund, F. (2008). Paradoxes of Social Policy Reform in South Africa. *Social Work Practitioner-Researcher*, 20 (2), 137–153.

Mavungu, E.M. (2013). Provider Expectations and Father Involvement: Learning from Experiences of Poor 'Absent Fathers' in Gauteng, South Africa. *African Sociological Review*, 17 (1), 65–78.

Mavungu, E.M., Thomson-de Boor, H. and Mphaka, K. (2013). *'So We are ATM Fathers'. A Study of Absent Fathers in Johannesburg, South Africa*. Johannesburg: Centre for Social Development in Africa.

Midgley, J. (2014). *Social Development: Theory and Practice*. London: Sage.

Molyneux, M. (2007). Change and Continuity in Social Protection in Latin America Mothers at the Service of the State? Gender and Development Programme Paper No. 1. Geneva: United Nations Research Institute for Social Development (UNRISD).

Morel, N., Palier, B. and Palme, J. (2009). *What Future for Social Investment?*. Institute for Futures Studies Research Report. Stockholm: Digaloo.

Motala, S. (2014). Equity, Access, and Quality in Basic Education. In T. Meyiwa, M. Nkondo, M. Chitiga-Mabubu, M. Sithole and F. Nyamnjoh (eds), *State of the Nation. South Africa 1994–2014: A Twenty-Year Review*. Cape Town: HSRC Press, pp. 284–295.

Neves, D., Samson, M., van Niekerk, I., Hlatshwayo, S. and du Toit, A. (2009). *The Use and Effectiveness of Social Grants in South Africa*. Cape Town: FinMark Trust, Institute for Poverty, Land and Agrarian Studies, and Economic Policy Research Institute.

Patel, L. (2010). Pointers for Future Research on Gender and Care in Voluntary Organisations in Southern Africa. *Social Work Practitioner-Researcher: Towards an African Social Development Research Strategy*, Special Issue, April, 39–53.

Patel, L. (2015). *Social Welfare and Social Development in South Africa*, 2nd edn. Cape Town: Oxford University Press Southern Africa.

Patel, L. and Hochfeld, T. (2013). Developmental Social Work in South Africa: Translating Policy into Practice. *International Social Work*, 56 (5), 688–702.

Patel, L., Hochfeld, T., Moodley, J. and Mutwali, R. (2012). The Gender Dynamics and Impact of the Child Support Grant in Doornkop, Soweto. CSDA Research Report. University of Johannesburg, Centre for Social Development in Africa.

Patel, L., Knijn, T. and Van Wel, F. (2015). Child Support Grants in South Africa: A Pathway to Women's Empowerment and Child Well-Being?. *Journal of Social Policy*, 44 (2), 377–397.

Patel, L. and Mavungu, E.M. (2016). Children, Families and the Conundrum about Men: Exploring Factors Contributing to Father Absence in South Africa and its Implications for Social and Care Policies. *South African Review of Sociology*, 47 (2), 19–39.

Plagerson, S., Patel, V., Harpham, T., Kielmann, K. and Mathee, A. (2011). Does Money Matter for Mental Health? Evidence from the Child Support Grants in Johannesburg, South Africa. *Global Public Health*, 6 (7), 760–776.

Posel, D. and Rogan, M. (2012). Gendered Trends in Poverty in the Post-Apartheid Period, 1997–2006. *Development Southern Africa*, 29 (1), 96–113.

Razavi, S. (2014). Revisiting the UNRISD Research on the Political and Social Economy of Care: Implications for Future Research and Policy. In V. Reddy, S. Meyer, T. Shefer and T. Meyiwa (eds), *Care in Context: Transnational Gender Perspectives*. Cape Town: HSRC Press, pp. 32–51.

Rogan, M. (2014). Poverty May Have Declined, but Women and Female Headed Households Still Suffer Most. *Econ 3x3*, May. Retrieved from www. econ3x3.org.

Sabates-Wheeler, R. and Devereux, S. (2012). From Seasonal Lives towards A-seasonal Living: Building Seasonality into Risk Management Response. In S. Devereux, R. Sabates-Wheeler and R. Longhurst (eds), *Seasonality, Rural Livelihoods and Development*. Abingdon: Earthscan, pp. 278–298.

Shefer, T. (2014). Narratives of Gender and Practices of Care among Young People in Contemporary South Africa. In V. Reddy, S. Meyer, T. Shefer and T. Meyiwa (eds), *Care in Context: Transnational Gender Perspectives*. Cape Town: HSRC Press, pp. 308–325.

Southern Africa Labour and Development Research Unit (2016). *National Income Dynamics Study 2008, Wave 1* (dataset). Version 6.1. Cape Town: Southern Africa Labour and Development Research Unit (producer), DataFirst (distributor). Retrieved from http://www.nids.uct.ac.za.

Statistics South Africa (2011). *Census 2011 Report*. Retrieved from http:// mobi.statssa.gov.za/census2011/HouseholdIncome.html.

Statistics South Africa (2014). *Work and Labour Force*. Retrieved 6 July 2015 from http://beta2.statssa.gov.za/?page_id=737andid=1.

UNICEF (2006). *State of the World's Children 2007: Women and Children – the Double Dividend of Gender Equality*. New York: UNICEF.

UNRISD (2010). *Combating Poverty and Inequality: Structural Change, Social Policy and Politics*. Geneva: UNRISD.

Van der Meer, M. (2016). 'If They See You're Going to Hang their Underwear, They Start Saying Names: "Hey, this one is gay, man!"'. Male Child Support Grant Beneficiaries' Constructions of their Masculine and Paternal Identities in the Light of Perceived Dominant Gender Norms. Masters thesis, Utrecht University, Netherlands.

Vorster, J. and de Waal, L. (2008). Beneficiaries of the Child Support Grant: Findings from a National Survey. *Social Work Practitioner-Researcher*, 20 (2), 233–248.

World Bank (2015). *The State of Social Safety Nets*. Washington, DC: World Bank.

7. Investing in communities in the United States: social capital, asset building and local enterprise

James Midgley

It was noted earlier in this book that the social investment literature has been primarily concerned with policies formulated and implemented by governments at the national level. These policies prioritize budgetary allocations to education, job training, employment tax credits, family leave and similar programmes. However, little if any attention has been given to the way social investments operate at the community level. Indeed, it can be argued that the community is the missing link in the scholarly literature between national social investment policies and their effects on individuals and households. And yet, as explained in Chapter 1 of this book, community-level social investments are commonplace, particularly in the Global South where community development has featured prominently for many years. Social investments in communities have also expanded rapidly in Western countries. These community-level investments need to be incorporated into the social investment literature if a comprehensive and globally useful conception of social investment is to be formulated.

This chapter contributes to this goal by discussing how the federal and state governments of the United States, supported by nonprofit organizations and increasingly by commercial enterprises, have invested in low-income communities by allocating substantial resources to local social and economic development programmes. It begins by tracing the origins of the community social investment approach in the late nineteenth century, when the settlement house movement introduced various initiatives designed to deal with the social problems associated with industrialization, urbanization and international migration. These activities were subsequently augmented by the Johnson administration's War on Poverty in the 1960s which laid the foundation for current community economic development programmes around the country. The chapter

reviews the evolution of these programmes and shows how social
investments have been used to mobilize local residents for community
building, foster local economic development and promote community
well-being. It then discusses the contribution of more recent theoretical
innovations that have direct implications for social investment. They
include social capital, community asset building and local enterprise
development. The chapter concludes by assessing the achievements as
well as limitations of the community social investment approach in the
United States.

HISTORICAL ROOTS

The idea of community has played an important role in American social
and political thought ever since the nation's founding. The early colonial
settlers established tightly knit farming communities marked by a common religious and linguistic identity and a shared commitment to
collectively meet the challenges of living on a new and unfamiliar
continent. Although the indigenous peoples whose lands they appropri-
ated had an equally strong community identity, this was unappreciated by
the settlers, who readily justified the oppression of native people by
condemning their supposedly heathen and barbaric ways. As more
immigrants settled the land and displaced or annihilated indigenous
peoples, the country's European population eventually spread across the
continent, populating thousands of villages and homesteads with the
towns, including the major capitals, being comparatively small.

This development was celebrated by some of the nation's independence leaders and particularly Thomas Jefferson who idealized rural life
and envisioned a future society based on independent smallholders who
would be self-sufficient and able to exercise their democratic rights
through local participatory institutions. The rise of the Southern planta-
tions and the spread of slavery undermined this idyllic imagery, but a
belief in the virtues of community living continued to exert a powerful
influence. Although de Tocqueville famously reported that Americans
placed a very high value on voluntary association and community
participation when he toured the United States in the 1830s, the subsequent ravages of the civil war and the emergence of industry in the
Northern towns undermined the community as a primary unit of societal
organization. Nevertheless, the ideal of community has persisted up to
the present time.

By the end of the nineteenth century, industrialization, the destruction
wrought by the civil war and a rapid increase in migration from Europe

fostered the explosive growth of urban centres which accommodated large numbers of people who lived in conditions of poverty, deprivation, ill-health and substandard housing accompanied by crime, family dis-integration, substance abuse and other social problems. It was in this context that social reformers began to address the challenge of urban poverty by creating poor relief societies which dispensed charity to those in need. Multiple organizations of this kind emerged in American cities, and although they were paternalistic and drew a sharp distinction between the deserving and undeserving poor, they helped many families in desperate need. Other reformers took a different position, contending that the social problems arising from urbanization could best be met at the community level. By creating community centres where poor people could meet, benefit from educational and recreational services and collaborate to improve local conditions, an effective solution to the poverty problem could be found. Drawing on earlier ideals about community living, this approach was pioneered by the 'settlement houses' which recruited university students, who were primarily from wealthy and middle-class families, to 'settle' in deprived communities and provide services that would set an example to the poor and show them the prospect of a better life (Leiby, 1978). Supervised by salaried staff, and based on Toynbee Hall, the world's first settlement house established in London in 1884, settlement houses proliferated in the United States and recruited students to organize literacy classes, sports and recreational activities and visits to local parks and museums. Fisher (1994) reports that about 200 settlements were in operation at the beginning of the twentieth century; by 1911 when a national association to represent the settlements was founded, this number had doubled to more than 400.

A major aspect of settlement work was 'socializing' the millions of immigrants who settled in the cities, looking for work and a better life. Through group activities, education and outreach, it was believed that immigrants would learn American ways and be assimilated into the dominant culture. Settlement workers also motivated community resi-dents to engage in political activism by lobbying municipal authorities to remove garbage, build playgrounds and repair drains and streets. Jane Addams, the legendary leader of Hull House in Chicago, was a particu-larly strong advocate of local activism which she and her followers combined with political engagement at the national level. Their efforts fostered the subsequent emergence of national social policies particularly in the field of child and maternal welfare (Herrick, 2009).

The spread of the settlements was accompanied by the creation of community centres which did not rely on student volunteers but engaged in similar activities. The community centres were less dependent on a paternalistic mission to uplift the poor and they focused instead on providing opportunities for local groups and voluntary organizations to meet, for adult education and literacy classes to serve local people, and particularly for youth to participate in sports and recreational activities. They often collaborated with other associations such as the Boy Scouts and Girl Guides or with municipal libraries and adult education services. Their youth activities were designed to divert young people from the lure of gang life and engage them in constructive alternatives. In time, the settlement houses became less vibrant and many ceased to be places where university students provided services to local people. In addition, many merged with the community centre movement, and Yan et al. (2009) report that today the many thousands of local community centres that operate throughout the country have their roots in the settlement movement. They embody the community ideal, and although only a minority of local people utilize their services, they remain a focal point for many community activities.

The rise of the settlements and community centres was accompanied by the growth of academic publications on what became known as community organization. One of the earliest books on the subject by Hart (1921) was inspired by the settlements and emphasized the importance of promoting participation in civic life especially among poor people and immigrants who he argued needed to be educated in the virtues of local participation. Lindeman's (1921) highly influential book provided a practical guide for community workers and local leaders who engaged in community organizing. Like Hart, he stressed the need for local demo-cratic participation and outlined ten steps that community workers should adopt to promote the involvement of local people in community affairs. In addition to promoting participation in local decision-making, the contribution of community workers in fostering social solidarity through a process known as 'community building' was emphasized. This was particularly important in communities where immigrants comprised a significant proportion of the local population and needed to be integrated into society.

Another approach stressed the need to coordinate the services of local nonprofit organizations. As voluntary organizations proliferated in the inner-city areas, community practitioners urged that coordinating bodies be created to harmonize their activities, prevent duplication and engage in collective fundraising. These activities became known as 'community social services planning' and are today exemplified by the work of the United Way, which operates throughout the country. By the 1960s, a large number of publications on community social services organizations

had become available and a significant number of community practitioners found employment in agencies responsible for social services
planning. Authoritative books on community organizations by writers
such as Dunham and Harper (Dunham, 1959; Harper and Dunham, 1950)
were widely prescribed in sociology departments and schools of social
work in the United States.

In addition, activism was an important theme in the scholarly literature,
which was reinforced with the popularization of Alinsky's (1946, 1971)
writings after the Second World War. As will be discussed later in this
chapter, community-level activism flourished during the Johnson administration's War on Poverty which provided federal funds for local activists to
promote community participation. These activities became known as
'community action'. Although the term 'community organization' was
widely used to connote all types of community practice, it comprised very
different interventions, including community action, strengthening local
participation through community building, the provision of services and
activities by local community organizations, and the coordination of local
nonprofits. Notably absent from the community organization literature
however was a recognition of the need for projects and programmes that
create employment or in other ways directly address the material needs of
local people. It was primarily because of the War on Poverty that economic
development began to feature prominently in the field, laying the foundations for the subsequent emergence of social investment as an important
theme in the community organization literature.

COMMUNITY INVESTMENT AND THE WAR ON POVERTY

The years following the Second World War are widely regarded as a time
of unparalleled prosperity in the United States. Contrary to predictions,
the millions of men and women who were demobilized at the end of the
war readily found work, as industries geared to war production successfully transformed into civilian manufacture. Together with the expansion
of the services sector and rising government spending on infrastructure,
education, construction, science and the military, plentiful employment
opportunities were created. Keynesian economic policies were adopted to
ensure stability, and with the steady increase of well-paying jobs, living
standards rose, particularly for the expanding white middle class. With
growing affluence, a new generation of young people moved to the
rapidly growing suburbs, which were linked to the urban centres through

new networks of highways. Together with urban renewal and slum clearance policies, the construction of new roads, parking garages and office blocks resulted in the demolition of older housing, further encouraging suburbanization. In many cities, low-income families and particularly those of colour remained behind in the inner cities which were increasingly characterized by blight and poverty.

African Americans began to move from the Southern states to the Northern and Midwestern cities in search of work in the 1930s, and while few secured remunerative industrial employment, the low-wage jobs available to them provided a steady income and an attractive alternative to the rural poverty in which they were raised. In addition, farm mechanization in the South as well as continued racial oppression fostered the migration of African Americans. However, growing racial tensions between newly arrived African American migrants and white residents in the Northern cities accelerated the suburbanization process, creating ghettos of deprived people who were predominantly but not exclusively African American. In addition to blight and lack of employment, new challenges such as crime, gang activities, family disintegration, substance abuse and a rise in the number of single mothers emerged, exacerbating the growing problem of poverty and deprivation.

As the social problems of the inner cities became more acute, nonprofit organizations and government agencies intervened. Statutory child and family welfare services staffed by professional social workers increasingly focused attention on the inner cities, and urban poor relief organizations including food banks expanded rapidly. Like the settlements, community centres provided a variety of preventive services directed at youth and poor families. A particularly important development was the adoption of community activism by local civic and church leaders, who were inspired by the civil rights movement and the work of Alinsky to campaign for the empowerment of local people and the creation of organizations that would represent their interests. One of the first of these, in which Alinsky himself played a leading role, emerged in Chicago in the 1950s and attracted considerable national attention. However, it was soon recognized that these efforts were uncoordinated and poorly funded, prompting the Ford Foundation to launch a major initiative known as the Gray Areas Program which it was hoped would serve as a model for local community development. Another important initiative known as Mobilization for Youth, established in New York by faculty at Columbia University with federal research money, was designed to test the proposition that juvenile delinquency was, as two leaders of the project, Cloward and Ohlin (1960), claimed, largely the result of the lack of opportunities available to low-income families. The

Gray Areas Program and Mobilization for Youth subsequently exerted considerable influence on policy-makers responsible for the War on Poverty.

Although President John F. Kennedy decided to make poverty eradication a priority, his assassination prevented the implementation of his anti-poverty proposals and it was his successor President Lyndon Johnson who in January 1964 declared an 'unconditional war on poverty', which together with other social programmes such as Medicare and Medicaid would create the Great Society (Reich, 2009). The enactment of the Economic Opportunity Act in the same year created a new federal agency called the Office of Economic Opportunity, which launched a variety of programmes which it was believed would eradicate poverty. The legislation's emphasis on creating opportunities that would raise people out of poverty reflected the influence of Mobilization for Youth, while the focus on inner-city communities and their problems owed a debt to the Ford Foundation's Gray Areas Program. A new and important federal agency called the Department of Housing and Urban Development (HUD) was established, and one of its first responsibilities was the implementation of a 1966 statute that authorized a national demonstration project known as the Model Cities Program. This legislation provided federal funding to cities which were competitively chosen to implement major urban renewal initiatives.

However, the most widely discussed and controversial initiative of the War on Poverty was the Community Action Program (CAP). Patterson (2000) reports that this programme reflected the activism that had influenced community practice in the 1950s and was based on the principle that local people should be organized and empowered to address their own problems. Unusually, federal funds were allocated directly to local community organizations instead of municipal governments, to promote what was described as the 'maximum feasible participation' of local people in community decision-making. In this way, the tendency of poor people to adopt a fatalistic view would be challenged, and through empowerment they could be mobilized to pressure municipal governments to provide resources to meet their needs. However, by bypassing both the state and city governments, the programme prompted a fierce backlash that had national political ramifications. Immerwahr (2015) observes that well-connected local politicians pressured the federal government to rein in the programme, and in time its funding was significantly reduced. The problem was exacerbated by serious riots in cities such as Los Angeles, Newark and Detroit, which critics claimed were orchestrated by local activists. On the other hand, the programme contributed to the election of African Americans and other people of colour to municipal office, and to the subsequent increase in their representation in state and national politics. By the 1990s, many cities had African American mayors and a growing number of African Americans were elected to Congress.

The controversy over what Moynihan (1969) described as the Community Action Program's 'maximum feasible misunderstanding' also fostered the emergence of a less activist style of community development, as exemplified in the Model Cities Program and the creation of new local nonprofits known as 'community development corporations'. The first of these was established in the Bedford Stuyvesant neighbourhood in Brooklyn, New York with the support of Senator Robert Kennedy who was eager to champion his brother's commitment to eradicate poverty. Halpern (1995) reports that Kennedy visited the community and, inspired by local leaders, campaigned for federal funds to be allocated to a local nonprofit organization engaged in local infrastructural improvements, employment creation and the construction of affordable housing, rather than activism. In addition to sizeable donations from the business community, in 1966 he secured an amendment to the Economic Opportunity Act which established the Special Impact Program (SIP), which authorized the creation of community development corporations. Since then, the programme has funnelled sizeable resources to community economic corporations and has served as the focal point for community economic development.

During the Nixon presidency an effort was made to abolish the Community Action Program, but faced with a loss of funds for urban renewal, local politicians together with their congressional allies vigorously opposed the administration's proposals. Although the programme was weakened, it continued into the 1970s but with funds being directed through local municipal governments rather than activist organizations. Political support for the Special Impact Program and relatively generous federal funding for local economic development and housing programmes facilitated the spread of community development corporations throughout the country. Green and Haines (2008) report that more than 2000 community development corporations had been established by the end of the twentieth century. All are local nonprofit organizations which access federal funds for housing, urban infrastructure, business development, job training and other economic projects. Most are comparatively small and serve their immediate neighbourhoods, and in addition to their economic activities many also engage in lobbying for improvements in municipal services.

The introduction of Community Development Block Grants (CDBGs) in 1974 consolidated a number of federal funding streams into a single budgetary allocation to urban communities which has since been a major source of community investment. The Reagan administration formally abolished the Community Action Program in 1981, but despite retrenchment, federal funding for urban initiatives and particularly for community development corporations continued. This was partly due to the Ford Foundation, which together with several large business corporations increased funding for community development corporations by creating the Local Initiatives Support Corporation (LISC) in 1980 (Keating, 1999). Today, LISC provides grants, loans and professional advice to local community development corporations. It has branch offices all over the country which assist local community development corporations to implement local development projects and also to raise funds from local sources. Although not all corporations have been successful at fundraising, Green and Haines (2008) note that many have mobilized significant private resources.

Another important development was the enactment by the Carter administration in 1977 of the Community Reinvestment Act, which requires financial institutions holding federal deposit insurance to abandon the practice of 'redlining' geographic areas so that mortgages are made available only to whites seeking to purchase properties in these communities. This statute also required that financial institutions assess the credit needs of local communities and make credit available for local housing, business development and urban projects. Subsequently amendments to the legislation have further encouraged financial institutions to provide credit to underserved households and community organizations, and they have also facilitated the expansion of local financial institutions such as credit unions and banks. Among these was the famed South Shore Bank which was founded in Chicago in 1973, and subsequently renamed the Shore Bank. Although its mortgages and loan services to low-income people were widely admired, it faced serious financial difficulties during the recent Great Recession which began in late 2007 and was taken over by another financial institution.

In 1994, the Clinton administration launched the Empowerment Zones and Enterprise Community initiative (also known as EZ/ECs) that augmented the War on Poverty legacy by creating 11 large empowerment zones around the country. They received tax incentives and subsidies of up to US$100 million each to promote local economic development. Smaller Enterprise Communities receiving similar incentives were also established in 95 communities. An important element of the programme was the provision of an annual subsidy of US$3000 for each local person employed by businesses in the zones. Although funding for the programme expired in 2004, it was reactivated by the Obama administration during the Great Recession and, combined with other initiatives, was designed to stimulate the economy. In addition, Peters and Fisher (2002) observe that many states have established their own enterprise zone programmes which continue up to the present time.

Since the 1960s, these different initiatives have invested significant resources in deprived communities in the United States, and together they comprise a major attempt to decrease urban poverty and address social problems. They have been accompanied by other national cash transfers, nutritional and medical care programmes targeted at low-income house-holds, many of which live in deprived communities. They have also augmented the community investment resources allocated by both the state and federal governments. In addition, the nature and causes of inner-city poverty have been more extensively analysed, and a number of theoretically based policy proposals for addressing inner-city problems through community investment have been produced.

THEORETICALLY BASED PERSPECTIVES ON COMMUNITY INVESTMENT

American social scientists have made a major contribution to understanding the nature, extent and causes of urban poverty. Drawing on the formative work of sociologists such as Park and Burgess at the University of Chicago in the 1920s, they have sought to explain why so many American cities have neighbourhoods with high concentrations of poverty and social problems. Their analyses also led to the formulation of policy proposals for dealing with these problems. Some theoretical perspectives have been particularly relevant for policy purposes and are currently widely used in the community development field. They include Putnam's (2000) work on social capital, Kretzmann and McKnight's (1993) proposals for asset building in poor communities, and Porter's (1995, 1997) argument that inner-city poverty can best be addressed by establishing businesses that create employment and foster a local culture of enterprise. These perspectives provide a more coherent basis for community social investment than the incremental and uncoordinated initiatives of the War on Poverty.

These developments should be seen in the context of a number of explanatory theories of urban poverty that were formulated in the 1980s, a time when the War on Poverty facilitated greater scholarly work in the field. A major development was the conceptualization of inner-city poverty as a constellation of problems that many argued could best be captured by the notion of the underclass. Drawing on Lewis's (1966) theory of the culture of poverty, and far older characterizations of the urban poor by Mayhew in London in the 1830s and subsequently by Marx's notion of the lumpenproletariat, social scientists claimed that an impoverished and deviant underclass dominates American inner cities and that this class is responsible for the problems of poverty, crime, substance abuse and family disintegration that characterize inner-city life. To address these problems, they have sought to identify causal factors that give rise to the underclass.

Wilson's (1987) widely acclaimed research into this question concluded that the primary reason for the emergence of an underclass of what he calls 'truly disadvantaged' people is economic and social change resulting from a lack of opportunities and employment in the inner city. In particular, the export of jobs to the suburbs created a spatial mismatch that prevents inner-city people from finding work and earning a decent living. Massey and Denton (1993) agree that a lack of employment opportunities is a major factor, but they argue that this interpretation downplays the role of racism which has isolated African Americans in segregated urban ghettos. They contend that the problems facing the underclass can only be solved if the underlying problem of racism is addressed. A radically different explanation comes from social policy writers on the political right such as Murray (1984) and Mead (1986, 1992), who claim that the payment of generous welfare payments to poor inner-city people has created a culture of dependency, deviance and worklessness that demands radical solutions including the requirement that welfare recipients are weaned off benefits and obtain work. Otherwise, the self-perpetuating underclass will continue to be responsible for poverty and a host of related inner-city social problems.

Although the findings of studies into the underclass still resonate with community development scholars, more recent research that has direct policy implications for community investment now arguably exerts greater influence in the field. As mentioned earlier, Putnam, Kretzmann and McKnight and Porter have all promoted the idea that social investments are needed to promote the well-being of inner-city people. Putnam (2000) popularized the idea that social capital, as reflected in robust networks and social bonds, is required to promote economic development. Drawing on research he undertook with colleagues in Italy (Putnam et al., 1993), he found that areas in the country with well-developed social networks recorded higher rates of economic growth than areas where civil society participation was limited. To create vibrant and economically prosperous communities, social capital investments are needed, particularly in urban areas where social bonds are weak.

Social capital offers a uniquely sociological perspective on community social investment that stresses the role of social relationships in community development rather than individual capabilities as emphasized by the human capital approach. In addition, social capital advocates believe that local economic development is a function not only of entrepreneurship and financial capital but also of social networks that foster and support economic development. For this reason, policies and programmes should be introduced to strengthen local relationships and build trust among community members, particularly in deprived inner-city communities marked by social disorganization, crime and conflict. Although conventional community development interventions that build local civic organizations, empower local people and establish economic projects all mobilize social capital, Midgley and Livermore (1998) argue that community practitioners need to link these activities directly to economic projects in ways that promote social capital. They stress the importance of creating, strengthening and sustaining local networks known as 'bonding' ties that build social networks and solidarity. In addition, 'bridging' ties that extend beyond the community and access external resources should be strengthened. These ideas have exerted considerable influence and the social capital approach has become popular in community practice in the United States. Today, many urban community development initiatives have introduced programmes that strengthen local networks and foster civic participation in local economic initiatives. In addition, the Ford Foundation's Local Initiatives Support Corporation (LISC) mentioned earlier has, as Gittell and Vidal (1998) report, used social capital theory to frame its activities. The technical assistance it provides to local community development corporations emphasizes the need to maximize local participation and decision-making not only to mobilize community support for local development but also to build social capital.

A second conceptual perspective that has informed community social investment is Kretzmann and McKnight's (1993) asset building community development (or ABCD) approach, which has become very popular in community development circles in the United States. Building on Sherraden's (1991) pioneering work on financial assets as well as their own experience of community work, they recognized the importance of asset accumulation in low-income communities. They also became critical of the tendency among practitioners, journalists, politicians and academics to focus attention on the 'pathologies' that allegedly characterize inner cities. This tendency has fostered a pessimistic view of what community development can achieve, when in fact poor communities have many strengths which if recognized and developed can promote a more positive and successful approach. In addition to local schools, churches, libraries, clinics, community centres and other tangible resources, poor communities have human and social assets in the form of local knowledge and social networks that can be used constructively by community practitioners.

Reflecting the negative bias that has historically characterized community practice, formal needs assessments that identify the major deficits of inner-city communities have been routinely employed to form the basis for programmatic responses. However, this practice has simply reinforced negative stereotypes and should, Kretzmann and McKnight argue, be abandoned in favour of a process they call 'asset mapping'. Using asset mapping, practitioners are able to identify local community strengths and introduce projects and programmes that build on these strengths. However, they caution that asset mapping should not be undertaken by outside professionals but in close collaboration with local people. For this reason, community practitioners need to identify and reach out to community members who are active in local associations, churches and social clubs. Another important requirement is that close collaboration between different local organizations and their members be forged. These formative steps lead to a greater awareness of possibilities and a growing enthusiasm for asset building in the community. It also helps community members to unite behind efforts to access external resources.

Green and Haines (2008) observe that the ABCD approach has been particularly popular among community development corporations which are primarily committed to housing construction and other infrastructural development projects. These organizations, they point out, provide a set of concrete and achievable goals that are highly compatible with the asset building approach. In addition, the asset approach encourages community development corporations to reach out to community residents who do not serve on their governing boards. By involving local people more extensively in asset building, support for new initiatives can be mobilized. In addition to constructing new housing, community centres and similar facilities, existing infrastructural resources can also be repaired and modernized. Of course, people's involvement in asset building has the added advantage of strengthening human, cultural and social assets. By mobilizing local people to build community assets, the ABCD approach exemplifies the role of social investment at the community level.

A third theoretical perspective that provides a basis for community investment is Porter's (1995, 1997) proposals for promoting business investment in poor communities. Although not welcomed in left-wing academic circles or by many grass-roots community activists, his ideas have attracted attention for arguing that the problems of inner-city communities will only be solved if the material needs of poor people are addressed through large-scale employment creation by commercial firms. Although Porter recognizes that many community development corporations and nonprofits have established small businesses, they have seldom been successful, nor have they created employment on a significant scale. A major problem is that few have operated on a profit-making basis, and to be successful, businesses that are motivated by profits rather than an altruistic concern for inner-city problems should be established. This usually requires policies that invite established firms to move into inner-city neighbourhoods, but entrepreneurs can also be enticed to establish new businesses through incentives, subsidies and other advantages. In either case, the entrepreneurs who own or operate these businesses, rather than local bureaucracies or nonprofit organizations, are best placed to assess the prospects of investing in the inner city and launching profitable initiatives. Because of their experience, business acumen and desire to succeed, they can determine whether there are profits to be made in the inner city.

Porter is optimistic that many firms will recognize that inner-city communities have competitive advantages that are conducive to business investment. He highlights these advantages and provides case examples of how they can be exploited. Although it is widely believed that the main advantage of the inner city is its low rental property values, Porter disagrees, and instead emphasizes the strategic location of inner cities which, he points out, provides ready links to regional as well as local markets. The concentration of offices in the central business district reveals that cities are the hub of regional economies which inner-city businesses can also access. In addition, inner-city businesses are well placed to serve local people and office workers in nearby central business districts. He also believes that inner cities have untapped human resources which need to be cultivated through education and training programmes. However, the right priorities should be set. Profit-seeking must be recognized as the primary motivation for business investment, which should then be accompanied by programmes designed to produce skilled and knowledgeable workers. Many urban initiatives have failed because they invest in education and job training without having readily accessible employment opportunities. By first launching profitable commercial ventures, employment will increase and appropriate training opportunities can then be established.

Despite his strong emphasis on profit-making, Porter does not dismiss the need for social services and related welfare programmes. However, he argues that community development has for many years emphasized resource redistribution by accessing federal funds and the largess of foundations, rather than generating resources through local entre-preneurship and creating viable businesses in inner-city communities. The switch from wealth redistribution to local wealth creation will necessitate a different role for welfare programmes, which should support business development rather than providing resource transfers. It is by recognizing and exploiting the inner city's competitive advantage, and establishing vibrant businesses that create employment, that poverty and its related social problems will be addressed.

THE IMPACT OF COMMUNITY INVESTMENT

Since the War on Poverty, hundreds of millions of dollars have been spent on poor inner-city communities in the United States by the federal, state and municipal governments, large foundations and nonprofit organ-izations. In addition to community development corporations which have spearheaded these investments, urban planners, social workers, com-munity activists and many others employed by governmental and non-profit organizations are engaged in a variety of programmes that promote community well-being. Taken together, these resources amount to a significant investment that has sought to improve local infrastructure, build affordable housing, promote community participation, establish local businesses and provide health, education and other social services.

These investments have undoubtedly produced positive results, but despite well-documented evaluations of particular community develop-ment programmes, little research into their overall impact has been undertaken. Although many examples of successful community invest-ment programmes can be given, it is painfully obvious that inner-city poverty and its attendant social problems persist. Most American cities still have concentrations of poor people living in communities with inadequate public and social services, and many are characterized by high rates of violence exacerbated by police brutality. In addition, substance abuse, unemployment, crime and family disintegration remain widespread. The loss of many young people and especially African American and Latino men to gang violence, random shootings and drug overdoses deprives these communities of vital human resources. Just one recent manifestation of the problems that continue to plague many inner cities was the riot in Baltimore in 2015 following the killing of an unarmed African American man by the city's police. As a result of the riot, many small businesses were destroyed, housing was damaged and local support for community building was undermined.

On the other hand, there is scope for optimism. Writing at the end of the last century, Grogan and Proscio (2000) contend that urban renewal policies and programmes were having a positive effect and that many examples of 'comeback cities' could be given. In addition to successful inner-city community development initiatives, van Agtmael and Bakker (2016) observe that several cities which have been in decline because of deindustrialization are attracting new business start-ups, especially by high-tech firms. Concerted effort by the state and municipal governments, together with the support of private investors and foundations, is also helping to rebuild Detroit, a city that has become emblematic of urban decline in the United States. Although gentrification has also played a role as several municipal governments have revitalized abandoned waterfronts and warehouse districts, attracting middle-class residents, it has already been shown that many poor communities have also benefited from community development initiatives. One example is the Bedford Stuyvesant neighbourhood mentioned earlier, which was the location of the country's first community development corporation. Over the years, it has attracted substantial investments and is now a prosperous community.

However, much more needs to be done to formulate a coherent basis for community investment. The three theoretical approaches to community investment discussed earlier are being used by community practitioners around the country, but they could be more effective if synthesized into a unitary approach that combines their different recommendations. Social capital, asset and enterprise theories need to be integrated and adopted by local community development programmes to maximize their potential. The current practice of applying their insights to separate projects is wasteful and fails to fully exploit their policy proposals. This provides a unique opportunity for academics to respond and contribute to the formulation of a holistic community investment approach that can benefit communities both in the United States and around the world.

REFERENCES

Alinsky, S. (1946). *Reveille for Radicals*. Chicago, IL: University of Chicago Press.
Alinsky, S. (1971). *Rules for Radicals*. New York: Random House.
Cloward, R.A. and Ohlin, L.E. (1960). *Delinquency and Opportunity: A Theory of Delinquent Gangs*. Glencoe, IL: Free Press.
Dunham, A. (1959). *Community Welfare Organization: Principles and Practice*. New York: Thomas Crowell.

Fisher, R. (1994). *Let the People Decide: Neighborhood Organizing in America.* New York: Twayne Publishers.

Gittell, R. and Vidal, A. (1998). *Community Organizing: Building Social Capital as a Development Strategy.* Thousand Oaks, CA: Sage Publications.

Green, G.P. and Haines, A. (2008). *Asset Building and Community Development.* Thousand Oaks, CA: Sage.

Grogan, P. and Proscio, T. (2000). *Comeback Cities: A Blueprint for Urban Neighborhood Revival.* Boulder, CO: Westview Press.

Halpern, R. (1995). *Rebuilding The Inner City: A History of Neighbourhood Initiatives to Address Poverty in the United States.* New York: Columbia University Press.

Harper, E.B. and Dunham, A. (eds) (1950). *Community Organizing in Action.* New York: Association Press.

Hart, J.K. (1921). *Community Organization.* New York: Macmillan.

Herrick, J.M. (2009). Social Policy and the Progressive Era. In J. Midgley and M. Livermore (eds), *Handbook of Social Policy.* Thousand Oaks, CA: Sage Publications, pp. 114–132.

Immerwahr, D. (2015). *Thinking Small: The United States and the Lure of Community Development.* Cambridge, MA: Harvard University Press.

Keating, W.D. (1999). Federal Policy and Poor Urban Neighbourhoods. In W.D. Keating and N. Krumhotz (eds), *Rebuilding Urban Neighbourhoods: Achievements, Opportunities and Limits.* Thousand Oaks, CA: Sage Publications, pp. 14–32.

Kretzmann, J. and McKnight, J.L. (1993). *Building Communities from the Inside Out: A Path Toward Finding and Mobilizing Community's Assets.* Evanston, IL: Institute for Policy Research, Northwest and University.

Leiby, J. (1978). *A History of Social Welfare and Social Work in the United States.* New York: Columbia University Press.

Lewis, O. (1966). The Culture of Poverty. *Scientific American*, 214 (1), 19–25.

Lindeman, E.C. (1921). *The Community: An Introduction to the Study of Community Leadership and Organization.* New York: Association Press.

Massey, D.S. and Denton, N.A. (1993). *American Apartheid: Segregation and the Making of the Underclass.* Cambridge, MA: Harvard University Press.

Mead, L.M. (1986). *Beyond Entitlement: The Social Obligations of Citizenship.* New York: Free Press.

Mead, L.M. (1992). *The New Politics of Poverty: The Nonworking Poor in America.* New York: Basic Books.

Midgley, J. and Livermore, M. (1998). Social Capital and Local Economic Development: Implications for Community Social Work Practice. *Journal of Community Practice*, 5 (1–2), 29–40.

Moynihan, D.P. (1969). *Maximum Feasible Misunderstanding: Community Action in the War on Poverty.* New York: Free Press.

Murray, C. (1984). *Losing Ground: American Social Policy, 1950–1980.* New York: Basic Books.

Patterson, J. (2000). *America's Struggle Against Poverty in the Twentieth Century.* Cambridge, MA: Harvard University Press.

Peters, A.H. and Fisher, P.S. (2002). *State Enterprise Zones: Have they Worked?* Kalamzaoo, MI: Upjohn Institute.

Porter, M.E. (1995). The Competitive Advantage of the Inner City. *Harvard Business Review*, 73 (3), 55–71.

Porter, M.E. (1997). New Strategies for Inner-City Economic Development. *Economic Development Quarterly*, 11 (1), 11–27.

Putnam, R.D. (2000). *Bowling Alone: The Collapse and Revival of American Community*. New York: Simon & Schuster.

Putnam, R.D., Leonardi, R. and Nanetti, R.Y. (1993). *Making Democracy Work: Civic Traditions in Modern Italy*. Princeton, NJ: Princeton University Press.

Reich, M. (2009). Social Policy and the Great Society. In J. Midgley and M. Livermore (eds), *The Handbook of Social Policy*. Thousand Oaks, CA: Sage Publications, pp. 151–168.

Sherraden, M. (1991). *Assets and the Poor: A New American Welfare Policy*. Armonk, NY: M.E. Sharpe.

van Agtmael, A.W. and Bakker, F. (2016). *The Smartest Places on Earth: Why Rustbelts are the Emerging Hotspots of Global Innovation*. New York: Public Affairs Press.

Wilson, W.J. (1987). *The Truly Disadvantaged: The Inner City, The Underclass and Public Policy*. Chicago, IL: University of Chicago Press.

Yan, M.C., Lauer, S. and Sin, R. (2009). Issues in Community Rebuilding: The Task of Settlement Houses in Two Cities. *Social Development Issues*, 31 (1), 39–54.

8. Cash transfers as social investments: the Brazilian case

Anthony Hall

Although the notion of social investment has gained prominence in Western Europe and the Organisation for Economic Co-operation and Development (OECD) nations, it is by no means confined to the more industrialized countries. Some observers suggest that there has been a convergence in such thinking between developed and more advanced developing countries around the globe. It is claimed that this 'new development welfare thinking' (Jenson, 2010) has essentially diffused from Europe as the single major influence on social policy-making. This supposedly 'new' approach is geared towards employment creation and raising incomes through productive activities supported by social programmes that encourage investments in human capital and stimulate individual advancement rather than encouraging undue reliance on social protection.

According to Jenson (2010), the diffusion of a social investment perspective from Europe to Latin America, for example, has been facilitated by several factors. These include the spread of neoliberalism; the advent of a supposedly less central role for the state; the influence of international agencies such as the United Nations Children's Fund (UNICEF) with its pro-human capital message; and the transmission of such ideas through networks of communication and alliances amongst like-minded development actors. Draibe and Riesco (2009, pp. 328, 335) support this notion, suggesting that in Latin America a "new developmental welfare state model seems to be in the making ... based on the models of Western Europe and other advanced regions". Incorporating a regulatory role for the state, with private enterprise directing economic affairs and active civil society institutions, they optimistically predict that a regional social policy modelled along these lines could soon emerge, at least in Latin America.

Conditional cash transfer (CCT) programmes are sometimes presented as a form of social investment that has its origins in anti-poverty strategies developed by Western multilateral aid agencies such as the World Bank (2000). While the neoliberal policy context that has emerged since the 1990s has undoubtedly influenced the direction of change, however, it would be oversimplistic to see this as a totally one-way process. The contention in this chapter is that the design and implementation of cash transfers have also been strongly influenced by national circumstances and policy priorities. There is a strong argument for suggesting that many basic tenets of the conditional cash transfer, social investment model owe their origins, at least in part, to domestic influences from the developing countries themselves as much as to direct stimuli from the West.

In fact, it could be said that national policy-makers might be doing themselves something of an injustice by seriously overplaying the influence of Western thinking and underemphasizing their own impact on this process. Several years before Mexico's conditional cash transfer programme *Oportunidades* (now known as *Prospera*), the first in the world, was conceived, its creator Santiago Levy (1991) had suggested the idea of an integrated national scheme for the country combining nutrition, health and education initiatives targeted at the poorest citizens. Furthermore, there is clear evidence that home-grown thinking from the South has directly informed new policy-making in the industrialized world. For example, New York City authorities, based on the Mexican experience, introduced the 'Opportunity NYC – Family Rewards' scheme in 2007 to reduce poverty amongst six of the most deprived boroughs (Riccio et al., 2010).

CASH TRANSFERS AS SOCIAL INVESTMENT

It is enlightening to briefly examine some of the historical influences on development thinking in order to set the stage for the emergence of the social investment model. While the origins of this approach can be traced back in large measure to Keynesian economics in the pre- and post-war period, in development discourse it emerged somewhat later. As noted in Chapter 1 of this book, four decades ago, Robert McNamara focused attention on promoting integrated rural development, to link poverty alleviation with improved productivity and employment generation, together with investments in health and education (World Bank, 1975).

By the 1990s, the need for anti-poverty programmes was based on enhancing the productivity of labour with investments in basic social services such as education for the world's poor supplemented by targeted programmes and safety nets (World Bank, 1990). Ten years later, the

international anti-poverty discourse had become focused more specifically on investments in human capital and basic services, including a key
role for cash transfers and safety nets (World Bank, 2001). This evolution
in thinking on anti-poverty strategies and relevant social policies
undoubtedly influenced domestic policy-making in Brazil as the new
Constitution of 1988 challenged the old social policy agenda in the
country.

Long before social investment came to be considered a European
construct that had diffused to developing countries, many economists had
already drawn attention to the importance of investing in human capital
to enhance the productivity of individuals and society in poorer countries;
for example, through education (Becker, 1964; Psacharopoulos, 1973).
Midgley and Tang (2001) traced the evolution of developmental welfare
from the 1970s as an initiative that linked welfare provision within a
broader and more comprehensive economic development approach. This
built upon earlier efforts to emphasize the importance of a 'unified
approach' to economic and social development that recognized the
importance of a balanced strategy to promoting development in the South
(Hardiman and Midgley, 1982). Similarly, the livelihoods-based approach
to conceiving social policy envisaged integrating social welfare and
productive activities (Hall and Midgley, 2004).

Thus, in many respects, the antecedents of a social investment
approach can be traced back several decades in the writings of development scholars and policy-makers. In this sense, they can be said to have
originated to a large extent outside Western policy circles, and more
within a global intellectual community focused on analysing the specific
conditions of the South and drawing upon the attributes and potential of
these countries for their inspiration. A case in point concerns the
introduction of the conditional cash transfer, now considered a major
weapon in the armoury for implementing a social investment strategy in a
developing-country context.

Until Brazil's new Constitution was established in 1988, social policy
for its poorest citizens was fragmented and unsystematic, comprising
largely of charitable interventions such as the distribution of food baskets
and health assistance, administered largely by civil society actors, religious bodies and a handful of official agencies. These resources were
often consciously distributed according to electoral criteria by political
elites. Regular social protection applied only to formal sector workers
and was contribution-based.

All this was about to change in the 1990s. Following two decades of
military dictatorship, vigorous debates in the Constituent Assembly
allowed competing national views over the future direction of social

policy and nature of social protection to be fully aired. These competing internal political pressures and the growing strength of left-wing sentiments in Brazil signalled a new direction towards broader access to social services for the wider public and their increasingly non-contributory nature. The Congressional Joint Commission on Poverty, created through a Constitutional amendment, "helped to create a political consensus around the idea that conditional cash transfer programmes were the best policy to fight poverty in the country" (Soares, 2011, p. 56; Jaccoud et al., 2010). Thus, under Brazil's post-military 1988 Constitution, the responsibility of government to supply basic protection, social rights and public goods, irrespective of the ability to pay, was firmly established.

Once widely criticized as representing a minimalist, residual and almost Victorian approach to social policy, conditional cash transfers are now sometimes perceived as having almost transformative potential. They have also spread rapidly across the globe, numbering just three in 1997, rising to more than 30 by 2008, and 52 by 2014. This figure rises to more than 170 if unconditional cash transfers (UCTs) are included. Cash transfers are most popular in Latin America, which has 19 conditional and 25 unconditional cash transfer programmes, with Africa hosting 13 and 37 respectively (World Bank, 2014). In Latin America, all major countries have cash transfer schemes of variable sizes, including Mexico (*Prospera*) and Brazil (*Bolsa Família*, or family grant), the world's largest such programmes. Brazil's *Bolsa Família* now benefits 13 million families or more than 50 million people, fully one-quarter of the country's population.

Such transfers are relevant to the debate on social investment because they are perceived as strengthening 'human capital' and breaking the 'vicious cycle of poverty', rather than simply distributing cash to the needy (World Bank, 2000; Bastagli, 2011). In Brazil and other Latin American countries, conditional cash transfers entail creating mutual obligations between the state and participating citizens. Beneficiaries make a commitment, sometimes in the form of a written contract, as in the case of Chile, to meeting obligations in terms of minimal school attendance and participation in preventive health care programmes such as vaccination campaigns. Nowadays, this new 'developmental welfare thinking' should, as Midgley and Tang (2001, p. 247) put it, promote "social programmes that are investment oriented or 'productivist' by promoting economic participation and generating positive rates of return to the economy". In other words, "The focus is now on supporting the capacity of households in poverty, strengthening and protecting their consumption, agency and human capital" (Barrientos and Santinbáñez, 2009, p. 25).

It is worth pointing out, however, that in addition to the *Bolsa Família*, social assistance programmes in Brazil have a much wider reach, although these have no conditionalities attached. The 1988 Constitution established principles of social citizenship that revived and strengthened two nationwide pension schemes. The rural pensions scheme (*Previdência Social Rural*, PSR) can trace its origins to the 1960s and 1970s, and now reaches around 8 million workers. The continuous benefit scheme for the poor elderly and disabled (*Benefício de Prestação Continuada*, BPC) reaches a further 3.7 million.

Both programmes provide relatively generous benefits, amounting to one minimum wage per month (US$318). *Bolsa Família* individual benefits are much lower, ranging from US$40 to US$160 per month, depending on the number of children in a family, but it has a much wider influence through its impact on 50 million people (Barrientos, 2013). This is particularly relevant when considering how *Bolsa Família* might have influenced the political preferences and choices of the voting public. However, as far as the present discussion on social investment is concerned, *Bolsa Família* is especially relevant.

In addition to the above-mentioned national pension schemes, small-scale cash transfer programmes were introduced in several municipalities, including the capital Brasilia. Having spread to 1115 municipalities by 2000, the flagship *Bolsa Escola* (school grant) eventually became a federal programme in 2001 under the Ministry of Education. Other federal initiatives included the child labour eradication programme (PETI); the food grant scheme under the Ministry of Health, aimed at expectant mothers and infants; and a gas subsidy programme under the Ministry of Mines and Energy to compensate poor households for rising prices (Hall, 2006, 2008).

These separate initiatives were established during the administration of President Fernando Henrique Cardoso (1995–2002) but under his successor, Luiz Inácio Lula da Silva ('Lula'), the four programmes were combined in the first instance under the Zero Hunger (*Fome Zero*) umbrella. But the programme was relaunched as *Bolsa Família* after a few months, administered by the new Ministry of Social Development. During its inception, the programme received strong technical and financial support from the World Bank (2000). Brazil, along with Mexico, was one of the pioneers in adopting conditional cash transfers as part of its anti-poverty strategy, following a risk-based approach to social protection.

In 2004, the World Bank provided a sector loan of US$572 million, supplemented later by a further US$200 million, to strengthen programme management and implementation. At the same time, the

Inter-American Development Bank (IADB) provided support of more than US$1 billion (Hall, 2008). The World Bank thus provided the government of Brazil with vital assistance to implement and evaluate the programme, mainly via capacity building and training. Furthermore, this external support for the global spread of cash transfers to fight poverty has been very much in line with the Bank's risk-based approach to social protection (Hall, 2015).

The reborn *Bolsa Família* was launched as an integrated programme, its activities now coordinated and streamlined, designed to address mass poverty. Although the programme is centrally managed through a dedicated unit (SENARC) within the Ministry of Social Development, the programme implementation itself is decentralized to the country's 5564 municipalities. Functions include beneficiary identification and registration, based on quotas set by central government. Local *Bolsa Família* administration units liaise with schools and clinics to monitor beneficiary compliance with education and health obligations. With this locally collected information to hand, the federal government administers a means test to determine eligibility for the programme and then informs municipalities of those applicants who have been selected. A publicly owned savings bank, the *Caixa Econômica Federal*, is responsible for disbursing transfers through its ATM system and for maintaining the *CadÚnico* central database, which can be remotely accessed by municipal authorities (Barrientos, 2013).

Household incomes in the poorest regions, and municipal revenues, depend significantly on such transfers from the centre. There are several ways in which conditional cash transfers can in theory contribute towards social investment. These could be identified in terms of various dimensions: tackling mass poverty, reducing inequality and strengthening human capital. Cash transfers have generally been regarded primarily as an effective instrument for tackling widespread poverty. In this respect, Brazil's *Bolsa Família* has a very respectable track record. According to official figures, absolute poverty (defined in Brazil as a household income of under one-quarter of the legal minimum wage, which in 2014 stood at US$318 per month) halved from 21 per cent in 2010 to under 11 per cent by 2008, with the largest fall being registered in the Northeast, the country's poorest region (IPEA, 2010). However, isolating the impacts of the programme is methodologically problematic (Barrientos, 2013).

Using national household survey figures to create counterfactual poverty rates, Soares (2013) found that social protection lifted 13.2 per cent of participants above the poverty line of roughly US$2 per day. He concluded that about 30 million people would have fallen into poverty without social protection. The elderly are the main beneficiaries of social protection programmes through the rural pensions (which cover almost 22 per cent of the population) and continuous cash benefits. However, because of the relatively low *Bolsa Família* benefit levels compared with other social assistance schemes, the programme offers little support for children. Having said that, its impact is quite broad, benefiting the poor Northeast in particular, as would be expected. There is some evidence to suggest that *Bolsa Família* has had a positive impact at the regional level (Silveira-Neto and Azzoni, 2012).

In addition to reducing absolute poverty levels, *Bolsa Família* is credited with having made a marginal contribution to the fall in inequality, a process that has been under way for more than a decade. The Gini coefficient of income distribution dropped from 0.600 in 2000 to 0.534 by 2009. Income transfers in Brazil rose from 12 per cent of gross domestic product (GDP) in the early 1990s to 16 per cent by 2009, and have been accompanied by a decline in inequality. Social protection in general accounts for one-quarter of this fall over the period. It is claimed that *Bolsa Família* specifically is responsible for 14 per cent of this drop, reducing the Gini coefficient by 0.8 per cent (Soares, 2013).

The remainder is due to labour market factors such as regular, above-inflation increases in the legal minimum wage, alongside a credit-fuelled consumer boom and general macroeconomic growth. According to some analysts, the general increase in disposable income levels in Brazil has given rise to the emergence of a so-called 'new middle class'. The 'C-class', as it is known, grew from around 66 million in 2006 to about 115 million in 2011, in a population of more than 200 million (Neri, 2011). However, during 2015 there was no increase in *Bolsa Família* monthly payments, which has probably helped to undermine these positive trends evident during the past decade. Combined with Brazil's economic downturn during 2015–2016, it is highly likely that these economic gains resulting from cash transfers have to some extent been neutralized.

BOLSA FAMÍLIA AS SOCIAL INVESTMENT?

Rhetorical pronouncements by optimistic policy-makers often claim a range of benefits arising from conditional cash transfer programmes such as *Bolsa Família* that go far beyond simply handing out cash to the poor. Indeed, meeting certain prerequisites has been considered essential, both to confirm people's worthiness to receive such advantages, while at the same time strengthening human capital. In Latin America, including

Brazil, such demonstrations of mutual obligation were considered important in order to convince the wider public and voters that the poor 'deserved' such assistance and could not expect something for nothing (de Britto, 2008). Although income transfers targeted at the poorest are now increasingly identified as an integral component of basic citizens' rights in many countries, this moral sentiment requiring mutual obligation to be fulfilled is still commonly expressed.

At the same time, conditional cash transfer programmes would contribute directly to national development by strengthening the stock of human capital. Based on modernization theories put forward in the 1960s, the productive capacity of the population would be enhanced by investing in people, principally through interventions in education, health and nutrition. This risk-based approach to social protection would target the vulnerable, breaking the vicious cycle of poverty and acting as a 'springboard' for development (World Bank, 2000). In order to examine the supposed links between *Bolsa Família* and social investment goals, it is worth considering impacts in education, health and nutrition, as well as related aspects such as citizenship.

Education

The *Bolsa Família* was consolidated from a number of originally subnational cash transfer programmes, the most prominent of which was the *Bolsa Escola*, or 'school grant' scheme. Starting as a municipal and state initiative, the *Bolsa Escola*, in 2001, was the first to be taken up as a national programme by the federal government. Under *Bolsa Família*, children have a minimum attendance requirement of 85 per cent. This is probably the easiest regulation to record and monitor in the programme. The earliest evaluations by the Ministry of Social Development show improved primary and secondary school attendance and a fall in dropout rates (Soares et al., 2010).

Subsequent longitudinal studies by the Washington-based International Food Policy Research Institute (IFPRI) show similar results, with increased participation rates for children aged 6–17 years of 4.5 per cent. These improvements were particularly striking for girls, with increases in enrolments (8.2 per cent) and grade progression (10.4 per cent) compared with non-*Bolsa Família* participants (de Brauw et al., 2014; Glewwe and Kassouf, 2012). Impacts also varied by region. In the poorer Northeast, the effect of the programme was more marked, stimulating enrolments by 11.7 per cent. The grant was found to be especially effective in retaining girls older than 14 at school, and slightly increasing the age of boys entering the labour market.

In terms of human capital strengthening through boosting school enrolments, there is some evidence to support conditional cash transfers as a vehicle for promoting educational investments in terms of the quantity of education delivered. However, this says little or nothing about the quality of these educational inputs and their effectiveness in enhancing people's productive capacity. This effect can only be very marginal at best as a consequence of the *Bolsa Família*, although girls and the poorest rural regions may benefit disproportionately and this may have a multiplier or demonstration effect on local populations.

To what extent the educational component of *Bolsa Família* can be considered a tool of social investment is a moot point. In theory this is a possibility; but in practice it is difficult, if not impossible, to demonstrate. To the extent that the programme fits within the country's mainstream education policy as an add-on to boost enrolments at the margin, there is some cause for optimism. Since 2006, public spending on basic education has risen steadily as a proportion of GDP, from 4.1 per cent to 4.9 per cent by 2010 (da Silva Gomes, 2013).

However, although educational reforms have redistributed resources more equitably, no provision has been made for guaranteeing standards of educational quality under the law. On the basis of figures compiled by the National System for the Evaluation of Basic Education (SAEB), it was concluded that the proportion of children reaching minimum standards of achievement was 'very small' (Matos Diniz et al., 2013). It has been estimated, for example, that in order to ensure that minimum standards are met, public spending on educational investment per pupil should be two-thirds higher than is currently recommended by official guidelines (Ximenes, 2013).

This discrepancy may help to account for the fact that, despite a 92 per cent enrolment rate for children up to age 14, Brazil underperforms quite markedly on international assessment indices. The quality of public education in Brazil has come under intense criticism for many years for failing to reach standards that match the country's economic status. The system is adversely affected by several factors; these include underinvestment in school infrastructure, the high proportion of unqualified teachers, unacceptable levels of grade repetition, poor access to early childhood education, and heavy government subsidies to the tertiary sector at the expense of basic education (Birdsall and Sabot, 1996; Arnold and Jalles, 2014; ABPM, 2013).

Health and Nutrition

In addition to encouraging school attendance, the *Bolsa Família* is intended to improve the take-up of preventive health care facilities. The first round of evaluations, published in 2007, found no evidence of a positive impact on child immunizations (cited in Soares et al., 2010). This was attributed to the lack of health care facilities and medical staff. It has undermined service delivery in the health sector, which is chronically underfunded. It received the equivalent of 4 per cent of GDP, compared with 6.5 per cent for OECD countries (Arnold and Jalles, 2014).

But there is evidence from the later IFPRI study (Soares, 2011; Hunter and Sugiyama, 2013) that *Bolsa Família* has increased the use of prenatal care, while there has also been a 12–15 per cent rise in the likelihood that the children of beneficiary families will receive the required set of vaccinations within the first six months. There is also some evidence of longer gestation periods and fewer premature births by beneficiary mothers. Similar conclusions were reached by a study of children's health care in a squatter settlement within a large urban area, where improved rates of immunization, growth monitoring, check-ups and other primary care services were recorded. Diminished rates of under-five child mortality were observed in other areas and were noted in the same analysis (Shei et al., 2014).

One of the most striking, if contradictory, impacts of *Bolsa Família* has been upon child nutrition. Initial evaluations from the early stages of the programme showed no positive impact upon chronic (stunting) or acute (wasting) malnutrition for children aged 12–36 months (Soares et al., 2010). Although the programme was implemented in a context of generally rising standards of living, it has probably played a part by increasing food consumption. The scheme has increased expenditure on food, education and children's clothing, which seems to have contributed to a decrease in under-fives mortality living in the poor rural semi-arid Northeast. More recently, evaluations have recorded a significant increase (of almost 40 per cent) in the body mass index of beneficiary children compared with non-beneficiaries (Soares, 2011). However, a routine observation made by several studies is the constraint on programme effectiveness that arises from a failure to invest in basic primary health care facilities.

Citizenship

In addition to what could be called the more tangible benefits generated by cash transfers in the fields of education and health (human capital), there is another potentially very positive gain from the *Bolsa Família* and similar programmes. This is more political in nature. Often for the first time, the poorest segments of society, rather than being confined to the margins or manipulated through the clientelistic manoeuvrings of powerful elites, are occupying a more central political role, both through their newly acquired social rights under the Constitution and through their voting power. This amounts to no less than a transformation that, together with the other wider changes taking place, is at least as significant as any direct benefits of cash transfers and, arguably, is a form of social investment.

Brazil's Constitution of 1988, coming after two decades of military rule, incorporated many advances brought about by lobbying from trade unions, new social movements, progressive middle classes and liberal professions. As already discussed, among the victories of the Constituent Assembly was a major change to social security policy, which for the first time complemented traditional social insurance with noncontributory schemes for the poor, elderly and disabled as a right. This paved the way for the introduction of targeted cash transfer schemes from the late 1990s, culminating in the creation of *Bolsa Família* (Jaccoud et al., 2010).

There is much evidence to show that *Bolsa Família* became a powerful electoral tool in the hands of the Workers Party (PT) and, in particular, its charismatic leader, President Lula. His personal and well-publicized 'ownership' of *Bolsa Família*, especially in the run-up to the 2006 presidential elections, undoubtedly helped him to secure a second term in office with support from a grateful North and Northeast of the country (Hunter and Power, 2007; Zucco, 2010; Singer, 2012). Arguably, this has helped to create a policy 'lock-in' or path dependence on the *Bolsa Família*, which nowadays all candidates from right across the political spectrum publicly endorse (Hall, 2013). Woe betide any politician who openly questions the programme. This has given the voting poor a tool for exerting powerful leverage through the ballot box.

Citizenship has also been strengthened through the single national unified registry (*CadÚnico*), a product of *Bolsa Família*. This collects socio-economic data on all beneficiary families to calculate risk and vulnerability, and increase programme efficiency, as well as to reduce duplication and fraud. This has encouraged many poor Brazilians previously outside the formal system to acquire basic identity documents such as birth certificates, identification (ID) cards and voter registration cards. Increased grassroots demand due specifically to the *Bolsa Família* has prompted the government to rise to meet this growing need, especially in the case of women. Other gains upon which research has thrown light suggest that women's position in the family and community may have been strengthened as a direct consequence of the programme. This includes greater control over contraception, autonomy in decision-making over household purchases, greater freedom from indebtedness, and enhanced status within the family (Hunter and Sugiyama, 2013).

According to field evidence, *Bolsa Família* has helped to weaken the traditional clientelism typical of the past. However, local patronage remains a complex issue that pervades personal and political relationships. Cash transfer programmes such as *Bolsa Família* have helped formerly rigid arrangements evolve into more fluid dealings. Participants have gained more independence from local patronage politics, while avoiding any feelings of social stigma (Ansell, 2014). There is an increasing sense on the part of beneficiaries that *Bolsa Família* is an entitlement to which recipients have a 'right', a far cry from the situation of just a few years ago (Hall, 2013). While these observations must be treated with some caution, they possibly represent the early stages of a gradual transition towards a more rights-based system of social policy. In this process, the programme has in all probability helped to strengthen the notion of citizenship for poor Brazilians.

SOCIAL INVESTMENT BEYOND CASH TRANSFERS

Bolsa Família has recently attempted to expand its impact by linking cash transfers with other more 'productive' initiatives, under the umbrella programme known as *Brasil Sem Miséria* (Brazil Without Extreme Poverty). Launched in 2011, it encourages *Bolsa Família* recipients to become involved in productive activities. These involve multi-ministry collaboration in, for example, vocational education and training, a micro-enterprise and microcredit scheme, a preschool building programme, agricultural extension, water storage, and the *Bolsa Verde* or 'green grant' conservation initiative for forest peoples (Brazil, n.d.). While this could be said to represent a move in the right direction, it is still small-scale and results remain to be demonstrated. Recent research in Brazil on the connections between *Bolsa Família* and rural credit programmes, for instance, has revealed the insurmountable obstacles that seem to hinder institutional cooperation and attempts at creating such 'productive' links (Rufino de Aquino et al., 2016).

As the preceding sections have shown, *Bolsa Família* has in some respects contributed both directly and indirectly to investing in people's welfare. It has achieved this mainly through encouraging or incentivizing the demand for education and health care to boost human capital accumulation among the poorest groups, in the expectation that this will lead to gains in economic productivity and improvements in social indicators. Yet this assumption begs the question of whether the supply of basic services is adequate for meeting this enhanced demand. Only if such demands are effectively catered for can they be considered a legitimate form of social investment in the wider sense.

To demonstrate this would require evidence of greater political and public spending commitment to making concomitant sector investments in education, health care delivery and nutrition programmes, as well as related sectors. Hoping that increased demand will somehow automatically stimulate greater supply is wishful thinking, to say the least. Another interpretation, as will be discussed below, is that using cash transfers as an increasingly mainstream approach to social policy allows decision-makers to opt for politically rewarding, short-term measures that allow major social sector investments to be postponed indefinitely. One of the consequences of this strategy is the neglect of basic infrastructure investment in those key social areas that are pivotal to maintaining the rate and quality of economic progress, namely, the education and health of its population.

It is difficult to accurately document trends in public spending in sectors in Brazil such as education, health and sanitation. Responsibility for expenditure is divided between federal, state and municipal levels of government, following decentralization measures introduced by the 1988 Constitution. Furthermore, there is no necessary correspondence between levels of spending and the efficiency or effectiveness of service delivery. In Brazil, however, the general picture on broader social investments is not encouraging. Several authors point to the discrepancy between Brazil's high rate of economic growth in recent years, and its disproportionately low levels of investment into social infrastructure.

From 1995 to 2006, as cash transfer schemes were being expanded and consolidated, there was a significant fall in the proportion of GDP allocated to education (from 1.14 per cent to 1.0 per cent) and health (from 1.81 per cent to 1.76 per cent) sectors (Costa, 2009). A similar trend was documented for sanitation (Souza and Costa, 2013). Lavinas (2013) also observes that while spending on welfare benefits (including *Bolsa Família*) rose by 300 per cent from 2001 to 2010, that on education doubled, and public health spending increased by just 60 per cent. Access to clean drinking water and adequate sanitation provision improved little over this period.

Castro et al. (2012) drew attention to a similar trend. They demonstrated that health spending fell from 16 per cent to 11.5 per cent of the social budget from 1995 to 2005, while education spending dropped from

8.5 per cent to 5.5 per cent over this period. Education spending then rose to 7.2 per cent by 2010 as the result of educational reforms that increased capitation spending for basic education and for technical schools. Alongside this apparent slowdown in wider social investment levels across key sectors, there has been a major shift in funding towards social protection in Brazil. In 1995, 0.7 per cent of the social budget went to this sector, rising to 3.2 per cent by 2000, and 6.8 per cent by 2009. Around 1 per cent of GDP now comprises income transfers, while *Bolsa Família* itself accounts for around 0.4 per cent (Castro et al., 2012; Barrientos, 2013).

Different reasons have been advanced to explain this growing emphasis on cash transfers. One explanation sees this shift essentially as a fiscal matter: the need to tighten social spending as the result of fiscal constraints. From 1999, the Brazilian government came under pressure to reduce the primary fiscal surplus to help manage the country's debt burden. There was a push to reduce overall social spending and adopt a policy of targeting poorer groups, which was considered more effective for reducing poverty. As noted already, conditional cash transfers are a relatively inexpensive social policy option, taking up around 0.4 per cent of GDP in Brazil's case.

From 1999, as international financial organizations such as the World Bank and the IADB were starting to support conditional cash transfers as part of their risk management strategy for addressing poverty, the Brazilian government sought their substantial technical and financial support for the development of conditional cash transfers (Hall, 2015). This new emphasis on cash transfers "directly affected the availability of resources of the central government for basic social areas – health, education and sanitation … [and] Brazilian society still maintains a high social deficit in basic areas" (Costa, 2009, p. 10).

Closely linked to this argument is a second reason, which is more political-ideological in nature. As mentioned above, the vote-winning potential of *Bolsa Família* among the poor majority meant that President Lula had a strong interest in expanding programme coverage. This benefited him personally, the governing party and his successor Dilma Rousseff. It could be speculated that this has helped to create a vested interest in prioritizing short-term social assistance programmes rather than long-run social investment, whose political returns would become evident only much further down the line. One consequence could be that these high political returns have encouraged the creation of a short-term planning horizon in the Executive. In this vision, more immediate political rewards take precedence over long-run investments serving the public good.

THE GROWING TENSION BETWEEN SOCIAL PROTECTION AND SOCIAL INVESTMENT

The recent focus on cash transfers as a poverty alleviation strategy has gradually encroached upon the social policy space in Latin America. Far from being peculiar to Brazil, it has been noted as typical over Latin America as a whole, where the rise of conditional cash transfers has been accompanied by the neglect of social infrastructure investments, whether by coincidence or design (Lavinas, 2013). This funding gap or 'social debt' is universal across the continent. Furthermore, according to a recent World Bank study, lack of access to basic services contributes to a 'disabling context' that perpetuates chronic poverty (Vakis et al., 2015).

Attempts to overlay *Bolsa Família* with a veneer of more 'productive' social investment through programmes such as *Brasil Sem Miséria* (Brazil Without Extreme Poverty) is testament to the realization amongst policy-makers wishing to promote sustainable development that alleviating absolute poverty is not enough. Linking *Bolsa Família* with broader, cross-sector development challenges is a necessary progression. In Brazil, evidence of government failure to invest adequately in basic health, education and sanitation services has created much popular discontent. Yet it should come as no surprise that this contradiction exists, due to the ways in which the structure of vested interests in Brazil serves to perpetuate inequities in basic service access. The fact that Brazilians themselves, rather than outsiders, have played a major role in establishing cash transfers as a key social policy instrument post-1988 does not mean that it has been any easier to overcome these fundamental obstacles.

It should not be forgotten that the pattern of social spending itself contributes strongly to inequality in Brazil (Hunter and Sugiyama, 2009). For example, the top 20 per cent of income earners receive 65 per cent of pension payments, while the bottom quintile receive just 2.4 per cent. Any pension reform proposals are strongly resisted in Congress by the better-off. Brazil has a strong bias towards tertiary education, with one-quarter of the education budget benefiting just 2 per cent of all students. The wealthy are strongly subsidized, since only they can access the higher-quality private secondary education necessary to qualify for low-cost public universities; while poorer students must resort, paradoxically, to the more expensive private university sector. Although the public health system has improved medical services for the poor, access and the quality of services is often questioned, while the private health sector receives some public subsidies.

The situation has been exacerbated by alleged manipulation of the social budget in Brazil. According to Gentil (2006), successive Brazilian governments have perpetuated the myth of a bankrupt social security system in the country, whereas in reality it has enjoyed a substantial primary surplus since the late 1990s. According to this analysis, such tactics have allowed funds to be diverted from needy areas such as health and social protection to others serving different priorities, such as servicing the national debt. Some social security funding has been made available through legal budgetary channels and other means that are illicit, while further funding has been diverted anonymously through the national budget. Although in theory financially self-sustaining, social security has thus become something of a 'black box', with surplus funds being diverted for other purposes while serving to boost international investor confidence at the same time. Unfortunately, there has been a high opportunity cost to these financial adjustments in terms of foregone social security spending that could have been used to greatly expand coverage for poorer Brazilians.

Weighing up the social policy scenario in Brazil, there is clear evidence of an emerging tension between the politically appealing *Bolsa Família* on one hand and, on the other, the pressing need to expand universally accessible basic services. It seems that the short-term political rewards accruing from the programme's expansion are taking precedence over the less attractive option of investing in social infrastructure, the public benefits of which take much longer to come on-stream. Yet even in terms of *Bolsa Família* itself, however, this is somewhat contradictory since the demands on health and education cannot be satisfied if the supply of basic services is not being adequately funded.

There is thus a clash "between draining social services to poor people and the legally guaranteed universality of these services to all Brazilians" (Kerstenetzky, 2014, p. 74). Tackling this fundamental inequity through a more comprehensive programme of social investments for the benefit of all Brazilians would at least help to address some of the country's entrenched disparities. Put another way: are conditional cash transfers an effective way to address poverty and build human capital in the long term, or do they also allow governments to avoid making difficult decisions to restructure education and health in ways that would have a more fundamental and enduring impact? It may be impossible to escape the conclusion that any serious expansion of social investments in Brazil will depend on effective grassroots political pressure being mobilized to challenge entrenched interests, enhance social citizenship and strengthen people's rights.

REFERENCES

ABPM, Todos Pela Educação (eds) (2013). *Justiça pela Qualidade na Educação.* São Paulo: Editora Saraiva.
Ansell, A. (2014). *Zero Hunger: Political Culture and Antipoverty Policy in Northeast Brazil.* Chapel Hill, NC: University of North Carolina Press.
Arnold, J. and Jalles, J. (2014). Dividing the Pie in Brazil: Income Distribution, Social Policies and the New Middle Class. OECD Economics Department Working Papers, No. 1105. Paris: OECD Publishing.
Barrientos, A. (2013). The Rise of Social Assistance in Brazil. *Development and Change*, 44 (4), 887–910.
Barrientos, A. and Santinbáñez, C. (2009). New Forms of Social Assistance and the Evolution of Social Protection in Latin America. *Journal of Latin American Studies*, 41, 1–26.
Bastagli, F. (2011). Conditional Cash Transfers as a Tool of Social Policy. *Economic and Political Weekly*, 21 May, 61–66.
Becker, G. (1964). *Human Capital: A Theoretical and Empirical Analysis with Special Reference to Education.* New York: Columbia University Press.
Birdsall, N. and Sabot, R. (eds) (1996). *Opportunity Foregone: Education in Brazil.* Washington, DC: Inter-American Development Bank/Johns Hopkins University Press.
Brazil (n.d.). *Plano Brasil Sem Miséria: 2 Anos de Resultados.* Brasília: Ministério do Desenvolvimento e Combate à Fome.
Castro, J., Ribeiro, J., Chaves, J. and Duarte, B. (2012). Gasto Social Federal: Prioridade Macroeconômica no period 1995–2010. Nota Téchnica No. 9, IPEA, Brasília.
Costa, N. (2009). Social Protection in Brazil: Universalism and Targeting in the FHC and Lula Administrations, *Ciência e Saúde Coletiva*, 14 (3), 1–12.
da Silva Gomes, E.C. (2013). O Financiamento da Educação Básica no Brasil. In ABPM – Todos pela Educação (ed.), *Justiça pela Qualidade na Educação.* São Paulo: Saraiva, pp. 266–287.
de Brauw, A., Gilligan, D.O., Hoddinott, J. and Roy, S. (2014). The Impact of Bolsa Família on Women's Decision-Making Power. *World Development*, 59, 487–504.
de Britto, T.F. (2008). The Emergence and Popularity of Conditional Cash Transfers in Latin America. In A. Barrientos and D. Hulme (eds), *Social Protection for the Poor and Poorest.* London: Palgrave Macmillan, pp. 181–193.
Draibe, S. and Riesco, M. (2009). Social Policy and Development in Latin America: The Long View. *Social Policy and Administration*, 34 (4), 328–346.
Gentil, D.L. (2006). A Política Fiscal e a Falsa Crise da Seguridade Social Brasileira – Análise financeira do period 1990–2005. PhD thesis, Institute of Economics, Federal University of Rio de Janeiro.
Glewwe, P. and Kassouf, A.L. (2012). The Impact of the Bolsa Escola/Família Conditional Cash Transfer on Enrollment, Dropout Rates and Grade Promotion in Brazil. *Journal of Development Economics*, 97, 505–517.

Hall, A. (2006). From Fome Zero to Bolsa Família: Social Policies and Poverty Alleviation under Lula. *Journal of Latin American Studies*, 38 (4), 689–709.
Hall, A. (2008). Brazil's Bolsa Família: A Double-edged Sword? *Development and Change*, 38 (5), 799–822.
Hall, A. (2013). Political Dimensions of Social Protection in Brazil. In J. Midgley and D. Piachaud (eds), *Social Protection, Economic Growth and Social Change: Goals, Issues and Trajectories in China, India, Brazil and South Africa*. Cheltenham, UK and Northampton, MA, USA: Edward Elgar Publishing, pp. 166–183.
Hall, A. (2015). It Takes Two to Tango: Conditional Cash Transfers, Social Policy and the Globalising Role of the World Bank. In S. McBride, G. Boychuk and R. Mahon (eds), *After '08: Social Policy and the Global Financial Crisis*. Vancouver, BC: UBC Press, pp. 140–160.
Hall, A. and Midgley, J. (2004). *Social Policy for Development*. Sage: London.
Hardiman, M. and Midgley, J. (1982). *The Social Dimensions of Development: Social Policy and Planning in the Third World*. Chichester: John Wiley & Sons.
Hunter, W. and Power, T. (2007). Rewarding Lula: Executive Power and Social Policy in the Brazilian Elections of 2006. *Latin American Politics and Society*, 49 (1), 1–30.
Hunter, W. and Sugiyama, N.B. (2009). Democracy and Social Policy in Brazil: Advancing Basic Needs, Preserving Privileged Interests. *Latin American Politics and Society*, 51 (2), 29–58.
Hunter, W. and Sugiyama, N.B. (2013). Assessing the Bolsa Família: Successes, Shortcomings, and Unknowns. Paper presented at 'Democratic Brazil Emergent', Brazilian Studies Programme, University of Oxford and the Brazil Institute, King's College London, 21–22 February.
IPEA (2010). Políticas Sociais: Acompanhamento e Análise. Boletim de Políticas Sociais No. 18. Brasília: IPEA.
Jaccoud, I., Hadjab, P. and Chaibub, J. (2010). The Consolidation of Social Assistance in Brazil and its Challenges, 1988–2008. IPEA Working Paper 76, December.
Jenson, J. (2010). Diffusing Ideas for After Neoliberalism. *Global Social Policy*, 10 (1), 59–84.
Kerstenetzky, C.L. (2014). Approximating Intent and Action: Bolsa Família and the Future. In T. Campello and M. Neri (eds), *Bolsa Família Program: A Decade of Social Inclusion in Brazil. Executive Summary*. Brasília: Secretariat of Strategic Affairs of the Presidency of the Republic/IPEA, pp. 73–74.
Lavinas, L. (2013). 21st Century Welfare. *New Left Review*, 84 (November–December), 1–31.
Levy, S. (1991). *Poverty Alleviation in Mexico*. Washington, DC: World Bank.
Matos Diniz, H.D., Fontanive, N.S. and Klein, R. (2013). Indicadores de Qualidade na Educação Básica. In ABPM – Todos Pela Educação (ed.), *Justiça pela Qualidade na Educação*. São Paulo: Saraiva, pp. 537–612.
Midgley, J. and Tang, K.-I. (2001). Social Policy, Economic Growth and Developmental Welfare. *International Journal of Social Welfare*, 10, 244–252.
Neri, M. (2011). *A Nova Classe Media: o Lado Brilhante da Base da Pirâmide*. FGV: Editora Saraiva.

Psacharopoulos, G. (1973). *Returns to Education: An International Comparison.* Amsterdam: Elsevier.

Riccio, J., Dechausay, N., Greenberg, D., Miller, C., Rucks, Z. and Verma, N. (2010). *Towards Reduced Poverty Across Generations: Early Findings from New York City's Conditional Cash Transfer Program.* New York: MDRC.

Rufino de Aquino, J., Castillo, C., Neves, J., Lima, J. and Schneider, S. (2016). A Articulação de Políticas para a Superação da Pobreza Rural. Final Report, CNPQ.

Shei, A., Costa, F., Reis, M. and Ko, A. (2014). The Impact of Bolsa Família Conditional Cash Transfer Program on Children's Health Care Utilization and Health Outcomes. *BMC International Health and Human Rights*, 14 (10), 1–9.

Silveira-Neto, R. and Azzoni, C. (2012). Social Policy as Regional Policy: Market and Nonmarket Factors Determining Regional Inequality. *Journal of Regional Science*, 52 (3), 433–450.

Singer, A. (2012). *Os Sentidos do Lulismo: Reforma Gradual e Pacto Conservador.* São Paulo: Companhia das Letras.

Soares, S. (2011). Brazil's Bolsa Família: A Review. *Economic and Political Weekly*, 21, 55–60.

Soares, S. (2013). The Efficiency and Effectiveness of Social Protection against Poverty and Inequality in Brazil. In J. Midgley and D. Piachaud (eds), *Social Protection, Economic Growth and Social Change: Goals, Issues and Trajectories in China, India, Brazil and South Africa.* Cheltenham, UK and Northampton, MA, USA: Edward Elgar Publishing, pp. 153–165.

Soares, F., Ribas, R.P. and Osório, R.G. (2010). Evaluating the Impact of Brazil's Bolsa Família: Cash Transfer Programs in Comparative Perspective. *Latin American Research Review*, 45 (2), 173–190.

Souza, A.C. and Costa, N. (2013). Incerteza e Dissenso: Os Limites Institucionais da Política de Saneamento Brasileira. *Revista de Administração Pública*, 47 (3), 1–9.

Vakis, R., Rigolini, J. and Lucchetti, L. (2015). *Left Behind: Chronic Poverty in Latin America and the Caribbean.* Washington, DC: World Bank.

World Bank (1975). *The Assault on World Poverty.* Baltimore, MD, USA and London, UK: World Bank and Johns Hopkins University Press.

World Bank (1990). *World Development Report 1990: Poverty.* Oxford, UK and Washington, DC, USA: World Bank.

World Bank (2000). *Social Protection Strategy Paper: From Safety Nets to Springboard.* Washington, DC: World Bank.

World Bank (2001). *World Development Report: Attacking Poverty.* Washington, DC and New York: World Bank and Oxford University Press.

World Bank (2014). *The State of Social Safety Nets 2014.* Washington, DC: World Bank.

Ximenes, S.B. (2013). Custo Aluno-Qualidade: Um Novo Paradigma para o Direito à Educação e Seu Financiamento. In ABPM – Todos pela Educação (ed.). *Justiça pela Qualidade na Educação.* São Paulo: Saraiva, pp. 312–334.

Zucco, C. (2010). The President's 'New' Constituency: Lula and the Pragmatic Vote in Brazil's 2006 Presidential Elections. *Journal of Latin American Studies*, 40, 29–49.

9. Pension reform in China: towards social investment

Joe C.B. Leung and Yuebin Xu

Most countries have strived to establish a diversified and multi-pillar pension system. While the public pillar (defined benefits) serves primarily to reduce and prevent old-age poverty, as well as to achieve income redistribution, the mandatory and voluntary private pillars (defined contribution) encourage individual savings and investment to improve the quality of life in retirement. To ensure financial sustainability and income adequacy, recent pension reforms encourage individuals to work more and longer, so as to strengthen the productive capacities of the economy and thereby improve the scope of pension systems to deliver adequate retirement income promises (OECD, 2015). More importantly, they encourage early preparation for retirement, particularly through private savings and investment. As such, pension systems have shifted from a traditional focus on providing passive cash transfer toward active social policy or social investment orientation for greater social and economic inclusion.

After decades of phenomenal economic growth, China has entered a new stage of economic and social development, known as the 'new normal'. The transition is marked by a slowing down of economic growth, increased globalization, a shrinking workforce, an ageing population and the degradation of the environment. Indeed, the previous developmental strategy that focused primarily on economic growth has led to greater social inequalities and risk of instability. To face these formidable challenges, the Chinese government has prepared for the Thirteenth Five-Year Plan for Social and Economic Development (2016–2020). Since 2002, the government has pledged to achieve a *xiakang* (moderately well-off) level of economic and social development by 2020. This involves a different developmental strategy.

Economically, China can no longer rely solely on cheap labour and foreign investment to sustain growth. A high-quality, mobile and dynamic workforce, together with increased domestic consumption, is essential to facilitate this new economic transition. Putting inclusive and balanced development, or a social investment perspective, on the policy agenda, greater developmental emphasis has been placed on human capital building which includes job creation for university graduates and low-skilled workers, improvement in quality education, enhancement of labour market flexibility, relaxation of the one-child policy, and integration of rural migrants into the cities. In social protection, the government has significantly extended the coverage of the programmes on pensions, health care and social assistance. In addition, individual savings accounts have been introduced into pension and health care insurance, which can enhance programme sustainability and encourage individual asset building. These programmes will improve human capital and encourage the integration of vulnerable groups, such as landless peasants, the unemployed, economically inactive women, the informally employed, older workers and the disabled, into the changing labour market (Leung and Xu, 2015). In essence, pension reform in China exemplifies a social investment approach fostering balanced and quality economic and social development, moving away from the previous developmental model emphasizing solely the quantity of economic growth.

CHINA'S PENSION POLICY

Current social security arrangements for the urban population in China consist of two major systems: social insurance and social assistance. Social insurance comprises five programmes: old-age pensions, unemployment insurance, medical care insurance, workers' injury and compensation benefits, and maternity benefits. Combined with the housing fund programme, these are often referred to as the 'five insurances and one fund' and are the standard provision for employees in the formal sector. Residents of rural areas and economically inactive urban dwellers are entitled to the newly developed pension and health care insurance programmes. Social assistance (*dibao*) in both urban and rural areas provides means-tested cash assistance to families living in poverty as well as subsidies for medical services, children's education and housing.

In terms of the pension system, there are currently three major schemes covering urban and rural areas and different social sectors:

- Pension System for Employees in Government Offices and Public Institutions (1955), which is a non-contributory, publicly funded defined benefit scheme.

- Urban Employee Old Age Pension System (1997), which is contributory, partially funded, and offers a mix of a defined benefit (employer contribution) and defined contribution (individual account) scheme for employees of urban enterprises.
- Residents' Old Age Pension System for rural (2009) and urban (2011) residents, which is contributory, partially funded, and a mix of a defined benefit (government contribution) and defined contribution (individual account) scheme.

The current pension system has been described as "uncoordinated, unsustainable, and segmented" (Leung and Xu, 2015, p. 45). Key challenges of pension reform include the ageing population, rapid urbanization, a shrinking workforce, system fragmentation, informalization of the labour market, and pension fund deficits. Facing changing economic structures and social needs, further substantial reforms are required to ensure pension integration, risk pooling, portability and sustainability. There have been numerous international reviews of the evolution and emerging issues of the urban old-age pension system (Chow and Xu, 2001; Leung, 2003; Beland and Yu, 2004; Sin, 2005; Salditt et al., 2007; Frazier, 2010; Gao, 2010; Herd et al., 2010; Zhang and Xu, 2012; China Development Research Foundation, 2012; Dorfman et al., 2013; Giles et al., 2013; Johansson and Cheng, 2016). Reviews of old-age support in rural areas include Shi (2006), Giles et al. (2010), Shen and Williamson (2010), Cai̇ et al. (2012) and Dorfman et al. (2013). These works focus on describing the reform process, the challenges encountered and outcomes. It has been suggested that China should develop a universal (Johansson and Cheng, 2016) or social pension scheme (Dorfman et al., 2013). Others criticize the regressive nature of China's pension system (Gao, 2010; Liu et al., 2016).

Thirty Years of Pension Reform

Under the centrally planned socialist system, the pension system was divided between urban and rural areas. Urban employees were universally covered by the non-contributory, individual work unit-based, defined benefits social insurance scheme. In other words, all welfare expenses were considered to be part of the operational costs of each work unit. In contrast, rural residents could receive residual relief assistance (the so-called 'five guarantees scheme') from the commune only if they were destitute, unable to work, received no support from their children and had no other source of income. By providing the 'iron rice bowl' of basic livelihood security to the Chinese people, the socialist system of social security served primarily to enhance political unity and the legitimacy of Party rule, but at the expense of economic development (Leung, 1994, 2003).

In the 1980s, the 'iron rice bowl' system began to be considered as an impediment to productivity and market-oriented reforms, and social security reform was perceived as an essential route to liberating state-owned enterprises (SOEs) from their social welfare responsibilities and enhancing their market competitiveness. At this early stage, the overall strategy was to turn the work unit- and employment-based labour insurance system into a pay-as-you-go defined benefit social insurance system based on employer and employee contributions. In pilot projects, enterprise contributions were pooled to share pension responsibilities. Without fund accumulation, the system would be unable to cope with the rapidly ageing workforce. To avoid the shock to the state-owned enterprises, social and economic reforms were introduced gradually.

Based on local pilot projects on fund pooling and individual accounts, the basic structure of the reformed retirement insurance system for urban enterprise workers was formulated in 1997 (State Council Decision on the Establishment of a Unified Basic Pension System for Enterprise Workers). Since then, enterprises have had to contribute an average of 20 per cent of their wage bills to a unified account which pays a basic pension for retirees with a minimum of 15 years of contributions. The basic pension pays 1 per cent of the average of the indexed individual wage and the province-wide average earnings for each year of coverage. The pension in payment is indexed to a mix of wages and prices. The modelling assumes 50 per cent indexation to wages (OECD, 2015).

Each individual employee is required to contribute 8 per cent of their wages to an individual account. On retirement, a retiree can receive a monthly payment based on the accumulated savings and interest, divided by a government-determined annuity factor with reference to the national life expectancy and individual retirement age. The factor is 139 if the employee retires at the age of 60. By 2006, a retiree was able to receive a monthly payment of 1 per cent of the average wage for each year of individual contribution. According to government regulations, individual accounts should pay a higher rate of interest than the bank rate, and such interest is tax free. On the death of the employee, family members can inherit these benefits. Those who have less than 15 years of contribution can pay up the remaining sum required in contributions in order to be eligible for the pension, or receive a lump-sum payment of the funds that have accumulated in their individual accounts.

In summary, under the two-tier pension system, retirees have been able to receive their pension benefits from these unified accounts based on employer contributions, which are linked to the local average wage, and from personal savings accounts, which are linked to the amount of individual contributions. Both accounts are managed by the government. As such, the reformed pension model is a hybrid, combining both a pay-as-you-go and a funded system. Parametric reforms seek to link the length of contribution to the level of benefits, inviting participation from migrant workers and the self-employed.

In rural areas, peasants have had to rely mainly on their children for support in old age. This has been eroded due to the one-child policy and the increased migration of young people into cities as migrant workers. Rapid urbanization has also led to the loss of farmland due to redevelopment. Without an effective pension system, continuous labour mobility and urbanization will be restricted. Previous attempts to introduce a pension system in the rural areas, particularly in less-well-off provinces, have been unsuccessful. This is largely due to a lack of support from central government. In 2009, central government proposed a pension system mixing a social pension-based central government allocation with a savings account based on individual and local government contributions. Central government subsidies basically covered the basic pension in full in the central and western provinces, and 50 per cent in the eastern provinces. There were five contribution standards ranging from 100 to 500 yuan (US\$1 = 6.47 yuan) a year. In some local government areas, contributions could be based on the proportion of the average household income, ranging from 5 to 30 per cent. As such, each rural peasant reaching the age of 60 with 15 years' contributions could receive a basic pension of 55 yuan (70 yuan by 2015), and a monthly pension derived from the balance of the accumulated individual account (individual savings and local government subsidies) divided by 139. Participation is based on the household, not the individual. Those aged over 60 can participate in the scheme and receive benefits immediately if they can deposit a lump sum amounting to 15 years of contributions in the individual account.

CHALLENGES AND RESPONSES

As described above, the Chinese pension system is segmented with different schemes catering for different target groups. Future reforms are based on the principles of a scheme that has "broad coverage, protects at the basic level, is multilayered, and is sustainable" (Dorfman et al., 2013, p. 15). Key future challenges include the rapidly ageing population, shrinking workforce, high contribution rates, low retirement age and pension fund deficits. Continuous reforms are essential to enhance sustainability, portability, labour mobility and human capital development.

Demographic Challenges

With the implementation of the one-child policy in 1980, China benefited initially from a demographic dividend structure. The demographic structure of a large workforce and low-dependency population facilitated economic growth. However, rapid ageing has begun to diminish this dividend. The Chinese population reached 1368 million in 2015. The proportion of those aged over 60 soared from 8.6 per cent in 1990, to 10.5 per cent in 2000, 13.3 per cent in 2010, and 15.5 per cent in 2014. This represents a current figure (as of March 2016) of 212 million people (137 million of whom, or 10.1 per cent, are aged over 65) (China News Center, 26 March 2016). Furthermore, the population of those aged over 60 is projected to reach more than 243 million by 2020, 300 million by 2025, 400 million by 2034, and 450 million by 2050 (33 per cent of the total). The median age is projected to increase from 32.6 in 2005, to 44.8 in 2050. By then, the number of people aged over 80 will have reached 100 million (China News Center, 19 August 2013). Old-age dependency ratios are projected to rise from 13.5 per cent and 21.1 per cent in 2008 in rural and urban areas, respectively, to 34.4 per cent and 21.1 per cent by 2030. The urban pension system dependency rate will also rise from 34 per cent in 2001, to 100 per cent by 2030 (that is, one worker for each retiree) (Dorfman et al., 2013). The major characteristics of China's ageing population are its sheer extent; the rapidity of the overall ageing process; and the significant regional, gender and rural–urban differences. As the urbanization rate continues to accelerate, rural–urban migration, particularly among the young, will further increase the age dependency ratio in rural areas.

Following on from the rise in the dependency ratio is the inevitable shrinking of the workforce. In 2012, for the first time, the size of the economically active population declined. Facing a possible demographic deficit, the National Bureau of Statistics has predicted that the working-age population will decline by 29 million between 2012 and 2020 (China News Center, 28 January 2013). As a group, China's ageing population has been 'getting old before getting rich' (that is, premature ageing), and the shrinking workforce has become a formidable challenge. This affects not only continuous economic growth, but also rising social expenditure on health, pensions and long-term care. Recent efforts to remove the one-child policy represent an attempt to moderate the process of the ageing of society.

Postponement of the retirement age not only reduces pension costs and increases pension benefits, but can increase the labour supply. The current retirement age of 60 for men, 55 for female cadres, and 50 for female workers was formulated in the early 1950s when life expectancy was only 40 years. As life expectancy has now reached more than 75 years, postponement of retirement is seen as a measure that can reduce the burden on the pension system. Despite strong resistance from the general public, the Fifth Plenum of the Eighteenth Party Congress (2015) recommended the implementation of the policy on the gradual postponement of retirement age set out in the Thirteenth Five-Year Plan (2016–2020) (China News Center, 11 November 2015). The Chinese Academy of Social Sciences (CASS) has recommended a two-step approach. First, by 2017, all women employees should retire at the age of 55. By 2018, women employees would postpone retirement age by one year every three years, and men every six years. Accordingly, male and female employees will reach the same retirement age (65) in 2045 (China News Center, 5 December 2015). The government is expected soon to introduce a step-by-step postponement of retirement-age options for public consultation (China News Center, 1 March 2016).

A similar pilot scheme was introduced in urban areas in 2011, covering residents without formal employment, such as housewives, the unemployed, migrant workers and the informally employed. There are ten contribution levels ranging from 100 to 1000 yuan a year. The benefits arrangement is similar to the rural pension system. In 2012, the Residents' Old Age Pension System for rural and urban residents was unified. The average annual contribution level in 2015 was 230 yuan. Local government is expected to match individual contributions. Therefore, the higher the level of individual contribution selected, the more government subsidies will be received in the individual account. The scheme is still largely voluntary. However, as a non-wage-based 'social pension' with match funding from central and local government, high participation and individual contribution rates are expected (Leung and Xu, 2015). The government has promised to make an adjustment to the basic pension benefits every two years according to wage and consumer price increases.

The Chinese government has been aware of the need to develop the private pillar of the pension system, including enterprise and occupational annuity schemes. With taxation incentives, enterprises (2004) and government offices (2011) have been encouraged to set up annuity schemes with contributions from both employers and employees (Peng, 2016). The funds are managed by an enterprise-based fund governance structure. In 2014, around 73 300 enterprises had set up such annuities for their employees, with participants reaching 23 million and an accumulated fund of 769 billion yuan (MOHRSS, 28 May 2015).

Segmentation and Integration

To fill the gap and manage the social risks arising from market-oriented reforms, the Chinese government set up a segmented pension system catering to the needs of civil servants, urban employees, urban residents and rural peasants. Targeting different population groups, different schemes had different financing methods, contribution rates, and benefit levels. In 2011, the pension schemes for urban and rural residents were unified. According to the 'Decisions on Reforming Pension System in Government Organizations and Public Institutions' (2015), civil servants and employees in public institutions are now required to join the urban employee pension scheme, requiring employers and employees to contribute to the fund. Employees who were employed after 1 October 2014 and their employers have to pay 12 per cent and 28 per cent of their wages, respectively, into the pension fund. On retirement, the retiree can receive the basic and individual account pension plus the occupational pension (MOHRSS, 21 December 2015). This integration implies that both employees and the government have to make a contribution to the pension fund, instead of being covered by the financial allocation. In other words, central and local government will have to increase the budget allocation to their departments and raise the salaries of their employees in order to compensate for the losses due to these reforms.

Pension portability facilitates labour mobility. To reduce labour market gaps, places with a plentiful supply of labour are encouraged to export it to places with high demand. The current pension fund is, in principle, unified at the provincial level. However, because different provinces can have different contribution rates and benefit levels, the pension system is not actually portable or transferable. The government now aims to unify the pension system at the national level, not only to facilitate labour mobility but also to improve fund management.

Coverage

In the development of China's old-age pension system, "wide coverage and low benefit levels" has been the guiding principle (Leung and Xu, 2015, p. 75). By the end of 2015, 842 million people were participating in pension schemes, an increase of 23 million over the previous year. They included 255 million urban employees (plus 55 million migrant workers) and 86 million retirees. For the urban and rural resident scheme, the number of participants reached 505 million, with 148 million receiving benefits. In addition, 8 million civil servants and 32 million employees of public institutions are covered by the Pension System for Employees in Government Offices and Public Institutions. Excluding children, 150 million people are not covered by any pension scheme (a participation rate of 86 per cent) (China News Center, 29 February 2016). So far, there has been a continuous increase in enrolments and, therefore, pension contributions. Even though the rural pension system is largely voluntary and was only introduced in 2009, it has achieved almost full coverage already. The match funding from central and local government has been a major incentive to enrolment. While this is a remarkable achievement in terms of coverage, further expansion is needed to those in the private and informal sectors, as well as urban migrant workers. A survey shows that only about one-fifth of migrant workers or the informally employed are covered by existing pension schemes (Chin, 2015). Finally, the government has pledged to achieve 95 per cent coverage by 2020.

Fund Management and Deficits

By the end of 2015, income from the urban employee pension system amounted to 2762 billion yuan (including government subsidies) with an expenditure of 2333 billion yuan. The pension fund still has an overall reserve of 3565 billion yuan, which is sufficient to cover the expenditure for 17 months. However, without government subsidies, the fund is certainly facing a growing deficit. Income from the pension fund for urban and rural residents amounts to 231 billion yuan (67 billion yuan from individual contributions) and expenditure 157 billion yuan. The reserve stands at 385 billion yuan (China News Center, 29 February 2016).

The level of annual increases in pension contributions has been declining, from 23.4 per cent in 2008, to 9.7 per cent in 2014. This results from the slowdown in the rate of enrolment. It has been estimated that by 2025, the social security fund will no longer be in surplus (China News Center, 1 June 2015). Furthermore, the distribution of the reserves has been extremely uneven. Reserves in nine of the 32 provinces constitute two-thirds (66.3 per cent) of the total. Some provinces have enough in reserve to cover their pension payments for 40–50 months, whereas some could manage only one or two months. Seven provinces are in deficit. Guangdong has 512.8 billion yuan in reserve (enough to pay all its retirees for 50 months), 18 times that in Heilongjiang (3.5 months) (China News Center, 29 February 2016). This unevenness can largely be attributed to differences not only in the level of economic development of the provinces, but also in their labour mobility and demographic structures. Coastal provinces with a large population of young migrant workers moving in and making contributions, and a lower number of retirees, have pension surpluses. Provinces with more young people moving out will benefit from lower contributions to the fund. Inter-provincial transfers of funds are currently difficult. Moreover, according to the Chinese Academy of Social Sciences (CASS), non-accountable use of social security funds by local government is also a serious issue, amounting to 80 billion yuan in 2015 (China News Center, 22 January 2016).

To cover payments to existing retirees who made no or insufficient contributions in the past, the government has to tap into individual accounts. Even worse, pension benefits have been adjusted due to rising wages. Pension benefits for current retirees have been adjusted upward by an average of 10 per cent per year from 2004 to 2015. If the liabilities of individual accounts are included, pension fund deficits in 2015 amounted to 300 billion yuan (156 billion yuan in 2014) (China News Center, 11 November 2015). The pension fund shortage will reach 1.21 trillion yuan by 2019 (*Xinhua News*, 2015).

Together with other contributory social insurance schemes (health care, unemployment, injury at work, maternity and housing), the total con-tributory rate has reached more than 40 per cent of total wages. This is made up of 28 per cent from retirement (20 per cent from employers and 8 per cent from employees); 12 per cent from medical care (10 per cent from employers and 2 per cent from employees); 3 per cent from unemployment (2 per cent from employers and 1 per cent from employ-ees); 0.8 per cent for maternity (from employers); and 2 per cent for injury at work (from employers). According to the Ministry of Human Resources and Social Security (MOHRSS), China's total social security contribution rate ranks thirteenth-highest among 173 countries (China News Center, 18 May 2015). The high rate of contribution is considered to be a burden to enterprises and not conducive to economic develop-ment. Furthermore, it also encourages non-compliance.

To reduce the burden on companies, the Third Plenum of the Eighteenth Party Congress (2014) recommended a reduction in the contribution rates of all the social insurance schemes. Since then, 12 provinces have reduced social security contribution rates, particularly for unemployment, mater-nity and injury at work insurance (China News Center, 17 June 2016). In Shanghai, various social security contribution rates, including pensions, have been slightly reduced. It is estimated that the reduction will save firms in Shanghai 13.5 billion yuan in 2016. In Guangdong, the reduction is expected to save 5.3 billion yuan for enterprises and 2.4 billion yuan for employees. In other words, employees will have higher take-home pay (China News Center, 23 March 2016).

To cover the imminent deficits, the government has also initiated a series of reforms. In 2000, central government established the National Social Security Fund with initial funding of only 20 billion yuan. With allocation from central government funding, the fund would invest in deposits and government bonds, private bonds and shares. It exists to provide short-term subsidies to provincial social security funds. In 2015, the fund had accumulated 1500 billion yuan for future use. The Third Plenum of the Sixteenth Party Congress (2004) and the Third Plenum of the Eighteenth Party Congress (2014) both indicated the need to transfer some state assets to strengthen social security funds. State assets include central government financial allocation, sale of state shares, lotteries and investment returns (MOHRSS, 30 June 2015). Central government funds mainly target the western and central provinces, and such subsidies have been mounting. Central government allocated 302.7 billion yuan to the pension fund in 2014, accounting for 13 per cent of the total pension fund revenue (140.7 billion yuan in 2009) (*Economic References*, 31 December 2015). From 2002 to 2014, central government subsidies amounted to 2075 billion yuan, soaring from 40.8 billion yuan in 2002, to 354.8 billion yuan in 2014, and 367.1 billion yuan in 2015 (China News Center, 23 November 2015).

To reduce financial risks, social security funds have been required to invest mainly in government bonds and bank savings accounts. From 2007 to 2013, the average annual investment return of these funds was only 2.2 per cent, much lower than the average annual inflation rate (3.8 per cent). In other words, the social security fund has suffered from deflation (China News Center, 28 December 2014). To improve investment returns and stimulate the declining economy, an increased proportion of these funds are now to be invested in the stock market. According to *Methods on Managing the Investment of Social Security Pension Fund* (2015), around 30 per cent of the social security funds, or 600 billion yuan, will be invested in the stock market in 2016; according to the *Regulations on National Social Security Fund* (2016), the fund can also now invest overseas (see China News Center, 29 June 2015; China News Center, 28 December 2015).

Pension Benefits

According to data produced by the CASS, the amount of pension received by a retiree in August 2011 ranged from 200 to 10 000 yuan;

more than 75 per cent had pensions below 2000 yuan; and 77.3 per cent received less than the average of 2615 yuan (*People's Daily*, 2013). In 2012, the Urban Employee Old Age Pension System spent a total of 1556.2 billion yuan on 74.46 million pensioners, averaging a monthly pension of more than 1700 yuan. In contrast, the average monthly payment of the Residents' Old Age Pension System was around 110 yuan. According to a longitudinal survey conducted in 2015, the monthly pension benefits of government organizations and public institutions were 3175 yuan; of enterprises, 2400 yuan; of urban residents, 1387 yuan; and of rural residents, 141 yuan. The benefit received by civil servants is almost 23 times that of rural residents. Compared to the average monthly wage of 4695 yuan in the public sector, 3033 yuan in the private sector, and 3033 yuan for migrant workers in 2015, the replacement ratio is low (MOHRSS, 28 May 2015). As compared to the average social assistance (*dibao*) standard of 231 yuan in rural areas, this pension benefit is evidently too low (Ministry of Civil Affairs, 2016).

According to OECD estimates, the replacement rate of China's pension benefits in 2012 was around 60 per cent, above the OECD average of 54 per cent (OECD, 2013). However, the CASS estimates China's replacement rate in 2011 as only 50 per cent, down from 73 per cent in 2002, and 58 per cent in 2005 (China News Center, 11 September 2013). This drop is mainly attributed to rapid wage increases in recent years. The replacement rates of those in government offices and institutions can be maintained at a level of 80–90 per cent. On average, their pension benefits are two to three times higher than those of the average worker (China News Center, 1 November 2013). Even with the integration of the civil service pension scheme into the urban employee pension system, government workers will remain a privileged group in terms of retirement benefits.

FUTURE DIRECTIONS

Social welfare, especially pension reform, will be a pivotal issue in whether or not China can become a high-income economy complemented by a universal welfare state. The goal of pension reform is to create a more universal, fair and accessible social welfare system based on equal rights and citizenship. In short, the Chinese government is building a new welfare system that will match or be compatible with the development and reform of its market-oriented economy, as well as a stabilizing mechanism mitigating rising social dissatisfaction and tension (Leung and Xu, 2015; Ngok and Chan, 2016). Social development cannot be understood and interpreted as a separate aspect of economic and political development.

The Fifth Plenum of the Eighteenth Party Congress in October 2015 pledged to establish a relatively well-off society (*xiakang*) by 2020, with a fairer and more sustainable social security system offering universal coverage and national unification. By that time, the pension system will have achieved nearly full coverage, including more than 100 million migrant workers and the informally employed. The current pooling of funds at the provincial level can be moved upward to the national level, giving greater capacity to share risk and reduce regional differences. However, in view of the significant regional variations currently present in fund contribution rates and reserves, unification at the national level will take a long time. There should be more incentives and restrictions in the individual account system to encourage saving and discourage abuse. Gradual postponement of retirement is inevitable. The management of pension funds could be improved to enhance investment returns. Government subsidies to pension funds could be diversified and strengthened, especially through the transfer of state assets (China News Center, 29 February 2016).

Through the decades, pension reform has been considered an integral part of the continuous market-oriented economic reforms, and the achievements have been substantial. Without a blueprint, reform has been pragmatic and incremental. Effective pension reforms are not only paramount in offering retirees better social protection, but complementary to economic restructuring and maintaining continuous growth. The earlier pension reform agenda centred on reducing and sharing the welfare responsibilities of the state-owned enterprises in order to enhance their competitive advantage during the market-oriented reforms. In the late 1990s, the establishment of a partially funded system with individual saving accounts served to encourage individual asset building. Furthermore, the rapid expansion of the social assistance safety net in urban and rural areas in the 2000s represented a further attempt to reduce the risk of pensioner poverty (Leung and Xiao, 2016). Through setting up pension schemes for rural and urban residents, further efforts have been made to widen coverage and increase contributions. Match funding from government has encouraged participation. Indeed, China has succeeded in significantly increasing its pension coverage in recent years. Looking to the future, further reforms will centre on fund pooling at the national level, fund portability, fund management transparency, gradual reduction of contribution rates, further integration of segmented schemes, and extension of the retirement age. These reforms will facilitate not only pension sustainability but also labour mobility, economic participation, urbanization, human capital development and a reduction in rural–urban differences. Even though China has not officially endorsed the concept of social investment, its pension reform illustrates a precise social investment orientation.

REFERENCES

Beland, D. and Yu, K.M. (2004). A Long Financial March: Pension Reform in China. *Journal of Social Policy*, 33 (2), 267–288.

Cai, F., Giles, J., O'Keefe, P. and Wang, D. (2012). *The Elderly and Old Age Support in Rural China, Challenges and Prospects*. Washington, DC: World Bank.

Chin, L.J. (2015). Analysis on the Social Insurance Coverage and Factors of Mobile Population. *Statistical Studies*, 1, 68–72 (in Chinese).

China Development Research Foundation (ed.) (2012). *Constructing A Social Welfare System for All in China*. London: Routledge.

China News Center (28 January 2013). Working Age Population is on the Decline for the First Time, Appearance of the Turning Point of the Demographic Dividend. http://news.china.com.cn/2013-01/28/content_27808859. htm (in Chinese).

China News Center (19 August 2013). China's Population Aged over 60 Reaches 4 million, and Will Exceed 300 Million by 2025. http://news.china.com.cn/txt/ 2013-08/19/content_29763950.htm (in Chinese).

China News Center (11 September 2013). Figures on Declining Incomes of Retirees Indicate Serious Pension Gaps. http://finance.china.com.cn/news/gnjj/ 20130911/1803604.shtml (in Chinese).

China News Center (1 November 2013). China's Pension Benefits as a Proportion of the Wage Continue to Fall for Nine Years. http://china.com.cn/2013-11/ 01/content_30468147.htm (in Chinese).

China News Center (28 December 2014). Pension Insurance, Fund Management – Report of the State Council on the Progress of Construction of the Social Security System. http://finance.china.com.cn/roll/20141228/2876286.shtml (in Chinese).

China News Center (18 May 2015). Each Employee's Lifelong Social Security Contribution Amounts to over a Million Yuan. http://finance.china.com.cn/ news/gnjj/20150518/3122229.shtml (in Chinese).

China News Center (1 June 2015). Increase in Pension Fund Contribution is Declining. http://finance.china.com.cn/news/gnjj/20150601/3149529.shtml (in Chinese).

China News Center (29 June 2015). Options on Billion of Yuan will Enter into the Market. http://finance.china.com.cn/news/gnjj/20150629/3199977.shtml (in Chinese).

China News Center (11 November 2015). Interpreting the Fifth Plenum of the 13 Party Congress. http://news.china.com.cn/txt/2015-11/11/content_37030977. htm (in Chinese).

China News Center (23 November 2015). Inadequate Pension Incomes of 22 Provinces. news.china.com.cn/2015-11/23/content_37131160.htm (in Chinese).

China News Center (5 December 2015). Retired at 65?. http://shehui. china.com.cn/2015-12/05/content_37242283.htm (in Chinese).

China News Center (28 December 2015). MOHRSS: 2000 Billion Yuan Pension Fund will Move into the Stock Market Next Year. http://news.china.com.cn/2015-10/28/content_36909076.htm (in Chinese).

China News Center (22 January 2016). Pension Fund Should Not be Misused. http://opinion.china.com.cn/opinion_73_143473.html (in Chinese).

China News Center (29 February 2016). State Council News Office Report on Employment and Social Security. http://www.china.org.cn/china/2016-02/29/content_37899745.htm (in Chinese).

China News Center (1 March 2016). Ministry of Human Resources and Social Security, Gradual Postponement of Retirement Age Options will be Introduced This Year. http://news.china.com.cn/2016-03/01/content_37902095.htm (in Chinese).

China News Center (23 March 2016). By Reducing the Social Security Contribution Rate, Five Insurance will become Four Insurance. http://news.china.com.cn/2016-03/23/content_38089506.htm (in Chinese).

China News Center (26 March 2016). China's Population Structure Deteriorates. http://guoqing.china.com.cn/2016-03/26/content_38115015.htm (in Chinese).

China News Center (17 June 2016). Fourteen Provinces Reduce their Pension Contribution Rate by 1%. http://finance.people.com.cn/n1/2016/0617/c1004-28451800.html (in Chinese).

Chow, N. and Xu, Y.B. (2001). *Socialist Welfare in a Market Economy: Social Security Reforms in Guangzhou, China*. Aldershot, UK: Ashgate.

Dorfman, M., Holzmann, R., O'Keefe, P., Wang, D., Sin, Y. and Hinz, R. (2013). *China's Pension System, A Vision*. Washington, DC: World Bank.

Economic References (2015). Pension Benefits Continue to Rise in the Past 12 Years. 31 December. http://finance.china.com.cn/news/gnjj/20151231/3524256.shtml (in Chinese).

Frazier, M.W. (2010). *Socialist Insecurity: Pensions and the Politics of Uneven Development in China*. Ithaca, NY: Cornell University Press.

Gao, G. (2010). Redistributive Nature of the Chinese Social Benefit System: Progressive or Regressive?. *China Quarterly*, 201 (March), 1–19.

Giles, J., Wang, D. and Park, A. (2013). Expanding Social Insurance Coverage in Urban China. Policy Research Working Paper 6497. Washington, DC: World Bank.

Giles, J., Wang, D. and Zhao, C. (2010). Can China's Rural Elderly Count on Support from Adult Children? Implications for Rural-to-Urban Migration. Policy Research Paper 5510, December. Washington, DC: World Bank.

Herd, R., Hu, Y. and Koen, V. (2010). Providing Greater Old-Age Security in China. Economics Department Working Papers No. 750. Paris: OECD.

Johansson, S. and Cheng, S. (2016). Universal Old-Age Pension in an Aging China: Can China Learn from Sweden? *International Social Work*, 59 (6), 922–937.

Leung, J. (1994). Dismantling the Iron Rice Bowl: Welfare Reforms in the PRC. *Journal of Social Policy*, 23 (3), 341–361.

Leung, J. (2003). Social Security Reforms in China: Issues and Prospects. *International Journal of Social Welfare*, 12 (2), 73–85.

Leung, J. and Xiao, M. (2016). The Institutionalization of Social Assistance. In K.L. Ngok and C.K. Chan (eds), *China's Social Policy*. London: Routledge, pp. 33–51.

Leung, J. and Xu, Y.B. (2015). *China's Social Welfare, The Third Turning Point.* Cambridge: Polity Press.

Liu, J., Liu, K. and Huang, Y. (2016). Transferring from the Poor to the Rich: Examining Regressive Redistribution in Chinese Social Insurance Programmes. *International Journal of Social Welfare*, 25 (2), 199–210.

Ministry of Civil Affairs (2016). 2014 Social Service Statistics. http://http://www.mca.gov.cn/article/sj/tjgb/201506/201506008324399.shtml (in Chinese).

Ministry of Human Resources and Social Security (MOHRSS) (28 May 2015). 2014 Report on Human Resources and Social Security Development. http://www.mohrss.gov.cn/SYrlzyhshbzb/dongtaixinwen/buneiyaowen/201505/t2015 0528_162040.htm (in Chinese).

Ministry of Human Resources and Social Security (MOHRSS) (30 June 2015). 2014 Annual Social Insurance Report. http://www.china.com.cn/zhibo/2015-06/30/content_35933224.htm?show=t (in Chinese).

Ministry of Human Resources and Social Security (MOHRSS) (21 December 2015). Decisions on Reforming Pension System in Government Organizations and Public Institutions. http://www.ssf.gov.cn/flfg/fkgl/201601/t20160126_6996.html (in Chinese).

Ngok, K.L. and Chan, C.K. (eds) (2016). *China's Social Policy, Transformation and Challenges*. London: Routledge.

Organisation for Economic Co-operation and Development (OECD) (2013). *Pensions at a Glance 2013*. Paris: OECD.

Organisation for Economic Co-operation and Development (OECD) (2015). *Pensions at a Glance 2015*. Paris: OECD.

Peng, H. (2016). Old Age Pension. In K.L. Ngok and C.K. Chan (eds), *China's Social Policy, Transformation and Challenges*. London: Routledge, pp. 51–65.

People's Daily (2013). The Difference of China's Social Security Benefits Ratio Reached 0.86. 25 February. http://society.people.com.cn/n/2013/0225/c1008-20592477.html?_fin (in Chinese).

Salditt, F., Whiteford, P. and Adema, W. (2007). Pension Reform in China. OECD Social, Employment and Migration Working Papers 53. Paris: OECD.

Shen, C. and Williamson, J.B. (2010). China's New Rural Pension Scheme: Can It be Improved?. *International Journal of Sociology and Social Policy*, 30 (5–6), 239–250.

Shi, S.J. (2006). Left to Market and Family, Again? Ideas and the Development of Rural Pension Policy in China. *Social Policy and Administration*, 40 (7), 791–806.

Sin, Y. (2005). Pension Liabilities and Reform Options for Old Age Insurance. Working Paper Series on China, Paper No. 2005-1. Washington, DC: World Bank.

Xinhua News (2015). Aging Population has Limited Impact on China Growth: World Bank. 9 December. http://news.xinhuanet.com/english/2015-12/09/c_134900608.htm (in Chinese).

Zhang, X.L. and Xu, Y.B. (2012). Pensions and Social Assistance: The Development of Income Security Policies for Old People in China. In S.Y. Chen and J. Powell (eds), *Aging in China: Implications to Social Policy of A Changing Economic State*. New York: Springer, pp. 43–61.

10. A critical perspective on child care and social investment in Norway: what is in children's best interest?

Knut Halvorsen, Amy Østertun Geirdal and Anne Grete Tøge

A strong focus on social investment, to reduce new social risks such as changes in the labour market and new family formations, seems not only to be directed at adults, but first and foremost at children and young people: "Children and childhood are key to any successful investment strategy" (Van Lancker, 2013, p. 6). The parental role in implementing such a strategy is highlighted (Jenson, 2004). Industrial organizations are advocating that child care shall prepare children for the future through more formalized training, such as computer skills, at the expense of playing (Vassnes, 2015). Education is also seen as an important part of social investment in children (Clarke, 2006). In this light, and from a social investment view, a good parental role, child care and education are important for the child's well-being, as well as a prudent long-term investment. The question is whether the 'here and now' (well-being) can be reconciled with a long-term goal of making children as adults productive workers (becoming).

In this chapter, we critically discuss the impact of a social investment strategy on children by applying human rights, capability and citizenships perspectives. Tendencies to concentrate policies on children as future 'worker citizens' can conflict with their own best interests, such as having a good life in the present. Furthermore, social investment in parents (production) can have unintended negative effects on children, due to inability to reconcile work and family. The child's needs have to be set above the needs of its parents. A 'happy' childhood is not only an end in itself, but could also be a means: it may lead to better life outcomes (De Neve et al., 2013). Of three key features of child development (academic, behavioural and emotional), the emotional best predicts whether the adult will be satisfied with life (Layard et al., 2014).

A particular focus of this chapter is on children from poor and dis-advantaged backgrounds. A pertinent question is then how important it is to fight poverty through cash benefits versus in-kind benefits in a "child centered social investment strategy" (Hemerijck, 2013, p. 381).

A social investment strategy in its neoliberal version connotes a business-friendly, market-oriented, and dynamic entrepreneurship. It is a future-oriented, proactive approach whereby investing in human capital aims to raise employment levels and productivity levels, widen the tax base and improve the quality of work, not only more jobs, but also better jobs. By combining social and economic goals, social policy is becoming productive. Such a strategy is understood within an economic growth paradigm, where the question of sustainability, for example sustainable production and consumption, or other important goals are neglected. In a Nordic social democratic version, social investment is also seen as a means to reduce inequality, promote gender equality through reconcili-ation of work and family life, and increase social cohesion (Kvist, 2015). In reality, as underscored by Nolan (2013), it is hard to distinguish, in both theory and application, between social investment and social con-sumption programmes, between the 'productive' and 'unproductive' elements of social spending.

It has to be mentioned that this chapter is rooted in European experience. Unlike other parts of the world, the social investment perspective is likely to be strong already in, for example, Norwegian child and family policy. It has been argued that in a Nordic context the social investment strategy builds on an implicit contract between gener-ations resulting in a welfare state smoothing the resources over the life course, a 'horizontal redistribution', and at the same time redistributing resources from the those who 'have' to the 'have nots', a 'vertical redistribution' (Kvist, 2015). In that way a society's social capital, personal trust and social networks are improved. The rationale for our approach is that the ultimate goal of a nation-state should be to secure high and equal satisfaction with life, not economic growth, which should be regarded as a means to an end (Layard, 2005).

THE CAPABILITY AND WELL-BEING APPROACH

A social investment strategy aimed at children focuses on their healthy development and protection from harm (Qualtieri and Robinson, 2012), and development of their human capital such as their (marketable) skills through training and education. In that way, children as adults will contribute to the tax base and the growth of the economy. Social investments in children are needed for the sustainability of the welfare state (Commission of the European Communities, 2005). In this perspective, an idea behind social investment is to facilitate a shift from direct redistribution to investment in people's vocational qualifications, in order to strengthen the market's own equalizing abilities (Morel et al., 2012). Focusing on social investments in children means that they are not viewed as a cost but as an investment (Knijn and van Oorschot, 2008), producing financial, social and educational benefits (Weiss, 2011). However, to prepare young children for precarious work availability in an uncertain globalized and unsustainable future could be a disservice to them as well as the society to which they belong.

Can such a future-oriented strategy also provide benefits to the individual child 'here and now'? In order to discuss this question, we use a capability approach. A capability approach is primarily concerned about the benefits of the individual's quality of life, not the possible benefits for the society. Such an approach is based on human rights, and specifically the freedom to do and become; in other words, the individual's 'capability' to function, where 'functionings' refer to what people are and do. The society's primary responsibility is to develop human capabilities through, for example, the welfare state in order to avoid poverty and inequality. Freedom to achieve capabilities presupposes resources. According to Sen (1999), fundamental conditions for human development are "good health, basic education and encouragement and cultivation of initiatives" (p. 5). The quest for human development should not be seen as competing with the quest for increasing happiness, defined in terms of an individual's overall life evaluation (Hall, 2013). Yet, in contrast to subjective well-being, a capability approach does not focus only on outcomes, but also "on agency and a person's substantive opportunities" (Binder, 2014, p. 1198). Sen (1985) linked happiness to the fulfilment of functionings. As an alternative perspective to societal progress than economic growth, new indicators of well-being are suggested (Layard, 2005). Such indicators can be used to create more coherent public policy and to identify conflicting policy goals and other values (Binder, 2014). Individuals are not only concerned about outcomes, but also derive their subjective well-being from processes and the way outcomes are achieved (Frey and Stutzer, 2012). Sen's capability approach has been incorporated into a well-being framework: subjective well-being capabilities reflecting "the total of an individual's capabilities to achieve subjective well-being" (Binder, 2014, p. 1211). This perspective enables us to assess the personal freedoms and substantive opportunities that an individual has to strive for happiness within a given caring and educational system (the institutional framework), focusing on the role of learning for subjective well-being (Schubert, 2012) in a wide time frame (Binder, 2014). The capability approach seems thereby to include both the 'being' and 'becoming' approaches. A well-documented connection between well-being and mental health (see, e.g., Helliwell et al., 2013; Layard, 2005, 2013; Layard et al., 2013; Layard et al., 2014; Layard and Hagell, 2015) calls for some remarks on the effects of different forms of schooling on possible stressors among young students.

The Best Interest of Children: The United Nations Convention on the Rights of the Child

Another possible theoretical point of departure to discuss social investment directed at children is the concept of the 'best interest of a child', which is central in the United Nations Convention on the Rights of the Child (1989). What is meant by such a concept is not universally agreed. In the Preamble of the Convention, it is recognized "that the child for the full and harmonious development of his or her personality, should grow up in a family environment, in an atmosphere of happiness, love and understanding". In Article 3, it becomes clear that focus is on the child's well-being; and in Article 6, that it is about the development of the child. According to the Convention, the best interest of a child includes the child's right to express their view "freely in all matters affecting the child, the view of the child being given due weight in accordance with the age and maturity of the child" (Article 12). Lister (2006) has stressed the importance of implementing social investment without violating children's human rights, including their participatory rights. A children's rights perspective is about the present needs of children for developing their capabilities (Saraceno, 2011). The question is to what extent the child's 'best interest' shall count. In Article 3, it is stressed that it has to be a fundamental consideration in all situations that involve children (Sandberg, 2009).

Article 28 deals with the child's right to education. It says further that all appropriate measures shall be taken to ensure that school discipline is administered in a manner consistent with the child's human dignity and in conformity with the Convention. In Article 29a it is stated "that the education of the child shall be directed to: The development of the child's personality, talents and mental and physical abilities to their fullest potential". The best interest of a child is secured by taking a child's perspective, which is implemented by understanding of the particular young child's specific perspectives of the world. Children's perspectives mean giving them a voice to express their own experiences, perceptions and understandings of their life world. By adopting both perspectives, a carer or teacher will see a child as "being" and "becoming" (Prout, 2005, cited in Sommer et al., 2013, p. 468).

INFLUENCES ON CHILDREN'S WELL-BEING

Small children's needs are primarily to be safe, controlled, cared-for and loved, which ideally shall be provided by parents and, later on, by preschool teachers in kindergartens who are supposed to act in the child's best interest. To be sure, there might be opposing views on what is a child's best interest: the parents on the one hand, and the professional teacher on the other. A common understanding across cultures is that the child undergoes personality maturation during early childhood, partly genetically shaped (Bleidorn et al., 2013). An ultimate objective is to make children happy "throughout the school years and to emerge with capabilities to be happy throughout their lives, and to spread happiness to others", while the instrumental objective is to prepare them for employment (Thin, 2012, p. 167). According to the World Values Surveys (2006/2007), attitudes towards parenting differ on some dimensions between Norway and other European countries (Table 10.1). The question posed was: 'Here is a list of qualities that children can be encouraged to learn at home. Which if any, do you consider to be especially important? Please choose up to five!'

Table 10.1   Important child qualities mentioned by country (%)

	Norway	All European countries (18)
Independence	90	64
Hard work	13	37
Responsibility	89	80
Imagination	55	29
Tolerance and respect for others	91	77
Religious faith	9	22
Thrift (saving money and things)	14	38
Unselfishness	20	31
Obedience	29	31
(N)	1 025	19 742

Source: World Values Survey Association (2014).

Norwegian parents stress tolerance and respect for others, independence and responsibility, as the most important qualities. That is also the case in all European countries, although to a smaller extent than in Norway. What differs are the higher proportions in Europe stressing hard work, thrift (saving money and things), religious faith and unselfishness, and in Norway stressing imagination. In Norway, 'attachment parenting' is popular. The ideal represents close attachment with the child. Especially during the first two or three years it is regarded as essential for building strong emotional links and thus creating confident children (Howe, 2013; Szalavitz and Perry, 2010). A great majority (85 per cent) agree with the statement that 'parents' duty is to do the best for their children, even at the expense of their own well-being', in accordance with a child-centred social investment strategy (Ivan et al., 2015).

In 2010–2011, 42 per cent of Norwegian children below three years of age were in formal child care compared to a European Union (EU)-27 average of 33 per cent. In 2011, of children between the age of three and formal school age, 87 per cent in Norway were in formal child care, compared with an average of 84 per cent in the EU (European Commission, 2013). By 2012, 70 per cent of one-year-old children participated in kindergartens, and more than 95 per cent among 3–5-year-olds (Engel et al., 2015). Children in Norway have a legal right to kindergarten from age one and until start of school at age six. These kindergartens make ample room for children's free-chosen leisure activities, preferably outdoors in a natural environment, perhaps in accordance with what is called a child-oriented paradigm (Sommer et al., 2013). It seems that playing in natural landscapes is beneficial for the development of curiosity, play, desire to learn and improvement of motor abilities in children (Fjørtoft, 2004).

The quality of child care is in large part dependent on whether the staff is professionally qualified or not. The ratio of staff to children is 6:1 on average for all age groups in Norway (Ministry of Education and Research, 2015). In Norway, assistants undergo a two-year post-16 apprenticeship, and preschool teachers have three years' tertiary education (bachelor's degree). There is still a considerable lack of qualified staff in Norwegian kindergartens (Engel et al., 2015): the percentage was as low as 39 per cent in 2014 (Directorate of Health, 2015). The early childhood programmes are characterized by two divergent approaches: a socio-pedagogical approach, focusing on play, child-initiated activities and everyday real-life themes; and an academic approach with a similar focus to that in school, teaching subject areas such as literacy, mathematics and so on in an adult-structured environment (Sommer et al., 2013). The recent White Paper on the further development of kindergartens in

Norway underlines both the intrinsic value of a good childhood (the 'here and now') and future possibilities to conduct education and achieve stable employment. Nevertheless, whether facilitating these two dimensions involves substantive contradictions in concrete activities (free play versus learning), is not discussed (Norwegian Government, 2015–2016).

It has been shown that play with other children of the same age stimulates language skills better than through language teaching by adults in kindergartens among children aged 1–3 years (Oslo and Akershus University College of Applied Sciences, 2015). This finding is in line with Sommer et al. (2013) who conclude that children learn more and are better prepared for primary school and even secondary school when they have been in a play and socio-pedagogical learning environment, rather than an academic one, in their early years. It seems, for example, that "the foundations of both mathematical and verbal skills are acquired in the earliest years more effectively through informal interaction with adults than through formal training" (Putnam, 2015, p. 110).

When children are in "daydreaming mode" (in contrast to the brain's default, "the central executive mode"), imagination, creativity, inspiration and intuition are desirable outcomes (Levitin, 2014, p. 375). Such qualities seem to be neglected in a social investment strategy directed at small children. An academic approach may also ignore the importance of social capital for a society's economic development. A socio-pedagogical approach could therefore enhance interpersonal trust, social support networks and pro-sociality to a greater extent than an academic one (Sachs, 2015).

One may ask which nation secures 'the best start' for a child. From a future-oriented social investment perspective, perhaps early school start and grading, emphasis on hard work, thrift and obedience are most preferable. Yet, as in Norway, to promote independence, responsibility and imagination are qualities in accordance with a 'here and now' perspective, but may also be beneficial for the child's future role as a responsible citizen in an uncertain world, in line with expectations of post-industrial economies. Ideas of modernization have resulted in promotion of early learning, standardizing curricula and more educational testing (Lewis, 2006). An example of a future-oriented social investment perspective can be found in Norway. Field experiments are under way in about 150 daycare centres, with the aim through self-regulation, interpersonal, vocabulary and numeracy skills to 'systematically cultivate school readiness skills known to promote future learning' (Rege, 2014). Such an 'employability agenda' has been applauded by the Norwegian industrial organization (NHO), while for example researchers on kindergartens are strongly against such a development (Pettersvold and Østrem, 2014). It has been shown that children aged 1–3 years in kindergartens stimulate their language skills better through play with other children at their own will than through language teaching by adults. Not all kindergartens organize their activities accordingly (Oslo and Akershus University College of Applied Sciences, 2015).

Schooling

The mandatory school age in Norway is from six years old. Children enter upper secondary school at the age of 16 (Lamb et al., 2011). Pupils only get grades from the age of 13, but there is a tendency to emphasize grading at an earlier age as well. Looking at average school performance for 15-year-olds, according to the Programme for International Student Assessment (PISA) 2012 study (OECD, 2013), student performance in mathematics in Norway is around average, above average in reading, but below average in science. The teacher–student relation is less positive than on average across Organisation for Economic Co-operation and Development (OECD) countries (OECD, 2013). A documented lack of trained teachers (OECD, 2013) may explain poor teacher–student relations. According to OECD's PISA study, average scores in mathematics and science actually decreased in Norway between 1998 and 2008. There are worries that this unfortunate development may have a negative impact on future productivity in the economy (NOU, 2015). However, the gender gap, the gaps between socio-economic backgrounds, top performers and low performers, and between immigrant and non-immigrant students, are smaller in Norway than in many other countries (OECD, 2013).

School dropouts are also an indication of inadequacy of the schooling system (the learning environment) as well as social inequalities. In 2008 around two out of three Norwegian teenagers had completed upper-secondary education within five years. High dropout rates were prevalent especially among students on vocational education programmes (or apprenticeship training), in contrast to students on academic programmes (university preparatory courses) (Markussen et al., 2008); in 2010, 2.7 per cent of 15–19-year-olds were not in education or employment, while for example in France it was 14 per cent (Lamb et al., 2011). The percentage of youth aged 15–24 not in education, employment or training (NEET) was 6 per cent in Norway in 2013, while in France it was 11 per cent (Fanjul, 2014).

A comparative study of child well-being in 30 OECD countries from 2005–2006 shows that Norway is ranked as number 2 among 24 countries when it comes to quality of school life, consisting of two indicators: bullying and liking school. On all the other five indicators of

child well-being (material well-being, housing and environment, educational well-being, health and safety, risk behaviours), Norway is ranked
reasonably high (Chapple and Richardson, 2009). As mentioned previously, from a 'here and now' perspective the Norwegian educational
system seems to a certain degree to take care of children's best interest
(such as opportunities for leisure, to have fun and enjoy themselves).

Mental Health and Well-Being Among Children

A Norwegian national survey of the age group 14–17 years old shows
that in both 2010–2012 and 2013 a great majority enjoy school (Bakken,
2014). School-related unhappiness is nevertheless quite widespread in
industrialized nations (McReynolds, 2008), but to a greater extent in
other countries than in Norway, where 87 per cent feel happy at school
(OECD, 2013). On the other hand, at an early age children feel pressure
from parents and peers to perform well at school as well as in sports and
other leisure activities, and one out of three children aged 11, 13 and 15
felt pressured by school work (Bradshaw et al., 2013). School dissatisfaction is of great importance and strongly associated with high levels of
depressive symptoms among adolescents in Norway (Abebe et al., 2016).
From 1996 to 2015 there has been an increase in the prevalence of
depressive symptoms. The prevalence increases with school age, and is
higher among girls than among boys (Andersen and Bakken, 2015).

A national survey indicates that around 20 per cent in the age group
14–17 years old have symptoms of depression; 6–7 per cent say that they
have been bullied at school (Bakken, 2014). There is evidence that rates
of mental illness in young people have increased over time in many
modern societies (Eckersley, 2011; Norwegian Institute of Public Health,
2014). Yet, symptoms of depression are less prevalent among young
children in Norway than in other Western countries (Heiervang et al.,
2007). Since the best predictor of whether a child will become a satisfied
adult is emotional health in childhood (Layard and Hagell, 2015), the
high prevalence of depression symptoms among Norwegian children is
worrying.

Education is to improve not only children's cognitive competence, but
also their social and emotional competence (Lieberman, 2013), such as
learning agreeableness, this being an advantage for maintaining positive
social relationships (Levitin, 2014). This means that one has to be careful
about regarding parenting and early schooling solely in a future-oriented
social investment perspective. Children live 'here and now' (12 months in
the life of a 40-year-old person are experienced as half as long than a
similar period for a ten-year-old child) (Levitin, 2014), and therefore

their 'best interest' and well-being has to be the central focus. Further-more, it turns out that child happiness and joy can predict future life chances: a happy childhood gives a higher probability of being more productive and having a higher income than for those who are not so happy (De Neve et al., 2013; Halpern, 2010). Therefore, emphasizing 'being' is the best 'becoming'.

THE POTENTIAL CONFLICT BETWEEN SOCIAL INVESTMENT IN PARENTS AND THE WELL-BEING OF CHILDREN

In order to promote increased use of female labour in the formal economy, strong initiatives have taken place in most Western countries in order to reconcile paid labour for parents with parenting (Jeroslow, 2014). Government policy includes, for example, maternity and paternity leave, and other parental leave arrangements. Kindergartens are available in many countries for children from the age of one, while preschool programmes are expected to mitigate mechanisms of intergenerational inheritance (Pintelon et al., 2013).

Preschool, early school start and after-school care arrangements are meant to fit the child schedule with those of their working parents. According to Lewis (2006), the question is of how children have a voice in deciding how to create their own welfare, and who is to speak for the child and represent their best interest, as referred to in the United Nations Convention on the Rights of the Child. Work-time arrangements in line with a flexible workforce, such as irregular work (being on call), shift and night shift work, overtime and weekend work, are not in accordance with the child's need for regular time spent with his or her parents. To a greater extent the boundary between work and free time is blurred, also making it more and more difficult to engage in so-called 'quality time' with the child. Neither is the huge expansion of formal child care places, not followed up by more emphasis on quality, in accordance with the child's best interest (Lewis, 2006). Some would argue that "it is in the best interest of small children to be cared for at home, in their own environment, preferably by one of their parents" (Knijn, 1994, p. 204). On the other hand, kindergartens could be beneficial for parents, not only because they enhance their possibilities to take up paid work, but also in that as social meeting-places they can improve parenting (Sundnes and Andenæs, 2014). It also turns out that working mothers spend much more active time with their children now than they did in the 1970s, while spending less time on housework (Statistics Norway, 2010). Also the total time parents spend with their children has substantially increased since the 1970s (Kitterød and Rønsen, 2012). Child care is of importance from a gender perspective, since the gender pay gap among 30–34-year-old parents is smaller with greater enrolment rates in formal care of children under three years old (European Commission, 2013). It thus seems that it is possible to reconcile investments in parents with the well-being of children, provided that high-quality formal care is available.

SUPPORT TO POOR AND DISADVANTAGED FAMILIES

As early as in the 1930s, leading Swedish social scientists Gunnar and Alva Myrdal (1934) maintained that poor parents were unable to act in their children's best interest. Therefore, instead of cash transfers, such families should have support through in-kind services. We find similar arguments among sociologists today (see, e.g., Giddens, 1998). Justification of cutbacks in social transfers is made by stronger emphasis on targeted investment in children and their families. In most Western countries, paid work is regarded as the way out of poverty. In reality, social investment has so far failed to reduce relative poverty (Cantillon, 2011). As maintained by Kothari et al. (2014), work is not the only viable route out of poverty. In-work poverty is rising, although social transfers substantially reduce the risk of poverty (Fanjul, 2014). Yet, according to politicians, child poverty has to be combated not by higher cash transfers but through improving employment opportunities for parents. However, in many Western countries child poverty is on the increase; in Norway the rate is 5.6 per cent (Fanjul, 2014), not least due to high unemployment levels. Such a situation is not in the child's best interest. Apart from higher risk of bad nutrition (less healthy food) and inadequate housing, lack of money means less possibility to socialize with other children and take part in essential leisure activities (extracurricular activities) such as sports. Activities like these enhance non-cognitive skills such as sociability (Putnam, 2015).

According to Article 27 of the United Nations Convention on the Rights of the Child, children have the right to a satisfactory standard of living, when it comes to physical, mental, spiritual, moral and social development. Children are interested in the quality of life 'here and now'; they live in the present, not ten years from now. Growing up in poverty could also impair children's physical as well as mental health, which could have a lasting negative effect on their health as grown-ups, risking fewer healthy life years.

Recent research on the psychology of scarcity demonstrates that shortage of money makes the poor worse parents. In managing scarcity, their mental bandwidths (the speed limits for the traffic of information we can pay attention to at one time) are narrowed (Levitin, 2014). When scarcity is on one's mind, there is less mind for everything else. Being a good parent requires self-control. This is depleted when in poverty; scarcity forces the brain to focus on alleviating pressing shortages and thus reduces the mental bandwidth available to address other needs, plan ahead, exert self-control and solve problems (Mullainathan and Shafir, 2013). Therefore, the poor seem to have lower effective capacity than others, because their minds are captured by scarcity. There is simply less bandwidth available for other things, like life (Tirado, 2014).

Recent research demonstrates that children who have developed their ability for self-control have a greater chance of a good life compared to those who do not have that skill (Baumeister and Tierney, 2011). The famous 'marshmallow test' has shown that the child's ability to defer gratification makes for a better adult life in many respects (Mischel, 2014). Self-discipline – a dimension of conscientiousness (one of the big five personality traits) – is the best predictor of many human outcomes, including education attainment (Levitin, 2014); it is two times more powerful than IQ as a predictor of progress in school (Layard, 2013). Since parents are role models, it is of the utmost importance to promote such skills in their children. As shown by Lister (2006) it might be particularly hard for single mothers to both take part in the labour market, and at the same time control their children's behaviour and involve themselves in their education.

The annual cost of child poverty is reduced productivity and economic output, due to inequality of opportunity, shown in higher school dropout rates; disadvantaged children do not develop their full capacity. Investing in greater equality of opportunity, for example in the form of cash to disadvantaged families, will pay off. It is good for democracy as well, since civic involvement also increases when more youth are getting an education (Putnam, 2015).

There seems to be an increasing polarization of cognitive skills among children in several European countries, which is an argument for children from disadvantaged families receiving good pedagogical preparation for school via (free) early child care (Knijn and van Oorschot, 2008). In order to promote social justice and at the same time promote productivity in the economy, early intervention targeted at the disadvantaged, such as preschool programmes improving cognitive and non-cognitive skills, is essential (Heckman, 2006; see also Jeroslow, 2014; NOU, 2015). This means that affordable high-quality child care is a must for vulnerable families. It is also of importance that free child care is available for children of immigrant parents: an evaluation of pilot programmes with child care for 4–6-year-olds demonstrates that use increases when it is free of charge (20 core hours per week). Attendance in child care is beneficial for children's cognitive and social development, especially for children coming from families with low education and income (Drange, 2015). Increasingly, subsidized fees are offered for low-income families (Engel et al., 2015). This nevertheless means that cash support aimed at families with children can be regarded as part of a social investment strategy (Hemerijck, 2013). While poverty is a concern in itself, it also has damaging long-term consequences, particularly its scarring effects on children. These scarring effects of low-income periods mean that when the recession ends, its impact on children does not. Ensuring that the basic needs of children and youth are met can therefore be one of the most important social investments, and should be a central pillar of social protection.

The question is in what form such financial support shall be given: unconditional or conditional, unfocused or focused? In the conditional case, parents have to meet certain obligations (responsibilities) in order to change their own behaviour or that of the child, which could mean a violation of both children's and parents' rights according to the United Nations (UN) Convention on the Rights of the Child and the UN Convention on Human Rights (Lister, 2006).

ENSURING SOCIAL INVESTMENT IS IN THE CHILD'S BEST INTERESTS

In this chapter, we have regarded parenting and early kindergarten and schooling as important elements of social investment in children. When comparing Norway with other OECD countries, we do not find any support that early education and preschool significantly improves school performance. Thus, it is not obvious that academic-oriented child care is more beneficial, not even in the long run. To the contrary, it comes at a high price: too much stress on cognitive skills at an early age could have a negative impact on non-cognitive skills (social intelligence), and in addition could be of disservice to some, through impaired mental health and lower levels of happiness. Informal face-to-face contact with parents, peers and professional carers is more important than digital skills for personal development and social skills.

Kindergartens run by professional childminders could be especially beneficial for children (and their parents) from disadvantaged families.

Services should nevertheless be supplemented by cash transfers in order to avoid poverty and unequal life chances for these children. Growing up in scarcity makes parents poor role models, besides having negative consequences for health and quality of life in the sense of the happiness and well-being of such disadvantaged children. It therefore does not make much sense to create a (false) dichotomy between services and cash in distinguishing what can be understood as social investment. It all depends on the total package of cash transfers and (high-quality) parenting, kindergartens and schools.

One should also ask whether social investment programmes directed at children and/or parents are always in the 'best interest' of the child living in the 'here and now'. Good intentions might not always match outcomes (such as early childhood education). Children live in the 'here and now'; a happy childhood is a goal in itself; let children be children. Anyway, one should balance the best interest of the child's becoming in the long run, with that of the child being here and now, by taking seriously the United Nations Convention on the Rights of the Child. So, having children's becoming as a goal through focusing on their being and here and now life might be of the greatest importance. This means that a socio-pedagogical approach in a child perspective is preferable to an academic approach. Our impression is that the latter approach is unfortunately getting more support in Norway.

REFERENCES

Abebe, D.S., Frøyland, L.R., Bakken, A. and Von Soest, T. (2016). Municipal-Level Differences in Depressive Symptoms among Adolescents in Norway: Results from the Cross-National Ungdata Study. *Scandinavian Journal of Public Health*, 44 (1), 47–54.

Andersen, P.L. and Bakken, A. (2015). *Ung i Oslo 2015* (Young in Oslo 2015). NOVA-rapport (NOVA report), Vol. 8/2015. Retrieved from www.hioa.no/content/download/104307/2425558/file/Nettutgave-Ung-i-Oslo-Rapport-8-15-26-august.pdf.

Bakken, A. (2014). *Ungdata: nasjonale resultater 2013* Vol. 10/14. NOVA-rapport (NOVA report). Retrieved from www.hioa.no/content/download/65261/1372634/file/Ungdata%20nasjonale%20resultater%20NOVA-rapport%2010_14.pdf.

Baumeister, R.F. and Tierney, J. (2011). *Willpower: Rediscovering the Greatest Human Strength*. New York: Penguin Press.

Binder, M. (2014). Subjective Well-Being Capabilities: Bridging the Gap Between the Capability Approach and Subjective Well-Being Research. *An Interdisciplinary Forum on Subjective Well-Being*, 15 (5), 1197–1217. doi: 10.1007/s10902-013-9471-6.

Bleidorn, W., Klimstra, T.A., Denissen, J.J.A., Rentfrow, P.J., Potter, J. and Gosling, S.D. (2013). Personality Maturation Around the World. *Psychological Science*, 24 (12), 2530–2540. doi: 10.1177/0956797613498396.

Bradshaw, J., Martorano, B., Natali, L. and de Neubourg, C. (2013). Children's Subjective Well-Being in Rich Countries. *Child Indicators Research*, 6 (4), 619–635.

Cantillon, B. (2011). The Paradox of the Social Investment State: Growth, Employment and Poverty in the Lisbon Era. *Journal of European Social Policy*, 21 (5), 432–449. doi: 10.1177/0958928711418856.

Chapple, S. and Richardson, D. (eds) (2009). *Doing Better for Children*. Paris: OECD.

Clarke, K. (2006). Childhood, Parenting and Early Intervention: A Critical Examination of the Sure Start National Programme. *Critical Social Policy*, 26 (4), 699–721. doi: 10.1177/0261018306068470.

Commission of the European Communities (2005). *Green Paper. Confronting Demographic Change: A New Solidarity between the Generations*. Retrieved from http://ec.europa.eu/employment_social/social_situation/responses/e4578 63_en.pdf.

De Neve, J.-E., Diener, E., Tay, L. and Xuereb, C. (2013). The Objective Benefits of Subjective Well-Being. In J. Helliwell, R. Layard and J. Sachs (eds), *World Happiness Report 2013*. New York: Earth Institute, pp. 54–79. Retrieved from http://unsdsn.org/wp-content/uploads/2014/02/WorldHappinessReport2013_ online.pdf.

Directorate of Health (2015). *Folkehelsepolitisk rapport 2015. Indikatorer for det tverrsektorielle folkehelsearbeidet* (Public Health Policy Report 2015 – indicators for intersectoral health promotion). Retrieved from https://helse direktoratet.no/Lists/Publikasjoner/Attachments/1130/Folkehel.

Drange, N. (2015). Gratis barnehagetid – et vellykket forsøk? (Free kindergarten – a successful project?). *Samfunnsspeilet*, 2, 16–21. Retrieved from https:// www.ssb.no/utdanning/artikler-og-publikasjoner/_attachment/232072?_ts=14e 1ae312f0.

Eckersley, R. (2011). Troubled Youth: An Island of Misery in an Ocean of Happiness, or the Tip of an Iceberg of Suffering?. *Early Intervention in Psychiatry*, 5 (s1), 6–11.

Engel, A., Barnett, W.S., Anders, Y. and Taguma, M. (2015). Early Childhood Education and Care Policy Review. Norway. Paris: OECD.

European Commission (2013). Barcelona Objectives: The Development of Child-care Facilities for Young Children in Europe with a View to Sustainable and Inclusive Growth. Retrieved from http://ec.europa.eu/justice/gender-equality/ files/documents/130531_barcelona_en.pdf.

Fanjul, G. (2014). Children of the Recession: The Impact of the Economic Crisis on Child Well-Being in Rich Countries. Retrieved from http://www.unicef-irc.org/publications/pdf/rc12-eng-web.pdf.

Fjørtoft, I. (2004). Landscape as Playscape: The Effects of Natural Environments on Children's Play and Motor Development. *Children, Youth and Environment*, 14 (2), 21–44.

Frey, B., and Stutzer, A. (2012). The Use of Happiness Research for Public Policy. *Social Choice and Welfare*, 38 (4), 659–674. doi: 10.1007/s00355-011-0629-z.

Giddens, A. (1998). *The Third Way: The Renewal of Social Democracy*. London: Polity Press.

Hall, J. (2013). From Capabilities to Contentment: Testing the Links between Human Development and Life Satisfaction. In J. Helliwell, R. Layard and J. Sachs (eds), *World Happiness Report 2013*. New York: Earth Institute, pp. 138–153. Retrieved from http://unsdsn.org/wp-content/uploads/2014/02/WorldHappinessReport2013_online.pdf.

Halpern, D. (2010). *The Hidden Wealth of Nations*. Cambridge: Polity.

Heckman, J.J. (2006). Skill Formation and the Economics of Investing in Disadvantaged Children. *Science*, 312 (5782), 1900–1902.

Heiervang, E., Stormark, K.M., Lundervold, A.J., Heimann, M., Goodman, R., Posserud, M.B. and Gillberg, C. (2007). Psychiatric Disorders in Norwegian 8- to 10-Year-Olds: An Epidemiological Survey of Prevalence, Risk Factors, and Service Use. *Journal of the American Academy of Child and Adolescent Psychiatry*, 46, 438–447. doi: 10.1097/chi.0b013e31803062bf.

Helliwell, J.F., Layard, L.R. and Sachs, J.D. (2013). *World Happiness Report 2013*. Retrieved from http://apo.org.au/research/world-happiness-report-2013.

Hemerijck, A. (2013). *Changing Welfare States*. Oxford: Oxford University Press.

Howe, D. (2013). *Empathy: What It Is and Why It Matters*. Houndmills: Palgrave Macmillan.

Ivan, G., Da Roit, B. and Knijn, T. (2015). Children First? Changing Attitudes Toward the Primacy of Children in Five European Countries. *Journal of Family Issues*, 36 (14), 1982–2001.

Jenson, J. (2004). Changing the Paradigm: Family Responsibility or Investing in Children. *Canadian Journal of Sociology*, 29 (2), 169–192.

Jeroslow, P. (2014). Social Investment in Early Childhood Across OECD Countries: Human Capital-Building or Development as Freedom?. Paper prepared for the 12th Annual ESPAnet Conference, Oslo.

Kitterød, R.H. and Rønsen, M. (2012). Kvinner i arbeid ute og hjemme. Endring og ulikhet (Women at work outside and within the home. Change and inequality). In A.L. Ellingsæter and K. Widerberg (eds), *Velferdsstatens familier. Nye sosiologiske perspekter* (The welfare state's families. New sociological perspectives). Oslo: Gyldendal Akademisk, pp. 161–190.

Knijn, T. (1994). Social Dilemmas in Images of Motherhood in the Netherlands. *European Journal of Women's Studies*, 1 (2), 183–205. doi: 10.1177/135050689400100204.

Knijn, T. and van Oorschot, W. (2008). The Need for and the Societal Legitimacy of Social Investments in Children and Their Families: Critical Reflections on the Dutch Case. *Journal of Family Issues*, 29 (11), 1520–1542. doi: 10.1177/0192513x08319477.

Kothari, P., Whitham, G. and Quinn, T. (2014). A Fair Start for Every Child: Why We Must Act Now to Tackle Child Poverty in the UK. Retrieved from http://www.savethechildren.org.uk/sites/default/files/images/A_Fair_Start_for_Every_Child.pdf.

Kvist, J. (2015). A Framework for Social Investment Strategies: Integrating Generational, Life Course and Gender Perspectives in the EU Social Investment Strategy. *Comparative European Politics*, 13 (1), 131–149.

Lamb, S., Markussen, E., Teese, R., Sandberg, N. and Polesel, J. (eds) (2011). *School Dropout and Completion: International Comparative Studies in Theory and Policy.* New York: Springer Science and Business Media.

Layard, R. (2005). *Happiness: Lessons from a New Science.* New York: Penguin Press.

Layard, R. (2013). Mental Health: The New Frontier for Labour Economics. *IZA Journal of Labor Policy*, 2 (1), 1–16.

Layard, R., Chisholm, D., Patel, V. and Saxena, S. (2013). Mental Illness and Unhappiness. Discussion paper, IZA, No. 7620. Retrieved from http://ftp.iza.org/dp7620.pdf.

Layard, R., Clark, A.E., Cornaglia, F., Powdthavee, N. and Vernoit, J. (2014). What Predicts a Successful Life? A Life-Course Model of Well-Being. *Economic Journal*, 124 (580), F720–F738.

Layard, R. and Hagell, A. (2015). Healthy Young Minds: Transforming the Mental Health of Children. In J. Helliwell, R. Layard and J. Sachs (eds), *World Happiness Report 2015*. New York: Earth Institute, pp. 106–131. Retrieved from http://worldhappiness.report/wp-content/uploads/sites/2/2015/04/WHR15.pdf.

Levitin, D.J. (2014). *The Organized Mind: Thinking Straight in the Age of Information Overload.* New York: Dutton Books.

Lewis, J. (2006). *Children, Changing Families and Welfare States.* Cheltenham, UK and Northampton, MA, USA: Edward Elgar Publishing.

Lieberman, M.D. (2013). *Social: Why Our Brains are Wired to Connect.* New York: Crown.

Lister, R. (2006). An Agenda for Children: Investing in the Future or Promoting Well-Being in the Present?. In J. Lewis (ed.), *Children, Changing Families and Welfare States.* Cheltenham, UK and Northampton, MA, USA: Edward Elgar Publishing, pp. 157–181.

Markussen, E., Frøseth, M.W., Lødding, B. and Sandberg, N. (2008). Bortvalg og kompetanse: Gjennomføring, bortvalg og kompetanseoppnåelse i videregående opplæring blant 9749 ungdommer som gikk ut av grunnskolen på Østlandet våren 2002. Hovedfunn, konklusjoner og implikasjoner fem år etter (Dropout and qualification: completion, dropout and attainment in secondary education among 9749 adolescents who left compulsory education eastern part of Norway during spring 2002. Main findings, conclusions and implications five years after). Retrieved from http://www.nifu.no/files/2012/11/NIFUrapport 2008-13.pdf.

McReynolds, K. (2008). Children's Happiness. *Encounter: Education for Meaning and Social Justice*, 21 (1), 43–48.

Ministry of Education and Research (2015). *Budget 2015.* Oslo: Ministry of Finance.

Mischel, W. (2014). *The Marshmallow Test: Mastering Self-Control.* Boston, Mass.: Little, Brown & Company.

Morel, N., Palme, J. and Palier, B. (2012). *Towards a Social Investment Welfare State? Ideas, Policies and Challenges.* Bristol: Policy Press.

Mullainathan, S. and Shafir, E. (2013). *Scarcity: Why Having Too Little Means So Much.* London: Allen Lane.

Myrdal, A. and Myrdal, G. (1934). *Kris i befolkningsfrågan* (Crisis in the population question). Oslo: Tiden.

Nolan, B. (2013). What Use Is 'Social Investment'?. *Journal of European Social Policy*, 23 (5), 459–468. doi: 10.1177/0958928713499177.

Norwegian Government (2015–2016). *Meld. St. 19*. Melding til Stortinget. Tid for lek og læring. Bedre innhold i barnehagen. (Government White Paper. Time for play and learning. Improvement of child care).

Norwegian Institute of Public Health (2014). Folkehelserapporten 2014: helsetilstanden i Norge (Public Health Report 2014). Vol. 2014:4. Oslo: Folkehelseinstituttet (Norwegian Institute of Public Health).

NOU (2015). *Produktivitet – grunnlag for vekst og velferd* (Productivity – the basis for growth and prosperity). Oslo: Ministry of Finance.

OECD (2013). *PISA Key Findings*. Paris: OECD.

Oslo and Akershus University College of Applied Sciences (2015). Barnehagetilbudet til de minste barna dårligere enn forventet (Daycare centre facilities for the youngest children worse than expected). 26 October. Retrieved 12 January 2016 from http://www.hioa.no/Aktuelle-saker/Barnehagetilbudet-til-de-minste-barna-daarligere-enn-forventet.

Pettersvold, M. and Østrem, S. (2014). Millioner til ideologisk og politisert forskning (Millions to ideological and politicized research). *Aftenposten*, 17 June, p. 8.

Pintelon, O., Cantillon, B., Van den Bosch, K. and Whelan, C.T. (2013). The Social Stratification of Social Risks: The Relevance of Class for Social Investment Strategies. *Journal of European Social Policy*, 23 (1), 52–67. doi: 10.1177/0958928712463156.

Putnam, R.D. (2015). *Our Kids: The American Dream in Crisis*. New York: Simon & Schuster.

Qualtieri, S. and Robinson, S. (2012). Social Investment in Children: Comparing the Benefits of Child Protection Early Intervention and Prevention Programs in Canada, the United Kingdom and Australia. *Canadian Social Work*, 14 (1), 27–52.

Rege, M. (2014). Leveling the Playing Field: An Intervention to Promote School Readiness and Human Potential. Project Bank, Grant No. 237973. Oslo: Norwegian Research Council.

Sachs, J.D. (2015). Investing in Social Capital. In J. Helliwell, R. Layard and J. Sachs (eds), *World Happiness Report 2015*. New York: Earth Institute, pp. 152–166. Retrieved from http://worldhappiness.report/wp-content/uploads/sites/2/2015/04/WHR15.pdf.

Sandberg, K. (2009). Barns rettigheter og muligheter (Children's rights and possibilities). In R. Hjermann and K. Haanes (eds), *Barn* (Children). Oslo: Universitetsforlaget, pp. 32–51.

Saraceno, C. (2011). Childcare Needs and Childcare Policies: A Multidimensional Issue. *Current Sociology*, 59 (1), 78–96. doi: 10.1177/0011392 110385971.

Schubert, C. (2012). Pursuing Happiness. *Kyklos*, 65 (2), 245–261.

Sen, A. (1985). *Commodities and Capabilities*, Vol. 7. Amsterdam: North-Holland.

Sen, A. (1999). *Development as Freedom*. Oxford: Oxford University Press.

Sommer, D., Pramling-Samuelsson, I. and Hundeide, K. (2013). Early Childhood Care and Education: A Child Perspective Paradigm. *European Early Childhood Education Research Journal*, 21 (4), 459–475.

Statistics Norway (2010). Time Use Survey. Retrieved from: https://www.ssb.no/en/kultur-og-fritid/statistikker/tidsbruk.

Sundnes, A. and Andenæs, A. (2014). Hva med foreldrene? Barnehage, sosial mobilitet og utvikling. (What about the parents? Kindergarten, social mobility and development). *Tidsskrift for velferdsforskning*, 37 (3), 247–258. doi: 10.1002/imhj.21568.

Szalavitz, M. and Perry, B.D. (2010). *Born for Love: Why Empathy Is Essential – and Endangered*. New York: William Morrow.

Thin, N. (2012). *Social Happiness: Theory into Policy and Practice*. Bristol: Policy Press.

Tirado, L. (2014). *Hand to Mouth: The Truth about being Poor in a Wealthy World*. London: Virago.

United Nations (UN) (1989). UN General Assembly, *Convention on the Rights of the Child*, 20 November 1989, United Nations Treaty Series, Vol. 1577, p. 3. Retrieved from http://www.refworld.org/docid/3ae6b38f0.html.

Van Lancker, W. (2013). Putting the Child-Centred Investment Strategy to the Test: Evidence for EU27. *European Journal of Social Security*, 15 (1), 4–27.

Vassnes, B. (2015). *Homo Digitalis*. Tromsø: Margbok.

Weiss, E. (2011). Paying Later: The High Costs of Failing to Invest in Young Children. Washington, DC: Pew Center on the States. Retrieved from www.pewcentereonthestates.org.

World Values Survey Association (2014). *The World Values Survey Wave 5 2005–2008*. Official aggregate v.20140429 Aggregate File Producer Madrid: Asep/JDS. Retrieved from http://www.worldvaluessurvey.org/AJDocumentation.jsp?CndWAVE=5.

11. Social investment as a means of integrating immigrants in Europe

Steinar Stjernø

The total foreign-born population in the European Union constitutes 21 million persons, and in recent years, more than 1 million persons have been seeking asylum every year. A large share of immigrants are young people of working age. Such inflows of human beings raise normative, political and economic challenges for the Union. This chapter discusses the idea of social investment in European immigration policy. First, it describes the number and distribution of immigrants from non-European Union countries. Second, the development of the role of the idea of social investment in the Union's normative framework is analysed, with a particular focus on immigrants and the integration of immigrants into the labour market. Third, the relationship between declarations and actions is discussed.

The material is European Union documents and texts. High-level texts are treaties and documents that have been approved by the European Council and Council of Ministers. Medium-level texts are Commission directives, Commission documents following up treaties and Council agreements, whereas low-level documents have been formulated below this level, for instance by working groups and administrative staff. However, texts do not necessarily tell us anything about social investments in practice. The European Social Fund project database makes it possible to compare projects targeted at immigrants with projects targeted at other groups. Finally, data from European social surveys are used to compare attitudes in member countries to economic aspects of immigration.

Historical, social, political and ideological differences between European Union member states have made the development of a common immigration and integration policy a long and complicated process. Some countries have received immigrants from former colonies since the 1950s (the United Kingdom, France); others from the late 1960s or early 1970s (Germany, Sweden); some for only a few decades (Southern Europe).

Finally, immigration is a rather recent phenomenon in Finland and in Central and Eastern Europe (Eurostat, 2011). Thus, immigration into the member states varies, in terms of numbers, share of the population and the composition of the immigrant population.

Today, all European Union member states are receiving or transit countries of migration. Immigrants come as legal or illegal labour migrants, asylum-seekers or refugees, as students and for family reunion. Relative to the total population, Luxembourg, Ireland, Sweden, Belgium, Austria and Slovenia have a high share, with more than 14 per cent non-nationals (Table 11.1). In absolute terms, the largest numbers of non-nationals from countries within and outside the EU in 2014 were found in Germany (10.7 million persons), the UK (8.4), France (7.6 in 2012), Spain (6.2) and Italy (5.8) (OECD, 2016). Altogether, the numbers in these countries constituted 71 per cent of the total number of non-nationals. In most European Union countries, the majority of non-nationals are citizens of non-member states.

In 2014, European Union countries received almost 627 000 asylum-seekers from non-Union countries, and in 2015 the number increased to 1.3 million. The largest groups were Syrians escaping from the civil war, followed by citizens from Russia, Afghanistan, Serbia, Pakistan, Somalia, Iran, Iraq, and other states afflicted by war and/or dictatorship. The handling of asylum applications differs across the European Union member states, as laws and rules of asylum and migration policies vary. In 2015, the highest numbers of asylum applicants were recorded in Germany, Hungary, Sweden and Italy. Generally, immigrants are younger and more educated than the resident population. Adding to these differences, member states have met immigration with different political ideologies, ambitions of integration, economic and social interests, laws and regulations. This constitutes the context of European Union immigration and integration policy.

The flow of immigrants constitutes a humanitarian, social and economic challenge to both societies and governments of member states, as well as to the political institutions of the European Union. At the same time, it represents an influx of potential labour in nations with ageing and stagnating populations. The issue covered by this chapter is not the social and cultural challenges, but to discuss to what extent investing in immigrants is part of European Union policy. Immigration policy consists of two main elements: control policy and integration policy. Control policy consists of rules and procedures governing the selection and admission of foreigners. Integration policy is about facilitating access to housing, the educational system and labour market, eventually also making immigrants share cultural values with the inhabitants of the

Table 11.1   Immigrants and asylum-seekers to European Union and member states, 2012–2015

	Born in a non-member country, 2012 (in '000s)	Foreign-born population, 2013 (% of total population)	Asylum applicants (total numbers)	
			2014	2015
Total European Union	–	–	626 960	1 321 600
Belgium	737	15.5	22 710	44 630
Bulgaria	52	–	11 080	20 365
Czech Republic	154	7.1	1 145	1 515
Denmark	200	8.5	1 460	20 935
Germany	2 318	12.8	202 645	476 510
Estonia	14	10.1	155	230
Ireland	183	16.4	1 450	–
Greece	415	6.6	9 430	–
Spain	1 889	13.4	5 615	–
France	1 566	11.9	64 310	–
Croatia	65	–	450	210
Italy	2 269	9.4	64 085	84 085
Cyprus	66	–	1745	–
Latvia	27	–	375	330
Lithuania	26	–	440	315
Luxembourg	53	43.7	1 150	–
Hungary	153	4.3	42 775	177 135
Malta	31	–	1 350	–
Netherlands	503	11.6	24 495	44 970
Austria	340	16.2	28 035	–
Poland	574	1.8	8 020	12 190
Portugal	42	8.3	440	–
Romania	268	–	1 545	–
Slovenia	110	16.1	385	275
Slovakia	8	3.2	330	–
Finland	137	5.6	3 620	32 345
Sweden	622	16.0	81 180	162 450
United Kingdom	2 767	12.3	32 785	38 800

Notes: Share of total population for France and Italy from 2012, and for Poland and Portugal from 2011.
'Foreign-born population' includes citizens of both member states and states that are not members of the EU.

Source: Retrieved from: http://ec.europa.eu/eurostat/tgm/table.do?tab=tableandinit=1and language=enandpcode=tps00191andplugin=1. OECD International migration policies and data: http://www.oecd.org/els/mig/keystat.htm.

receiving country. The first three decades after the Treaty of Rome in 1957 was a period of non-existent European Union policy in both control and integration policy. In accordance with the subsidiarity principle, immigration policy was for a long time the exclusive domain of national governments. Member states continued to have exclusive regulatory power in this area until the 1990s, and European Union institutions were mainly concerned with removing obstacles for the free movement of labour within the European Union area. Only in the last couple of decades have immigration policy, border control and integration of immigrants become a responsibility for EU institutions as well.

SOCIAL INVESTMENT AND THE NORMATIVE FRAMEWORK OF THE EUROPEAN UNION

The distinguishing feature of the social investment perspective (Hemerijck, 2013) is that social policy can have a productive function. The Treaty of Rome referred briefly to two ideas that some decades later became part of the concept of social investment: productive re-employment and the importance of vocational training (Article 125). Besides, it established a European Social Fund in order to improve employment. The Single European Act in 1986 established the principle of free movement of people, services, goods and capital, with no internal borders. This meant immigration to each member state became of interest to other member states as well, and resulted in a growing acceptance that the European Union should have some regulatory power. In the late 1980s, attention was directed towards South European states because these countries now experienced pressures at their external borders.

After the Schengen agreement on the abolition of internal borders was made part of the European Union, member states accepted that a more common policy towards non-Union immigrants should compensate for the removal of internal borders, with some soft harmonization of visa policy and asylum laws. Member countries that were not at the edge of the European Union made a more restrictive control policy a European issue, and gradually this developed into a broader perspective on the relationship between immigration and integration, labour markets and welfare arrangements. From around 2000, the Commission took a more active role within decision-making on migration and asylum. The Commission's Directorate-General for Justice, Freedom and Security (DGJFS) became an actor in migration and asylum policy.

The Treaty of Maastricht in 1992 was a significant step in the development of a normative framework for the European Union. The same year, the umbrella organization of Christian democratic and conservative parties – the European People's Party – had adopted a platform with key Catholic and Christian democratic concepts such as freedom and responsibility, justice, subsidiarity and solidarity. It criticized neoliberalism, because neoliberalism ignored the social dimensions of the free market (Stjernø, 2004, 2011). The treaty reflected some of these values, as it declared the ambition to reconcile non-inflationary economic growth and convergence of economic performance on the one hand, with high level of employment and social protection and social cohesion on the other hand (Title II, Article G2). The subsidiarity principle was redefined. Vocational training, education and employment should now be a common responsibility for the member states and no longer be entrusted to national governments alone. European Union institutions should play an active role in the forming of a skilled labour force and labour market policy in general. Vocational training was important because it could facilitate mobility and integration into the labour market (Article 127). With the treaty, the member states committed themselves to intergovernmental collaboration in these areas.

The governance of immigration policy was changed. National governments largely preserved their authority in the area of immigration and asylum (Geddes, 2008), but the role of the European Union was strengthened, as the Council could now adopt joint decisions and actions in immigration policy with a qualified majority instead of requiring unanimity. The treaty devoted several articles to immigration control: rules of asylum and family reunion, border control and illegal immigration. However, it said nothing about the integration of immigrants (Title VI, Article K.1). In line with this high-level document, two dual tracks were developed in the following years. First, a normative framework was established. Here, social cohesion is found together with other key concepts such as social inclusion, solidarity and justice. These concepts were combined with the economic instrumental idea of social investment: that investing in training and education would contribute to economic growth and employment. Second, in the following years, the Union continued to develop a dual structure of governance in the fields of labour market policy and immigration, with shared responsibility between the European Union and national governments.

The idea of a social investment policy matured gradually in Europe from the 1990s (Morel et al., 2011). In the preceding years, a frequent diagnosis of Europe had been that Europe was suffering from 'euro sclerosis', with low job growth and long-term mass unemployment. Allegedly, this was due to rigidity in the labour market and general economic stagnation. In the European Employment Strategy (EES), which gradually developed from 1994, a key idea was that investing in people was crucial both to Europe's place in the knowledge economy and to combat unemployment, poverty and social exclusion. Other key ideas were an active labour market policy with investments in workers' skills and competencies, vocational training for the young and life-long learning, flexible working time, wage restraint, and reducing labour costs.

As discussed in Chapter 1 of this book, the idea of social investment came to denote a policy that aimed at making people employable by increasing their skills and competencies, which could assist European Union countries to meet challenges from increasingly globalized competition. The common core of different concepts of social investment is that expenditure on kindergarten, education and vocational training is seen as investment in the present and future labour force. Thus, it is not a burden on the economy, but contributes to economic growth. The idea comes in at least two different versions. Esping-Andersen (2002) wrote on social investments – particularly investments in children – in early papers for the Commission, and later in the book *Why We Need a New Welfare State*. He argued for what can be considered a social democratic version of the idea that social investments could be made without cuts in cash benefits. However, social investments can be included in a more neoliberal approach as well: social investments combined with cuts in cash transfers and emphasis on the flexibility of work contracts. This represents a modification of neoliberalism (Hemerijck, 2012; Jenson, 2011): it shares with neoliberalism a focus on the supply of labour; however, it differs from neoliberalism because it does not consider social policy to be a burden on the economy and does not share neoliberals' negative attitudes to government responsibility and activity. This ambiguity results in a flexible concept that makes it possible for governments and European Union institutions to drift from one of these meanings to the other.

The Amsterdam Treaty in 1997 made employment policy a more prominent issue for the European Union. It authorized the Commission to take an active role in employment policy and declared that the activities of the Community should include a coordinated strategy for employment

(Article 3i), and the promotion of a "skilled, trained and adaptable workforce" (Article 109n). The treaty represented another step in the development of European Union immigration policy by following up articles in the Maastricht Treaty. Control policy and rules for asylum and family reunion were still dominating issues, but now immigrants' rights and minimum standards for asylum seekers and for temporary protection (Article 73k) were emphasized as well. Labour migration and the integration of labour migrants were not yet themes. In the years to come, recognition grew that neoliberal promises had not been met, and centre-left parties were gaining electoral success. Social democratic politicians believed that the European welfare state had to be transformed from transferring cash benefits to social investments in human capital, reconciling economic efficiency and solidarity (Hemerijck, 2013).

After the approval of the Amsterdam Treaty, European Union institutions devoted more attention to the economic and political integration of immigrants. Two years later the European Council followed up with a meeting in Tampere, Finland, and called for common European measures in both control policy and integration policy. These should include asylum, fair treatment of immigrants, more equal rights between immigrants and European Union citizens, and measures to fight racism and xenophobia (Geddes, 2008; Kicinger, 2013).

The Lisbon European Council in 2000 declared the ambition to make Europe the most competitive and knowledge-based economy in the world. In the Lisbon Strategy, social investment was a key idea, together with social cohesion, a concept that has no important role in neoliberal ideology. More and better jobs should go together with social cohesion (de la Porte and Jacobsson, 2011). The Union introduced the Blue Card as a means to attract highly qualified migrants. Later, a Council directive (2009/50 EC) facilitated admissions for qualified persons by harmonizing entry and residence conditions and improving the legal status of those already in the Union (European Council, 2009).

Gradually, the attention was widened from employment for young persons to the unemployed in general. Finally, immigrants came on the list of target groups for social investment (de la Porte and Jacobsson, 2011). In 2001, the Treaty of Nice stated that European Union institutions might promote the integration of immigrants residing legally in a member state. The Union should "support and complement the Member States in conditions of employment for third-country nationals legally residing in its Union territory", in combating social exclusion, and in integrating persons excluded from the labour market (Article 137). All these treatises are high-level documents, reflecting that integration of immigrants in the labour market was a growing concern. In the succeeding years, the European Union budget allocated financial resources for promoting the integration of immigrants.

The Justice and Home Affairs Council – the ministers of the member states for these affairs – adopted the high-level text *Common Basic Principles for Immigrant Policy Integration*, which was intended to form the further foundation of European Union initiatives in the field of integration. Here, integration was defined as a two-way process of mutual accommodation by immigrants and resident members of member states. Employment and education were seen as critical factors for integration (European Commission, 2004).

As part of implementing these policies, the Directorate-General for Justice, Freedom and Security published *The Handbook on Integration for Policy-Makers and Practitioners*. Here, we find a fully developed idea of social investments in immigrants. The *Handbook* referred to human rights standards and to values that the European Union had declared as basic: equality, anti-discrimination, solidarity and participation, and tolerance. First, introduction programmes should improve immigrants' linguistic skills, labour market skills and knowledge about culture and society (Chapter 1). Second, inter-religious dialogues, local electoral rights and participation in consultative bodies should strengthen immigrant participation in civil society. Third, authorities should develop indicators of economic and political integration (employment, voting, and so on), which could function as comparative benchmarks (DGJFS, 2005).

In the succeeding years, European Union institutions adopted a range of documents and Acts concerning the integration of immigrants. The Treaty of Lisbon in 2007 elaborated on the Union's normative framework, referring to universal values of rights of the human person, non-discrimination, tolerance, solidarity and equality between men and women. The internal market should be a social competitive market economy based on balanced economic growth, price stability, with full employment and a high level of social protection (Article 1a and Article 2). Here, all the positive concepts in Christian democratic ideology were present. In sum, this vocabulary is clearly distinguishable from neoliberal language and has more in common with social democratic language. Besides, the treaty strengthened the European Union's role in immigration control with common rules and systems for the admission of immigrants. These documents and Acts constitute a normative framework for integration, with participation, management of diversity, social inclusion and education as key concepts.

In 2008, the Council adopted the European Pact on Immigration and Asylum. Although illegal immigration and border control were predominant themes, the pact was innovative. It stated that immigrants might contribute decisively to economic growth in member states because of the state of their labour markets and the ageing of their populations. It stated bluntly that "zero immigration is both unrealistic and dangerous", and that a common immigration policy was needed. Member states should "establish ambitious policies to promote the harmonious integration in their host countries of immigrants who are likely to settle permanently" (p. 6) (for an analysis of the Union's role in migration and asylum policy, see Boswell and Geddes, 2011).

The Commission started publishing annual reports on immigration and asylum in 2009. The first report was mainly about linking the skills of legal and highly qualified immigrants to European Union labour needs; restricting illegal immigration and strengthening border control; and the growing concern about the effect of the economic crisis on immigrants (European Commission, 2009). Young people with a migrant background are at greater risk of dropping out from school than others, and their risk of poverty or exclusion remains higher than the overall European Union population (European Commission, 2013). During the economic crisis from 2008 to 2012, immigrants' employment rate fell.

In the Commission's document *Europe 2020: A Strategy for Smart, Sustainable and Inclusive Growth* (European Commission, 2010), the term 'social investment' is not present, but the idea certainly is. The Commission called for an agenda for "new skills and jobs to modernise the labour markets and empower people by developing their skills throughout the lifecycle" (p. 4). Growth should be inclusive and be based on the values of solidarity and social cohesion. Among the new ambitious goals were that by 2020, 20 million less people should be at risk of poverty, 75 per cent of the population should be employed, and the share of early school leavers should be less than 10 per cent.

From at least 2009–2010, social investment has become a key idea in European Union policy documents at all levels, and this idea is entrenched in a normative framework with social inclusion, integration and solidarity as basic concepts. In the *Consolidated Treaties* (European Union, 2010), several articles underline the importance of investing in the labour force. The significance of vocational training and retraining in order to "facilitate vocational integration and reintegration in the labour market" (p. 121) is emphasized, but investing in immigrants is not a theme (Article 166).

This high-level document does not pay much attention to immigrants and the integration of immigrants in the labour market, except for a few statements. "The Union shall develop a common immigration policy ... fair treatment of immigrants residing legally in member states, and ... combat illegal immigration" (Article 71.1). It shall complement the member states in creating "conditions of employment for [immigrants]", in "combating social exclusion" and in "the integration of persons excluded from the labour market" (Article 153). In the area of immigration policy, as in labour market policy and social policy, the text balances carefully between the subsidiarity principle and creating space for European Union initiatives, and excludes "any harmonisation of the laws and regulations" (Article 79.4).

INTEGRATION, RIGHTS AND DUTIES

As the number of migrants and refugees has increased, integration policy has gradually become a more important concern. However, the long-term tendency is that immigration from countries outside Europe has become more disputed. Right-wing anti-immigration parties have gained increased support and influence in many member states. Politicians declare that multiculturalism has been a failure, and governments have introduced measures to restrict family reunion by means of income and language tests. In this change of political climate since the 1990s, a growing number of countries have established courses in language training and on their history, culture and political system. In some countries, such courses were the result of initiatives from far-right populist parties and/or conservative parties (Perchinig, 2012). Today, many member states have introduced such programmes with varying content and organization, in some countries voluntary and in others mandatory.

European Union policies have reflected this development. *The Handbook on Integration for Policy-makers and Practitioners* (Niessen and Huddleston, 2010) argued for introduction courses for improving immigrants' linguistics skills and knowledge about culture and society. The Union's programme on Solidarity and Management of Migration Flows (2007–2013) established a European Fund for the Integration of Third-Country Nationals. Here, introduction programmes and actions for specific immigrant groups were prioritized. Another priority was to improve the integration of immigrants in societies, values and ways of life of member states (European Commission, 2011). The European Pact on Immigration and Asylum of 2008 stated that immigrants should respect European values, such as human rights, tolerance, equality of men and women, and compulsory schooling for children. The pact called for a balance between migrants' rights (to education, work, security, and public and social services) and duties (compliance with the host country's laws) (Council of the European Union, 2008).

For the period 2014–2020, the Union has established the Asylum, Migration and Integration Fund (AMIF) with funding of €3.137 billion. These resources shall be spent on developing a Common European Asylum System. Illegal immigration shall be combated, and member states that receive more immigrants than other member states shall be assisted. Legal immigration to member states in line with labour market needs and promoting the effective integration of immigrants shall receive financial support.

It is difficult to assess to what extent these programmes may be regarded as social investments. Language training certainly is a way of investing in the integration of immigrants in the labour market. On the other hand, these programmes can be considered as 'aggressive integrationism'. Immigrants are accepted only if they accept the values of the host country and take part in courses to prove their motivation in this respect (Triadafilopoulos, 2011). These texts do not say much about reciprocal accommodation; see above on the *Common Basic Principles for Immigrant Policy Integration.*

SOCIAL INVESTMENTS: FROM DECLARATIONS TO IMPLEMENTATION?

To what extent has the increasing emphasis in European Union documents on social investments resulted in prioritizing economic resources for investing in immigrants? Despite the ambitious rhetoric in key European Union documents, analysts have not been able to track a significant change in policies towards social investments in the years before the financial crisis. Analyses of social expenditure from 1980 to 2007 have concluded that the share of gross domestic product (GDP) for education and active labour market policy decreased, and that resources for activation schemes are hardly in line with the idea of social investment (Jenson, 2011; de la Porte and Jacobsson, 2011). On the other hand, the share of GDP for family policy increased (Jenson, 2011). Within the Union and the European Economic Area, Denmark, Sweden, Belgium, France, Norway, the United Kingdom, Ireland and Hungary could be regarded as the most social investment-oriented, whereas Switzerland, Germany, and countries in Eastern and Southern Europe are least social investment-oriented (Nikolai, 2011). According to Hemerijck (2013) – a key analyst and advocate for the social investment approach –

the Nordic welfare states come closest to having developed a comprehensive social investment policy.

Whereas unemployment rates increased during the financial crisis, most European Union countries did not spend a greater share of their GDP on active labour market programmes in 2011–2012 than in 2005 (OECD, 2015). The share of GDP spent on education fell every year from 2009 to 2012 in most countries (Eurostat, 2012). However, according to the Organisation for Economic Co-operation and Development (OECD) Social Expenditure Database, investing in families became somewhat more highly prioritized in some European Union countries during the financial crisis (OECD, 2015). Altogether, it is difficult to trace a significant change in the direction of social investment policy in member states.

The European Social Fund

The European Social Fund (ESF) "works by investing in Europe's human capital – its workers, young people and all those seeking a job" (European Commission, 2015a). It co-finances projects in member states to increase workers' employability by giving them new skills or training, helping young people to make the transition from school to work, and assisting disadvantaged groups to find jobs and integrate in society. It contributes to projects with 15 million participants in the member states. Although it is difficult to assess the reliability of data in the fund's project database (ESF, 2014), Table 11.2 indicates that immigrants have not been a major target group for the fund's social investments.

From 2000 to 2008, the European Social Fund co-financed 1408 projects with migrants as a target group. This is not a small number, but projects targeting migrants constituted only 4 per cent of the total number of projects, which indicates that investing in migrants was not a highly prioritized goal. The share of such projects is particularly low in priority areas that typically indicate social investments, such as developing skills, education and lifelong learning. In the next four years to 2012, the projects targeting immigrants constituted approximately the same share of fund-financed projects on employment, mobility, education and social integration as in the 2000–2008 period. Besides, immigrants were one of several target groups in another 6 per cent of the projects in the four years to 2012. This does not mean that immigrants did not take part in other projects, but project descriptions did not mention immigrants (based on the author's analysis of the presentation of projects on the fund's website).

Table 11.2   European Social Fund projects, 2000–2008 (total number and projects with migrants as a target group)

ESF priority area	Total number of projects	Number of projects with migrants as a target group	% with migrants as a target group
All priority areas	34 272	1 408	4.1
Increasing migrants' participation in employment	554	500	90.0
Integration of disadvantaged people into employment	4 924	378	7.6
Improving equal access to employment	1 540	104	6.8
Active and preventive measures to support employment	4 542	136	3.0
Develop lifelong learning	1 012	26	2.6
Promoting education and training throughout working life	2 374	54	2.3
Employment and training support for workers and companies	5 651	50	0.9

Source: ESF (2015).

The European Union's Ambitions on Social Investments and Integration 2012–2020

The European Union's ambition for the period 2012 to 2020 is to reinforce the role of the European Social Fund. The budget shall increase at least by 20 per cent, and resources shall be allocated to social inclusion so that "people in difficulties and those from disadvantaged groups will get more support to have the same opportunities as others to integrate into society" (ESF, 2014). The Commission's Social Investment Package for Growth and Social Cohesion states that social policy has a productive function. The social investment approach shall be reinforced, with more investments in children, women and gender equality. However, immigrants are not mentioned as a target group (European Commission, 2014). Neither were immigrants devoted much interest in the working documents on social investments from the European Social Fund and the Commission staff (see European Commission, 2015b). This may indicate that investing in and integrating immigrants has become of less interest for the Union in recent years.

A GAP BETWEEN RHETORIC AND REALITY?

This chapter has demonstrated that the European Union has established a normative framework that, with its emphasis on human dignity, social cohesion and solidarity, is distinguishable from neoliberalism. These normative values go together with an economic theory in which market competition, knowledge economy, human capital and social investments are key concepts. This idea of social investment has become firmly established as a core idea in Union documents at all levels, from high-level treatises, Commission directives and other texts (medium level), to policy documents from commission staff and the Committee for Justice and Internal Affairs (low level). Thus, at the rhetorical level the European Union has a consistent policy for social investments. This applies to immigrants as well, although to a lesser degree. Immigrants came later than other groups on the list of groups targeted for social investments, and only in the last decade have immigrants been on the list of groups worthwhile investing in. However, immigrants are not on the list of target groups in the most recent policy documents.

It is difficult to assess the degree to which the presence of social investment in policy documents has resulted in practical politics. A complete picture of social investments in immigrants should include activities in the member countries. Unfortunately, no comparative data exist that make this possible. The analysis of European Social Fund projects demonstrates that immigrants are a target group for investments, but only to a low degree. Children, youth and gender issues have had a higher priority than immigrants. In action plans for the years to come, investing in immigrants has an even less prominent place than before. The historians Schulz-Forberg and Stråth (2010) conclude that there is a gap between what the European Union declares about European integration, and its institutional capacity to follow up what is mapped out by language. As we have seen, this is also the case for investing in immigrants (see also Stjernø, 2015).

Before discussing some probable reasons for this gap, it should be mentioned that some authors argue that social investments may result in more inequality and poverty. If resources to programmes of social protection with a strong distributive effect, such as unemployment benefits and health care, are transferred to programmes with a weaker distributive effect such as education, this could increase poverty. Investing in kindergartens could have the same effect if middle-class women find work, but not women with lower education. Thus, we cannot take for granted that social investments result in stronger social inclusion and cohesion, and that they contribute to solidarity and justice, as many European Union documents tend to suppose (Cantillon, 2011; Vandenbroucke and Vleminckx, 2011).

One reason for the observed contrast between rhetoric and reality in the field of immigration could be the type of governance in this area. National governments and the Union share responsibility for immigration policy and labour market policy. Coordination of European Union policy takes place partly at the ministerial level, and partly through soft governance: the 'open method of coordination'. The Commission and member states in partnership set the priorities and decide how the European Social Fund shall spend its resources, which is probably one of the reasons why activities increasing immigrants' skills vary strongly between countries.

Another and probably more important reason is that the financial aspect of investing in immigrants is controversial among economists. The OECD concludes that immigration has boosted the working-age population and accounted for 70 per cent of the increase in the workforce in Europe in the ten years from 2003 to 2013. Migrants fill jobs that natives are not willing to accept, and increase the flexibility in the labour market. Migrants contribute to government income, but employment determines their fiscal contribution. Research concludes that the fiscal impact of migration in European OECD countries, Australia, Canada and the United States in the past 50 years is close to zero. Hence, immigration is neither a burden nor a blessing for public finances (OECD, 2014).

The financial crisis limited the economic and political leeway for social investment policies and was a serious blow to the ambitions of the Lisbon strategy. German requirements for budgetary balance and reduced public debts resulted in austerity politics in crisis-ridden member states, such as Ireland and in Southern Europe. These states could not, as before the introduction of the euro, resort to Keynesian deficit budgeting or to devaluating their currency, but had to cut their budgets and expenditure for both consumption and investments. In recent years we have witnessed a tug of war between a German-led group of member states demanding that member states should stick to budgets within European Union parameters, and other member states – particularly Southern member states – requiring financial slack and the possibility to stimulate economic growth by investing in people, research, education and infrastructure. Thus, it should not come as a surprise that investing in immigrants was not a prioritized issue.

A further reason for the low priority on investing in immigrants is that immigration is controversial among the citizens of member states. In 2008, 2012 and 2014 the European Social Survey (ESS, 2016) included data on citizens' opinions of whether immigration is good or bad for their country's economy (Table 11.3). People were asked to express their opinion on a scale from 0 ('bad for the economy') to 10 ('good for the economy').

Surprisingly, the economic crisis from 2008 does not seem to have had a strong impact on opinions about the economic effects of immigration.

Table 11.3   *Share (%) who agree that immigration is good for the country's economy (mean score on a scale 0 = bad to 10 = good)*

	2008	2012	2014
Germany	5.3	5.8	5.9
Belgium	4.8	4.6	4.9
Netherlands	5.4	5.2	4.9
France	4.9	4.6	4.6
Denmark	5.3	5.1	4.9
Finland	5.5	5.5	5.3
Sweden	5.5	5.6	5.8
United Kingdom	4.7	4.5	4.8
Ireland	5.0	4.9	5.0
Poland	5.5	5.5	4.9
Lithuania	–	5.3	5.2
Latvia	4.1	–	–
Estonia	4.5	4.9	4.9
Czech Republic	4.2	4.0	3.7
Slovakia	4.3	3.9	–
Hungary	3.5	4.1	3.6
Slovenia	4.4	4.5	4.0
Romania	5.4	–	–
Croatia	4.3	–	–
Bulgaria	5.2	5.0	–
Italy	–	5.2	–
Spain	5.2	5.2	5.0
Portugal	5.0	4.3	5.0
Greece	3.5	–	–
Cyprus	–	3.0	–

Source: European Social Survey (2008, 2012, 2014).

In most of the European Union countries that participated in the European Social Survey in both 2008 and 2012, the mean score remained stable. It became slightly more negative in six countries, particularly in France, Portugal and Slovakia. On the other hand, it became more positive in three: Germany, Hungary and Estonia. The more positive attitudes in Germany should not be surprising, because unemployment decreased and there was a strong demand for labour in these years.

Generally, the attitudes in member states to the economic consequences of immigration are mixed or negative. In 2014, only in Germany, Sweden and Finland were attitudes generally positive to the economic effects of immigration (scores above 5.0 on the scale 0–10). Only in these countries was the share of those with a positive attitude to the economic effects of immigration greater than the share of those with an opposite opinion (table not shown). In France, Belgium, the Czech Republic and Slovenia, opinions were more negative. In the Netherlands, Poland and Denmark, the shares of those who were negative and those who were positive tended to be approximately the same. Thus, the economic effects of immigration are controversial not only among economists, but also among people in the member states.

Voter attitudes are not automatically transformed into political influence. In the election to the European Parliament in 2014, far-right parties with hostile attitudes to immigration increased their support in some countries – Austria, the United Kingdom, France, Greece, and in Scandinavian countries – but this did not happen in other countries (Halikiopolou and Vasilipoulou, 2014). It remains to be seen to what extent the increased support of these parties will influence European Union immigration policy.

Finally, the refugee crisis of 2014–2015 has made it more challenging for governments spending resources on immigrants. The massive influx from faraway countries has further increased the efforts to regain control over common borders and has eclipsed integration policy. At the time of writing in 2016, national governments and the Union have not agreed upon how to re-establish border control, and disagreements about to what extent and how to receive immigrants are increasing, both within and between European countries. Strengthening border controls, and the accommodation of refugees, will both require large financial resources. In this situation, there is a danger that national governments and European Union institutions will neglect or not sufficiently prioritize investment in the human capital of immigrants, thereby making immigrants a permanent underclass in or outside the labour market.

REFERENCES

Boswell, C. and Geddes, A. (2011). *Migration and Mobility in the European Union*. Basingstoke: Palgrave Macmillan.

Cantillon, B. (2011). The Paradox of the Social Investment State: Growth, Employment and Poverty in the Lisbon Era. *Journal of European Public Policy*, 21 (5), 432–449.

Council of the European Union (2008). *European Pact on Immigration and Asylum*. 13189/05 ASIM 68. Brussels: Council of the European Union.

de la Porte, C. and Jacobsson, K. (2011). Social Investment or Recommodification. Assessing the Employment Policies of the EU Member States. In N. Morel, B. Palier and J. Palme (eds), *Towards a Social Investment Welfare State? Ideas, Policies and Challenges*. Bristol: Policy Press, pp. 117–149.

DGJFS (2005). *The Handbook on Integration for Policy-Makers and Practitioners*. Brussels: Directorate-General for Justice, Freedom and Security/The European Commission. http://ec.europa.eu/ewsi/UDRW/images/items/docl_1212_616852085.pdf. Accessed 10 January 2015.

ESF (2014). European Social Fund 2014–2020, European Commission. http://ec.europa.eu/esf/main.jsp?catId=62&langId=en. Accessed 13 February 2015.

Esping-Andersen, G. (2002). Towards the Good Society, Once Again. In G. Esping-Andersen (ed.), *Why We Need a New Welfare State*. Oxford: Oxford University Press, pp. 1–25.

ESS (2016). European Social Survey 2008, 2012, 2014. http://www.europeansocialsurvey.org/. Accessed 15 June 2016.

European Commission (2004). *EU Actions to Make Integration Work. Common Basic Principles*. Brussels: European Commission. https://ec.europa.eu/migrant-integration/main-menu/eus-work/actions. Accessed 15 June 2016.

European Commission (2009). *Report from the Commission to the European Parliament and the Council. First Annual Report on Immigration and Asylum*. Brussels: European Commission.

European Commission (2010). *Europe 2020: A Strategy for Smart, Sustainable and Inclusive Growth*. Communication from the Commission. Brussels, 3.3 2010. Com (2010) 2020 final. http://ec.europa.eu/eu2020/pdf/COMPLET%20EN%20BARROSO%20%20%20007%20-%20Europe%202020%20-%20EN%20version.pdf. Accessed 10 December 2015.

European Commission (2011). *Report from the Commission to the European Parliament, the Council, the European Economic and Social Committee and the Committee of the Regions on the Results Achieved and on Qualitative and Quantitative Aspects of Implementation of the European Fund for the Integration of Third-Country Nationals for the Period 2007–2009*. Brussels: European Commission.

European Commission (2013). *Social Investment Package. Key Facts and Figures. Employment, Social Affairs and Inclusion*. Brussels: European Commission.

European Commission (2014). *Policy Roadmap for the 2014 Implementation of the Social Investment Package. September 2014 Version. Brussels, European*

Commission. *Employment, Social Affairs and Inclusion*. Brussels: European Commission.

European Commission (2015a). *What is the ESF?* Brussels: European Commission. http://ec.europa.eu/esf/main.jsp?catId=35&langId=en. Accessed 17 February 2015.

European Commission (2015b). Social Investment: Commission Urges Member States to Focus on Growth and Social Cohesion. Brussels: European Commission.

European Council (2009). *Entry and Residence of Highly Qualified Workers (EU Blue Card)*. EUR-Lex – 114573 – EN – EUR-LEX.

European Union (2010). *Consolidated Treaties: Charter of Fundamental Rights*. Luxembourg: Publications of the European Union.

Eurostat (2011). *Migrants in Europe: A Statistical Portrait of the First and Second Generation*. Luxembourg, Eurostat. http://ec.europa.eu/eurostat/documents/3217494/5727749/KS-31-10-539-EN.PDF/bcf27a60-7016-4fec-98c5-e8488491ebbd. Accessed 19 January 2015.

Eurostat (2012). Government Expenditure on Education – 2012 Results. http://ec.europa.eu/eurostat/statistics-explained/index.php/Government_expenditure_on_education_-_2012_results. Accessed 17 February 2015.

Geddes, A. (2008). *Immigration and the European Integration. Beyond Fortress Europe?*. Manchester: Manchester University Press.

Halikiopolou, D. and Vasilipoulou, S. (2014). Support for the Far Right in the 2014 European Parliament Elections: A Comparative Perspective. *Political Quarterly*, 85 (3), 285–288.

Hemerijck, A. (2012). Two or Three Waves of Welfare State Transformation?. In N. Morel, B. Palier and J. Palme (eds), *Towards a Social Investment Welfare State? Ideas, Policies and Challenges*. Bristol: Policy Press, pp. 33–60.

Hemerijck, A. (2013). *Changing Welfare States*. Oxford: Oxford University Press.

Jenson, J. (2011). Redesigning Citizenship Regimes after Neoliberalism: Moving Towards Social Investment. In N. Morel, B. Palier and J. Palme (eds), *Towards a Social Investment Welfare State? Ideas, Policies and Challenges*. Bristol: Policy Press, pp. 61–87.

Kicinger, A. (2013). Migration Policy from the European Perspective: A Primer for Forecasters. In M. Kupiszewski (ed.), *International Migration and the Future of Populations and Labour Force Resources in Europe*. Dordrecht: Springer, pp. 7–34.

Morel, N., Palier, B. and Palme, J. (2011). Beyond the Welfare State as We Knew It?. In N. Morel, B. Palier and J. Palme (eds), *Towards a Social Investment Welfare State? Ideas, Policies and Challenges*. Bristol: Policy Press, pp. 1–30.

Niessen, J. and Huddleston, T. (2010). *Handbook on Integration for Policy-makers and Practitioners*, 3rd edition. European Commission, Directorate-General for Justice, Freedom and Security. https://ec.europa.eu/home-affairs/sites/homeaffairs/files/e-library/docs/handbook_integration/docl_12892_16851 7401_en.pdf. Accessed 15 June 2016.

Nikolai, R. (2011). Towards Social Investment? Patterns of Public Policy in the OECD World. In N. Morel, B. Palier and J. Palme (eds), *Towards a Social*

Investment Welfare State? Ideas, Policies and Challenges. Bristol: Policy Press, pp. 91–116.

OECD (2014). Is Migration Good for the Economy?. *Migration Policy Debates,* May. http://www.oecd.org/migration/mig/OECD%20Migration%20Policy%20 Debates%20Numero%202.pdf. Accessed 20 January 2015.

OECD (2015). Social Expenditure Database. http://stats.oecd.org/Index.aspx? datasetcode=SOCX_AGG#. Accessed 5 March 2015.

OECD (2016). OECD International Migration Database 2016. https://stats. oecd.org/Index.aspx?DataSetCode=MIG. Accessed 15 June 2016.

Perchinig, B. (2012). The National Policy Frames for the Integration of New-comers. Comparative Report. WP 2. PROSINT Promoting Policies for Integra-tion. http://research.icmpd.org/1429.html. Accessed 16 March 2015.

Schulz-Forberg, H. and Stråth, B. (2010). *The Political History of European Integration.* London, UK and New York, USA: Routledge.

Stjernø, S. (2004). *Solidarity in Europe: The History of an Idea.* Cambridge: Cambridge University Press.

Stjernø, S. (2011). The Idea of Solidarity in Europe. *European Journal of Social Law,* 3, 156–176.

Stjernø, S. (2015). Solidarity Beyond Europe?. In J. Salomon (ed.), *Solidarity Beyond Borders.* London: Bloomsbury, pp. 1–26.

Triadafilopoulos, T. (2011). Illiberal Means to Liberal Ends? Understanding Recent Immigrant Policies in Europe. *Journal of Ethnic and Migration Studies,* 37 (6), 861–880.

Vandenbroucke, F. and Vleminckx, K. (2011). Disappointing Poverty Trends: Is the Social Investment State to Blame?. *Journal of European Social Policy,* 21 (5), 450–471.

12. Social investment and the international development organizations

Sarah Cook

This chapter explores the ways in which the ideas and terminology of 'social investment' are used by selected international development organizations (IDOs), particularly United Nations agencies and global non-governmental organizations. As pointed out in Chapter 1 of this book, social investment as a concept has a long history in development thought, but the meanings attached to it have changed over time. The current use of the term to refer to a paradigmatic restructuring of social policies in welfare states appears at first glance to have limited resonance in most development contexts where state welfare provision has generally been minimal. At the same time, parallels can be found across contexts in the drivers of social policy shifts and in the language used to describe or justify them. Common factors include a reaction to the neoliberal attack on the state and public welfare spending; adaptation to new types of risk in the global economy; the shifting balance between state and market; concerns about welfare dependency and the creation of entitlements, alongside debates on responsibility and social citizenship; and above all a prioritization of economic growth and productivity through human capital investments, particularly in children and youth. These concerns feature in contemporary debates on social policies and protection in development contexts, just as they do in debates about welfare elsewhere, and are reflected to different degrees in the statements and practices of the international development organizations.

The chapter starts by reviewing the role played by these organizations in the evolution of social investment ideas within development debates. A significant body of literature exists on the institutions, including United Nations agencies and non-governmental organizations, and ideas that countered the neoliberal Washington Consensus policies in low-income countries and relegitimized a role – albeit limited – for the state in the social sphere. More recently a growing body of literature has focused on the evolution of instruments to deliver on a post-Washington Consensus social agenda, most prominently through social protection in the form of cash transfers. Ideas of social spending as investment have been an important element in these debates, with international development organizations important actors given the roll-back of the state under adjustment programmes in many contexts. Less attention has been directed to the ways in which they have adopted or used the term, or the role they play in the diffusion of ideas and practices around social investment.

To understand the current thinking about social investment in the international development organizations, the chapter examines in particular how they conceptualize and implement social protection programmes, and particularly cash transfers as currently a dominant social policy instrument in low-income contexts. By focusing on these questions, the analysis sheds light on whether they play a role in shaping social policy ideas in development contexts, or in transferring ideas, policies and practices from welfare states or other industrialized or post-industrial economies to emerging or lower-income economies, or alternatively reflect debates and practices emerging in developing countries. It also highlights both the contestation among international development organizations underlying the language of social investment, as well as the limits to their influence in the current development context.

THE FALL AND RISE OF SOCIAL INVESTMENT IN DEVELOPMENT THOUGHT

Historically, social policies in development contexts have often been linked to strong productivist or economic development goals, with investments in education and health seen as inputs into human capital formation and the creation of a more productive labour force. Early proponents of an investment approach to social development, such as the Nobel laureate Gunnar Myrdal, were influential in putting social development firmly on the United Nations agenda from the 1950s, and in shaping the approach of agencies such as the United Nations International Children's Emergency Fund (UNICEF) and the United Nations Research Institute for Social Development (UNRISD) in the early development decades. Recognition of the role of nutrition, health and education for children as the most basic of human investments with life-long effects on productivity shaped the early agenda of UNICEF and other agencies, including the Food and Agriculture Organization (FAO) and the World Health Organization (WHO) (Jolly, 2011). Goals set out by the United Nations for the early decades of development and in Declarations such as the 1978 Alma Ata 'Health for All' agenda reflected both the investment case as well as the rights base of such goals. These claims returned to the United Nations' agenda in the twenty-first century, although in some sense more cautiously, with the Millennium Development Goals.

Productivist social policies in development contexts had a strong focus on supply-side interventions and often involved an aspiration to universal provision, particularly with regard to basic education and health. Research from UNRISD demonstrated how such social policies in general served multiple functions: protection and redistribution, as well as enhancing productivity and contributing to growth (Mkandawire, 2004). The links between social and economic policy were, however, strained, if not severed, by the rise of neoliberalism, transferred through so-called Washington Consensus structural adjustment policies to low-income contexts. Led by the International Monetary Fund (IMF) and World Bank, such policies emphasized macroeconomic stabilization, fiscal austerity, a minimal role for the state and the privatization of social services. Social expenditures were reframed as consumption, and thus unproductive, and primary responsibility for such expenditures was shifted from the state to individuals and households through the market. Public expenditures were reduced, and where possible user fees were promoted as a way to ensure that services were valued by the poor and that private expenditures were not 'crowded out'. The devastating social consequences of adjustment policies, and a 'lost decade' as a result of disinvestment both in infrastructure and in people, across sub-Saharan Africa and Latin America have been well documented. Even in South East Asia, a region that had largely escaped structural adjustment and was experiencing rapid growth, the 1997 East Asian Financial Crisis found governments unprepared to respond, having also absorbed ideas that expenditures on education, health and other social assistance measures represented direct consumption, were unproductive and fiscally unsustainable (Cook and Kabeer, 2010).

A number of international development organizations, including some United Nations agencies and non-governmental organizations, countered the consensus on a number of grounds, building evidence on the human, social and economic costs of adjustment policies. UNICEF's landmark *Adjustment with a Human Face* (Cornia et al., 1987) asked how one could believe that "the economy of a country was being strengthened if its children, the human capital of the future, were being weakened by cutbacks in expenditures on nutrition and education?" (Jolly et al., 2009,

p. 145). Arguments were made for the importance of human capital investment, alongside programmes designed to maintain and strengthen the productive assets of households and communities as routes out of poverty as well as to support economic growth. As most regions returned to growth in the 1990s, these ideas took hold with the international development organizations again playing a major role in the new poverty agenda, but initially with substantial differences in perspectives or approach among organizations.

The Return of Social Investment

Shifts in social policy approaches thus occurred in reaction to the high neoliberalism of the 1980s; both in welfare states and in developing economies struggling to recover from a decade of social disinvestment. Renewed attention to the 'social question', reflected for example in the 1995 Social Summit and the subsequent adoption of the Millennium Development Goals, saw poverty reduction return as a central pillar of development policy, alongside a gradual acknowledgement that states should play a stronger role in social spending and investment in basic infrastructure and services. The new poverty agenda, development goals and instruments of social policy have led over the past two decades to a remarkable consensus being forged around instruments that were unthinkable shortly before: the idea of giving cash to the poor, anathema under the neoliberal consensus, has emerged as the 'magic bullet' of poverty reduction. Its compatibility with a 'social investment' approach, which has enhanced its acceptability among different organizations, is based in part on ensuring that cash is used by households to invest in children (better nutrition, health care, education) or in productive activities. Behavioural conditions may be explicit (as in the conditional cash transfers that dominate in Latin America and increasingly in Asia), or implicit as in the unconditional transfers in many sub-Saharan African countries.

This radical shift and contestation among ideas can be traced through the flagship reports of leading development agencies. Following the World Bank (1990) *World Development Report* on poverty, deepening concern with social questions in development is seen in the reports covering issues including *Investing in Health* (World Bank, 1992), *The State in a Changing World* (World Bank, 1996), *Making Services Work for Poor People* (World Bank, 2003) and *Equity and Development* (World Bank, 2005). A more forceful statement of alternatives to neoliberal policies came in the UNDP's *Human Development Reports*, launched in 1990, which focused on the idea of human development as a process of enlarging people's choices and developing capabilities, with a necessary condition thus being social investments. At the same time, the renewed commitment by rich countries to development assistance and poverty reduction, combined with the hollowing-out of state capacities in many development contexts and an ongoing distrust of state involvement that might distort markets, ensured a significant role at least initially for the international development organizations, and particularly non-governmental organizations as local project implementers or service providers, assisting the poor in overcoming financial and other barriers to economic and social development.

New social policies were also responding to a changing global context and particularly to greater economic integration. Globalization of trade and finance generated new economic risks alongside opportunities; inequality was rising between and within countries; climate change and other environmental challenges as well as new health pandemics posed threats for many low-income countries or populations. Contemporary welfare policies in developing and emerging economies were thus being shaped by different ideological and policy contexts, and in response to different risks and economic opportunities, than their predecessors. Convergence in the discourse around social goals, particularly with the renewed global commitment to poverty reduction reflected in the Millennium Development Goals, helped to spur the development and spread of new instruments to deliver on the social agenda, with cash transfers emerging as the preferred instrument of social protection.

In practice the shift in policies and programmes has been gradual and contested. In the World Bank case, early efforts to adopt a softer neoliberal approach and move beyond minimal safety nets were seen in its Social Investment Funds. The funds aimed at investing in community-level social infrastructure through small-scale projects with a high level of community participation, with the objective of improving the access of the poor in relatively disadvantaged communities to basic social and economic infrastructure and services. From the launch of the first fund in Bolivia in 1986, social funds became an important tool for channelling assets and social services to the rural and urban poor. According to Siri (2000) in a review of the funds undertaken for the International Labour Organization (ILO), they became a new social technology for addressing social welfare issues, helping to bring issues of poverty and employment back onto the policy agenda, albeit in a limited way and with limited impacts on the poor or on wider welfare. The main responsibility for welfare remained with individuals and households through the market, while state or donor interventions were designed to support market access and asset building.

The World Bank thus moved cautiously towards the idea that transfers might be provided to individuals or households as a safety net of last resort. Steps in this direction came through its thinking on 'social risk management', responding to the realization that households and individuals faced risks that often could not be met through market instruments, and that state or other interventions were needed to insure or mitigate against risks, or to help households cope with the effects of shocks. The idea that social protection was only about protection against shocks was critiqued by many as neglecting the chronically poor and vulnerable, or those disadvantaged by status or identity (gender, caste) or other structural factors. It was however in governments in the South, and particularly in Latin America led by Mexico, where the major push towards an expansion of cash as an instrument for social protection emerged (see Chapter 1 and Chapter 8 in this volume). While many rights-based organizations (including the ILO, UNRISD and many non-governmental organizations) remained critical of the degree of targeting and conditionalities attached to the new cash transfers, these conditions assuaged the concern of organizations such as the World Bank, as well as ministries of finance, about the negative incentives and affordability of transfers. Conditionalities related in particular to child health and education helped to cement the link with the renewed investment focus.

The international development community has thus moved towards a remarkable degree of consensus around the need for expanded forms of social protection, with cash and related conditions emerging as a key mechanism for delivery. However, justifications vary for promoting social protection, including the weight given to its investment or productive function. Key arguments are made on the grounds of social justice and human rights (several United Nations agencies, many civil society groups and some academics); poverty reduction and risk management (the World Bank); inclusive economic growth and capital-based production; participation, political stability and state-building; reducing inequality and promoting social cohesion or solidarity. Among the international development organizations there is a growing emphasis on investment: in individuals at critical points in their life course (children and youth) to maximize productivity and well-being; in households and communities to promote resilience to shocks; and in supply-side interventions, social infrastructure and services, and institutions that can strengthen social cohesion and more inclusive development. At the same time, however, these points of agreement around the role of cash transfers as social protection instruments tend to obscure significant differences in goals, values and approaches among organizations, reflecting different views on rights, redistribution, universalism versus targeting, conditionalities, and the role of the market and the state.

While justified by some development actors in terms of investments that support economic growth, the evidence on the impacts of cash transfers is largely grounded in evidence of 'what works' for results linked to programme goals, notably poverty alleviation, impacts on specific groups (women, children) and behavioural change (such as use of health and education services). Evidence is increasingly based on the growing economic literature using experimental techniques such as randomized control trials. The 'investment case' particularly in relation to programmes affecting children has been bolstered by scientific advances in understanding early child and, more recently, adolescent brain development, and the critical windows of intervention that can affect long-term outcomes, including lifelong health and productivity. The evidence for systemic impacts or the investment case linked to growth remains more limited (Cherrier et al., 2013). Alderman and Yemtsov (2012), writing for the World Bank, remain cautious about the links with growth, noting that "Distortions created by fragmented and poorly coordinated social protection interventions may influence the behavior of economic agents, discourage efforts and lock beneficiaries into low productivity–low growth equilibrium" (p. 2).

SOCIAL INVESTMENT IN INTERNATIONAL DEVELOPMENT ORGANIZATIONS

As social protection has emerged as an important pillar of contemporary development policy and practice, in forms that are often closely linked to ideas of social investment, it provides a useful lens to examine how different organizations have adopted the language of social investment, and the ideas that underpin its use. This section explores such usage among a number of organizations, with reference particularly to social protection but recognizing that related social policies or sectoral interventions are also relevant. It focuses on a number of recent reports or policy documents, which may reflect the overall strategy of an organization or, more narrowly, its goals in relation to social protection, in order to explore how social investment is reflected in organizational priorities, programmes and activities.

The World Bank

The World Bank plays an important role in shaping debates and influencing practice by virtue of its resources and leverage with governments. In recent years, it has expanded its role in social sectors and social development, moving significantly into policy areas previously dominated by the United Nations or civil society organizations. This trajectory from architect of structural adjustment policies that marginalized social policies or investments, to a leading player in social sectors and social protection, has occurred incrementally, as discussed above. Its current approach reflects a strong focus on a market-led risk management approach, on building resilience to shocks, on targeting of the poorest, and on conditionalities that generate behavioural change and minimize perverse incentives that might affect growth. More recently, equity goals have gained prominence in the light of the Bank's overall 'shared prosperity' strategy.

The World Bank Social Protection and Labor (SPL) Strategy 2012–2022 (World Bank, 2012) goes further than previous documents towards integrating these elements, articulating a framework around resilience, opportunity and equity. The social investment role of social protection is explicit, while many other elements associated with social investment debates are recognizable in the document. The strategy recognizes the new risks associated with the twenty-first-century economy; the need to invest in individuals and families to enable them to take advantage of opportunities (through human capital, assets and access to jobs), as well as manage risks (through enhanced resilience). While the responses are largely about enabling individuals and families to engage in market opportunities or access commercially provided services, the state is seen as having an expanded role in ensuring that systems for social protection are harmonized, overcoming the fragmentation and 'projectization' of provision that has been a consequence of the withdrawal of the state and the expansion of provision by private and non-profit actors. The strategy retains a strong focus on the poor, thus advocating targeted interventions, while also recognizing the need for broad-based human capital and skills formation. It also takes a life cycle approach, recognizing diverse needs at different stages of life with an emphasis on investments in children, and the inclusion of youth and women in labour markets. Investing in children ('child sensitive social protection') is prioritized on the grounds of both poor children's vulnerability and the high returns to such investment (World Bank, 2012).

Key mechanisms for achieving these goals include social assistance or safety nets (cash transfers), social insurance and active labour market

programmes – a familiar set of policy interventions. The justifications
resonate with a social investment perspective: "Cash transfers incentivize
investments in human capital by promoting demand for education and
health … And public works programmes provide cash payments to the
poor, while increasing physical capital investments" (World Bank, 2012,
p. xiv). The strategy also reflects ongoing debates about the contribution
of social protection to growth, suggesting that it "provides a foundation
for inclusive growth which can have a transformational effect on people's
lives" (World Bank, 2012, p. 2) through a number of pathways including
building human capital, encouraging higher-risk activities, enhancing
productive assets and reducing inequality. It also emphasizes the central
role of improving labour markets and access to jobs. While cautious
about universal coverage, it does nonetheless recognize the need for
non-contributory support or special measures to achieve inclusion or
equity particularly in low-income and fragile settings, or for the most
vulnerable and the elderly (World Bank, 2012).

The International Labour Organization (ILO)

The ILO has been a leading proponent of a rights-based approach to
social protection, reflecting its founding charter, mandate and normative
role. It has spearheaded key initiatives to extend social security or social
protection, most recently in the establishment of the now globally
recognized Social Protection Floor. The Social Protection Unit under the
leadership of Michael Cichon worked to build a strong evidence base for
the affordability of expanding basic social protection, leading to ILO
Recommendation 202, the first international legal instrument that recognizes the triple role of social security as a universal human right and an
economic and social necessity (ILO, 2012a). Relatedly, the Social
Protection Floor Initiative led by the ILO, and in collaboration with other
key United Nations (UN) agencies including UNICEF and the World
Health Organization, reflects an emerging global consensus on "building
inclusive, productive, responsive social protection and labour programmes and systems tailored to country circumstances" (ILO, 2012b). It
has led to a number of initiatives that promote wider consensus around
universal approaches to social protection, including the interagency
coordinating board (the Social Protection Inter-Agency Cooperation
Board, SPIAC-B) composed of international organizations and member
states, and bilateral initiatives such as the joint World Bank–ILO plan of
action for achieving universal social protection.

The ILO's *Social Protection Report 2014/15* (ILO, 2014) reviews the
state of social protection in light of the global agreement on the Social

Protection Floor. Under its lead author and successor to Michael Cichon, Isabel Ortiz, it provides a compelling and comprehensive statement of the ILO perspective, along with the current state of empirical evidence. The report argues for a stronger focus on social security, noting the fundamental right to social security which "remains unfulfilled for the large majority of the world's population" (ILO, 2014, p. 1), while recognizing the contribution of social policies to fostering economic and social development, reducing poverty and insecurity, redressing inequality and acting as automatic stabilizers in the event of shocks (as in the global financial crisis). It reflects several key elements of social investment thinking while maintaining a strong rights focus. First, the report is organized in terms of the life cycle, starting with social protection for children and families; social protection for children is concerned with "realizing children's rights, ensuring their well-being, breaking the vicious cycle of poverty and vulnerability and helping all children realize their full potential", while "underinvestment in children jeopardizes their rights and their future, as well as the economic and social development prospects of the countries in which they live" (ILO, 2014, p. 5). For women and men of working age, social protection is justified as providing basic income security, coping with life events that "will help workers to find and sustain decent and productive employment" and "smoothing incomes and aggregate demand, thereby facilitating structural change within economies" (ILO, 2014, p. 25). Active labour market policies and public works programmes where the state acts as employer of last resort are seen as essential in coordination with other social policies, while the report examines the challenges of achieving the right to income security in old age and universal health coverage. Similar to many other ILO documents, the report thus presents a strong argument for social security based on universal rights, as well as economic arguments for social protection as investment.

UNICEF

The language of social investment lends itself particularly strongly to the work of UNICEF and other organizations focused on children (such as Save the Children), although most are grounded in a strong commitment to the rights of the child based on state obligations within the Convention on the Rights of the Child. Common justifications used by UNICEF and other child-focused organizations for investing in children include: legal arguments linked to the Convention; ethical or rights-based arguments, investments that create productive adults and break the intergenerational cycle of poverty; the civic and political participation of children, and investing in children as a route to social cohesion (Vandermoortele, 2012). Critical investments include a wide range of essential services from nutrition and health to early child development, education, care, water and sanitation. Many of these basic investments – in systems, infrastructure and services – are part of the basic functions of states in higher-income countries and would generally be unquestioned as part of the duties of states or entitlements of citizenship or residence.

The 2014–2017 UNICEF strategy has equity as its core, by which it means that all children should have the opportunity to survive, develop and reach their full potential, without discrimination, bias or favouritism. Its approach to equity is to ensure that the poorest or most marginalized child has a better chance in life, arguing for this both from a rights perspective, "To the degree that any child has an unequal chance in life – in its social, political, economic, civic and cultural dimensions – her or his rights are violated" (p. 2), but also presenting the 'investment' case: "There is growing evidence that investing in the health, education and protection of a society's most disadvantaged citizens – addressing inequity – not only will give all children the opportunity to fulfil their potential but also will lead to sustained growth and stability of countries" (UNICEF, 2013, p. 2). A focus on equity is thus considered vital because "It accelerates progress towards realizing the human rights of all children, which is the universal mandate of UNICEF, as outlined by the Convention on the Rights of the Child, while also supporting the equitable development of nations" (UNICEF, 2013, p. 2).

UNICEF has long argued for investing in early childhood as "the most opportune time to break the cycle of poverty, or prevent it from beginning … Programmes that invest in early childhood development could generate considerable cost savings for government. Investments in children are increasingly seen as one of the best and most valuable long-term investments we can make" (UNICEF, n.d.). More recently it has extended its focus to the second decade of life as a second critical window, drawing on increasing evidence about brain development in adolescence. Its 2016 flagship *State of the World's Children*, on equity, argues for investments that reduce gaps and provide opportunity to those left behind, including the productivity-enhancing benefits of investing in child and maternal health, and education. Social protection and specifically cash transfers are seen as among the key instruments to achieve these goals. As part of its operational presence, UNICEF also contributes to building the evidence base at national and subnational level in terms of the design, implementation and impact of social protection interventions (see, e.g., Davis et al., 2016).

UN Women

Also a strong voice in the Social Protection Floor debates under the leadership of Michelle Bachelet, UN Women has often used arguments about investing in women as a 'smart' investment, with a focus on enhancing entrepreneurship and productivity as well as women's rights, empowerment and well-being. Its flagship *Progress of the World's Women* report for 2015–2016 provides a strong, in-depth analysis on the role of social policy as a key instrument in achieving women's rights and substantive gender equality. Its subtitle, *Transforming Economies, Realizing Rights*, highlights a focus on the relationship between social and economic policies, and a rights perspective. The report draws on a large body of research on women and social policy both in welfare states and in development contexts, and on issues such as the care economy, including research undertaken or commissioned by the report's lead author, Shahra Razavi, in her prior position at UNRISD. Given the strong research base, the report takes a more reflective and critical view of the social investment approach than is found in many United Nations reports. In Chapter 3, 'Making Social Policy Work for Women', it supports arguments of UNRISD and others that "the best way to realise economic and social rights for all without discrimination is through a comprehensive approach to social policy that combines universal access to social services with social protection" (UN Women, 2015, p. 132). It reveals the biases in the design of targeted and conditional transfers, as well as in contributory benefits such as pensions, that often undermine women's rights and well-being. The benefits of social transfers for reducing poverty and inequality, and for outcomes such as keeping girls in school, delayed marriage and pregnancy, are recognized, although transfers are not viewed as necessarily empowering for women. Investments in services such as health and care provision are shown to be important for realizing the rights of women and achieving wider social and economic goals. The chapter concludes with a recognition that "The SPF [Social Protection Floor] initiative is an important step in the right direction, but care needs to be taken in the priorities for social investment", "including those around the needs of care-givers and receivers" (UN Women, 2015, p. 185). Overall the report's conclusions suggest some caution about a narrow investment approach that may neglect critical services or support for those groups where direct productivity-enhancing effects are limited (such as women in unpaid care work, the elderly or others unable to work). Conversely, investing in women as a key to development, as entrepreneurs or to increase their paid labour force participation and productivity, without addressing the constraints of gendered roles and care demands, can undermine progress towards the realization of their rights.

The United Nations Development Programme (UNDP)

UNDP documents rarely explicitly address social investment. However, the organization has adopted broadly consistent ideas in its approach to inclusive growth through employment and social protection, with social protection viewed as an effective tool for helping individuals, households and societies to weather and recover from shocks. In a multi-country review of social protection, growth and employment (Jahan, 2013), social protection is seen as a mechanism for preventing households falling into poverty and raising incomes. However, it also notes that social protection policies must be consistent with labour market mechanisms.

Stronger arguments for a more universal approach to social investment are seen in UNDP's *Human Development Reports*, noted earlier. The recent 2014 report on *Sustaining Human Progress: Reducing Vulnerabilities and Building Resilience*, for example, covers similar ground to other reports on social protection. It addresses vulnerability not only in a narrow form of exposure to shocks, but as also rooted in chronic poverty and deprivation and structural factors such as gender, ethnicity and social status. In identifying the types of investments that can address social, structural and systemic vulnerability, the report points to the need for human-centred investments through a comprehensive set of social services, social protection and insurance, across the life cycle, in order to build human capabilities (UNDP, 2014).

The World Health Organization (WHO)

Documents produced by the World Health Organization have long reflected a concern with health as a human capital investment as an argument for investing in health. Commissions on the social determinants of health, as well as macroeconomics and health, backed up by substantial evidence, have made the case for broad social and economic investments in health promotion and health systems as a critical contributor to economic and social development.

The Regional United Nations Commissions

The regional economic and social commissions of the United Nations also play an important role in sharing policies and ideas at regional levels. In Latin America, for example, the Economic Commission for Latin America and the Caribbean (ECLAC) has worked with governments on social policies and documented the initiatives being undertaken in the region which pioneered a range of innovations that underpin current social protection programmes globally. In a comprehensive volume on the Latin American experience of universalizing social protection (Cecchini et al., 2015), authors from ECLAC play a role in analysing and sharing these experiences. They document characteristics of social policy in the region, including an increasing role for the state in social matters, rights as a basis of public policy, a response to new social problems and risks, and the progressive construction of social citizenship – an element of the social investment state that has been less prominent in the language of most international development organizations – and efforts to strengthen solidarity. This quest for social citizenship and solidarity is reflected in rising social investments across the region.

The Organisation for Economic Co-Operation and Development (OECD) and the European Union (EU)

As might be expected given its strong European membership, the OECD in its development work has taken an explicit approach to social protection as an investment in people, that "helps them better manage the trade-offs between satisfying immediate needs and building better livelihoods for the future", and references "a growing body of evidence showing that social protection programmes are effective and there is now strong political interest in the contribution they can make to growth-enhancing strategies to lead developing countries out of the present global crisis" (OECD, 2009, p. 218). Similarly, as mentioned in Chapter 1 of this volume, the European Union's development strategy reflects the Lisbon Agenda in taking a more explicit social investment approach.

The International Non-Governmental Organizations

Finally, a number of international non-governmental organizations play a major role in both campaigning and advocacy around social protection, and in the delivery of programmes on the ground. Key organizations reflect a similar range of positions as those described above, often with a strong rights-based perspective. While organizations focused on children and to some extent women can readily adopt social investment arguments, these less easily translate into advocacy around social protection for groups such as the elderly or people with disabilities where productivity gains may be limited. Others remain more critical of the limits of the investment case, seeing the risks of commodification, the threat to rights or, particularly for feminist organizations, the tendency to instrumentalize women as the channel for social investment particularly in children at the expense of women's own rights and well-being. On the ground, the non-governmental organizations play a significant role in programme interventions or projects designed to achieve specific objectives, including incentivizing behavioural and social norm change, for example around health-seeking behaviour, sanitation practices, schooling for girls and age of marriage.

SHAPING DISCOURSE: THE ROLE AND LIMITS OF INTERNATIONAL DEVELOPMENT ORGANIZATIONS

This review of some of the key ideas in relation to social investment reflected in the documents of the international development organizations demonstrates a convergence of language and ideas, but often with significant ideological differences hidden by a common language. Shared language, issues and practices among organizations, whether multilateral agencies or non-governmental organizations, may reflect a number of wider factors. These include the overall development policy landscape, which has increasingly focused on building consensus among the global community around common goals, most recently in the formulation of the Sustainable Development Goals to replace the Millennium Development Goals. A second critical factor in shaping the justifications for social investment is the funding landscape: major bilateral development donors have pushed increasingly towards results-based and evidence-based programming, where impacts can be clearly identified and justified through 'value for money' considerations. Such considerations are equally important for many of the new, large-scale corporate philanthropies that have reshaped the development funding landscape in recent years. Making an 'investment case' for interventions thus becomes an important part of the international development organizations' pitch for funding. In a context where many major donor countries are themselves seeing a stronger policy focus on social investment at home, development funding may also reflect these domestic debates and priorities, although this assertion would need to be examined in greater depth.

In the face of some apparent consensus around language and practices, there is nonetheless clear evidence of the debates and lines of contestation that lie beneath the surface. The role of key individuals in critical positions within particular agencies, the alliances across organizations around common values, and the links with academic communities, have helped to ensure that debates around expanding social protection and thus a more inclusive and rights-based approach to social development, have remained on the global agenda. The international development organizations have played a role in framing the global discourse, negotiating among contested positions, sharing practices and building the evidence base in support of a range of views, from targeted and conditional transfers to more universal social protection systems.

Whether the international development organizations have played a significant role in sharing or translating ideas and practices of social investment from welfare states to development contexts is more questionable. They may help to forge a common language around diverse practices, but recent years have seen the direction of travel of development ideas shift, from policies often designed and initiated in the North, to a much greater degree of 'South–South' cooperation and sharing. As documented in this volume, some international development organizations have kept alive long-standing ideas of social investment in development thinking, and a few organizations have consistently argued for the need to link social policies with economic development. At the same time, the specific mechanisms of social protection that have emerged as a key instrument at the current time originated within developing economies recovering from adjustment. The conditional cash transfers which laid the foundations for the current social protection revolution came from Latin America. Other developing and emerging economies have led the way in other critical areas of social policy expansion, including for example the Thai 30 Baht health scheme that provided important evidence of the economic and political feasibility of a universal health programme, in opposition to then dominant policy advice. More innovatively, such economies have also played a role in developing mechanisms to address new risks, such as those associated with climate change or environmental threats, for example in schemes such as Brazil's *Bolsa Verde* and *Bolsa Floresta* programmes designed to protect incomes while also incentivizing good environmental practices (Cook et al., 2012). The international development organizations have played a role in analysing and sharing experiences, in piloting variations in other regions, and in some cases bringing similar ideas to the attention of governments in the North, but have rarely been responsible either for social policy innovations or for transferring ideas from welfare state contexts. Ideas and practices now travel through multiple channels including direct South–South sharing.

Areas in which the international development organizations may be playing a more innovative role in expanding a social investment approach through forms of social protection include humanitarian and emergency contexts, among displaced populations and populations on the move. Cash transfers are increasingly viewed as an effective mechanism for reaching such populations, both supporting immediate needs and facilitating investments in longer-term development opportunities. At the same time the nature of crises, from health pandemics such as Ebola to protracted conflict, highlights the limits of demand-side interventions in the absence of adequate supply-side investments in infrastructure and systems, including health and education, or well-functioning markets for relevant goods and services.

The limits of the international development organizations in leading a sustained shift towards more inclusive forms of social protection, and the risks associated with a neoliberal interpretation of social investment, are visible in the post-2008 financial crisis context. In welfare states, austerity or 'fiscal consolidation' policies have reduced social spending precisely in areas justified by an investment approach, despite the widely used arguments about such investments being a key to recovery, an automatic stabilizer and a route to growth. More worryingly, since 2010, austerity measures and reduced social spending have occurred in many developing countries which had not faced the same crisis conditions (Ortiz and Cummins, 2013), as fiscal adjustments being imposed by governments in the North became mainstream policy advice in a majority of countries (ILO, 2014). While domestic political imperatives and electoral cycles make it unlikely that social protection programmes can be rolled back in many low- and middle-income countries, nonetheless the progressive expansion of social investments, whether in broadening the coverage of transfers, or in supply-side infrastructure and services, remains an area of ongoing struggle. It is one in which the international development organizations will undoubtedly continue to be significant actors.

REFERENCES

Alderman, H. and Yemtsov, R. (2012). *Productive Role of Social Protection.* Background Paper for the World Bank 2012–2022 Social Protection and Labor Strategy, Washington, DC: World Bank. http://siteresources.worldbank.org/ SOCIALPROTECTION/Resources/SP-Discussion-papers/430578-1331508552 354/1203.pdf (accessed 23 August 2016).

Cecchini, S., Filgueira, F., Martínez, R. and Rossel, C. (eds) (2015). *Towards Universal Social Protection: Latin American Pathways and Policy Tools.* ECLAC Books, No. 136 (LC/G.2644-P). Santiago: Economic Commission for Latin America and the Caribbean. http://www.cepal.org/sites/default/files/

events/files/eclac-un-towards_universal_social_protection.pdf (accessed 23 August 2016).

Cherrier, C., Gassmann, F., Mideros Mora, A. and Mohnen, P. (2013). Making the Investment Case for Social Protection: Methodological Challenges with Lessons Learnt from a Recent Study in Cambodia. Innocenti Working Papers no. 2013-06. https://www.unicef-irc.org/publications/pdf/iwp_2013_06.pdf (accessed 23 August 2016).

Cook, S. and Kabeer, N. (eds) (2010). *Social Protection as Development Policy: Asian Perspectives*. New Delhi, India: Routledge.

Cook, S., Smith, K. and Utting, P. (2012). Green Economy or Green Society? Contestation and Policies for a Fair Transition. UNRISD Occasional Paper 10, November. UNRISD: Geneva.

Cornia, G.A., Jolly, R. and Stewart, F. (eds) (1987). *Adjustment with a Human Face. Volume 1, Protecting the Vulnerable and Promoting Growth*. Oxford: Clarendon Press.

Davis, B., Handa, S., Hypher, N., Winder Rossi, N., Winters, P. and Yablonski, J. (eds) (2016). *From Evidence to Action: The Story of Cash Transfers and Impact Evaluation in Sub-Saharan Africa*. Oxford: Oxford University Press.

ILO (2012a). Social Protection Floors Recommendation, R202, 14 June 2012. http://www.ilo.org/dyn/normlex/en/f?p=NORMLEXPUB:12100:0::NO::P1210 0_INSTRUMENT_ID:3065524 (accessed 23 August 2016).

ILO (2012b). The Social Protection Floor Initiative. Factsheet. Geneva: ILO. http://www.ilo.org/wcmsp5/groups/public/—ed_protect/—soc_sec/documents/ publication/wcms_207781.pdf (accessed 23 August 2016).

ILO (2014). *World Social Protection Report 2014/15: Building Economic Recovery, Inclusive Development and Social Justice*. Geneva: ILO. http://www.ilo.org/ wcmsp5/groups/public/—dgreports/—dcomm/documents/publication/wcms_ 245201.pdf (accessed 23 August 2016).

Jahan, S. (2013). Employment and Social Protection for Inclusive Growth. http://www.undp.org/content/undp/en/home/ourperspective/ourperspective articles/2013/08/30/employment-and-social-protection-for-inclusive-growth-selim-jahan.html (accessed 23 August 2016).

Jolly, R. (2011). UNICEF, Economists and Economic Policy: Bringing Children into Development Strategies. UNICEF Social and Economic Policy Working Briefs, October. http://www.unicef.org/socialpolicy/files/Jolly_PolicyBrief_ October2011_Final.pdf (accessed 23 August 2016).

Jolly, R., Emmerij, L. and Weiss, T.G. (2009). *UN Ideas that Changed the World*. Bloomington and Indianapolis, IN: Indiana University Press.

Mkandawire, T. (ed.) (2004). *Social Policy in a Development Context*. Basingstoke: UNRISD/Palgrave Macmillan.

OECD (2009). *Promoting Pro-Poor Growth: Social Protection*. Paris: OECD. http://www.oecd.org/dac/povertyreduction/43514563.pdf (accessed 23 August 2016).

Ortiz, I. and Cummins, M. (2013). The Age of Austerity: A Review of Public Expenditures and Adjustment Measures in 181 Countries. Initiative for Policy Dialogue and the South Centre Working Paper, March. New York, USA and Geneva, Switzerland: Initiative for Policy Dialogue and the South Centre.

http://policydialogue.org/files/publications/Age_of_Austerity_Ortiz_and_Cummins. pdf (accessed 23 August 2016).

Siri, G. (2000). Employment and Social Investment Funds in Latin America. Socio-Economic Technical Paper (SETP no 7). Geneva: ILO. http://www. ilo.org/wcmsp5/groups/public/—ed_emp/—emp_policy/—invest/documents/ publication/wcms_asist_7591.pdf (accessed 23 August 2016).

UNDP (2014). *Sustaining Human Progress: Reducing Vulnerabilities and Building Resilience.* New York: UNDP. http://www.undp.org/content/dam/undp/ library/corporate/HDR/2014HDR/HDR-2014-English.pdf (accessed 23 August 2016).

UNICEF (2013). *The UNICEF Strategic Plan, 2014–2017: Realizing the Rights of Every Child, Especially the Most Disadvantaged.* New York: UNICEF. http://www.unicef.org/strategicplan/files/2013-21-UNICEF_Strategic_Plan-ODS- English.pdf (accessed 23 August 2016).

UNICEF (2016). *The State of the World's Children 2016: A Fair Chance for Every Child.* New York: UNICEF. http://www.unicef.org/publications/files/ UNICEF_SOWC_2016.pdf (accessed 23 August 2016).

UNICEF (n.d.). *Importance of Investing in Children.* http://www.unicef.org/ socialpolicy/index_53294.html (accessed 23 August 2016).

UN Women (2015). *Progress of the World's Women 2015–2016: Transforming Economies, Realizing Rights.* New York: UN Women. http://progress. unwomen.org/en/2015/pdf/UNW_progressreport.pdf (accessed 23 August 2016).

Vandermoortele, J. (2012). Equity Begins with Children. UNICEF Social and Economic Policy Working Paper, January. New York: UNICEF. http://www. unicef.org/socialpolicy/files/Equity_Begins_with_Children_Vandemoortele_ JAN2012.pdf (accessed 23 August 2016).

World Bank (1990). *World Development Report 1990: Poverty.* New York: Oxford University Press. https://openknowledge.worldbank.org/handle/10986/ 5973 (accessed 23 August 2016).

World Bank (1992). *World Development Report 1993: Investing in Health.* Washington, DC: World Bank.

World Bank (1996). *World Development Report 1997: The State in a Changing World.* Washington, DC: World Bank.

World Bank (2003). *World Development Report 2004: Making Services Work for Poor People.* Washington, DC: World Bank. https://openknowledge. worldbank.org/handle/10986/5986 (accessed 23 August 2016).

World Bank (2005). *World Development Report 2006: Equity and Development.* Washington, DC: World Bank.

World Bank (2012). Resilience, Equity, and Opportunity: The World Bank's Social Protection and Labor Strategy 2012–2022. Washington, DC: World Bank. http://siteresources.worldbank.org/SOCIALPROTECTION/Resources/ 280558-1274453001167/7089867-1279223745454/7253917-1291314603217/ SPL_Strategy_2012-22_FINAL.pdf (accessed 23 August 2016).

13. Conclusion: lessons learned and future directions

James Midgley, Espen Dahl and Amy Conley Wright

As mentioned in the Introduction to this book, the social policy literature on social investment has expanded rapidly in recent years. This is largely because of the scholarship of European writers who view social investment as a new welfare paradigm and a distinctive stage in the historical evolution of statutory welfare. The new social investment paradigm, they contend, has replaced the field's conventional policy commitment to meet people's needs through social security and the provision of social services with a new and dynamic model that enhances the capabilities of citizens to function effectively in the productive economy. In this way, social investment promotes an 'active' rather than a 'passive' approach to social welfare which emphasizes policies and programmes that promote knowledge and skills development, job referral and work supports such as child care and family leave.

This book uses the social investment approach as articulated by European and other Western writers as a point of departure but notes that it has several limitations. These include its obvious Eurocentricity, contention that social investment is a new paradigm, focus on a limited range of policy fields and neglect of other interpretations of social investment articulated in academic subjects such as development studies, non-profit management and community studies. The book's editors and contributors seek to address these limitations not primarily to criticize the Western social investment literature but rather to augment its insights and enhance its global relevance. This is needed to promote a universally applicable approach which can end the uncritical transfer of inappropriate Western social policies to countries with substantively different social, cultural and economic characteristics. Although these issues have been raised before, much more needs to be done to promote what Midgley (2017) calls a One World perspective that integrates knowledge from different parts of the world within a universally applicable framework.

By broadening the social investment literature to incorporate the experiences of different countries, a step towards articulating a broader, international interpretation of social investment may be taken. Also, as will be shown, the book raises other issues that may foster a more nuanced understanding of the field. Hopefully, it will be helpful to those who are engaged in the analysis of social investment policies and programmes. To this end, the following provides a brief summary of some of the issues raised by the authors of the book's chapters. It is concerned, first, with a discussion of some of the lessons learned from these contributors, and second, with some future directions that scholarship should take to promote a broader, internationally relevant interpretation of the field.

LESSONS LEARNED

The most obvious lesson arising from this book is that social investment has been implemented in many different countries around the world, comprising a rich diversity of experiences. These experiences need to be incorporated into the Western social investment literature to augment the limited Eurocentric approach that pervades the literature. Most of the book's chapters are country case studies which are representative of the major world regions including Africa, Asia, Australasia, Europe, North America and South America. They provide extensive comparative information that can foster this goal. Of particular interest are the case studies of countries that are classified as belonging to the Global South. These chapters belie the popular misconception that the governments of these countries do not address the social needs of their citizens or otherwise have 'backward' welfare systems. In fact, many of them have adopted highly innovative social investment policies that offer lessons for Western nations. The book's contribution to promoting an international perspective is augmented by Cook's account in Chapter 12 of the role of the international organizations which have actively supported the efforts of their member states to promote social investment. Stjernø's contribution (Chapter 11) also adopts an international perspective by examining the role of social investment in integrating migrants in Europe, an issue that is currently highly topical.

Fortunately, social policy writers are much more engaged with international issues today, and the comparative literature has expanded significantly. However, much of this literature still views social policy in other countries, and especially the nations of the Global South, through a Western lens so that inappropriate constructs, causal explanations and normative preferences are widely used to analyse their social policies (Midgley, 2017). On the other hand, scholars such as Deacon and his colleagues (Deacon, 2007; Deacon and Stubbs, 2013) have made a major contribution by promoting a global perspective that transcends the limitations of Western approaches. Recent international initiatives by European researchers will undoubtedly build on this work. One comes from the Centre for Interdisciplinary Research (ZiF) at Bielefeld University in Germany and is concerned with a major study entitled 'Towards Understanding Southern Welfare', while another by the World Politics of Social Investment Project based in Paris focuses on the way social investment ideas are being adopted around the world (Garritzmann et al., 2016).

It is clear from the book's chapters that social investment is not a recent innovation but has been employed in different countries for many years. In some countries, and particularly those in the Global South, social investment forms an integral part of the social development approach which has been widely adopted in the developing world since the 1950s. As Midgley (2014) reports and Cook confirms in Chapter 12, international agencies such as the United Nations and World Bank played a major role in promoting this approach. Lee notes in Chapter 3 that in Hong Kong and Singapore, social investment ideas have been closely linked to housing policy and have formed a key element of their social and economic development strategies since the 1960s. In India and China (Chapters 4 and 9) the concept of social investment is of more recent origin, but here too it is rooted in development plans which have historically emphasized the importance of economic growth in raising standards of living.

The book's chapters also show that social investment ideas are not confined to a limited range of policy interventions such as employment, child care and skills development, but encompass other fields such as housing, community development and social protection. Chapter 7 by Midgley seeks to broaden social investment's scope by discussing the role that community investments have played in the inner cities of the United States for many years. Similarly, Lee's chapter on housing policy in Hong Kong and Singapore (Chapter 3) reveals the critical role of the housing sector in promoting social investment in these societies. Pellissery's contribution (Chapter 4) shows how social investment ideas are being used to address the problem of rural poverty in India in a highly innovative way; and in Chapter 11, Stjernø discusses how social investment ideas can inform novel policy initiatives that have not previously been discussed in the social investment literature. As will be discussed later, several chapters examine the way social protection cash payments contribute to social investment, challenging the view that these transfers typify consumption welfare.

Another lesson is that it is implausible to view social investment as a distinctive social policy paradigm which can be readily distinguished from conventional welfare interventions. The book's case studies show that policies and programmes promoting social investments coexist with conventional, consumption-focused interventions and that in no country included in the book has social investment dominated the policy landscape to comprise a distinctive paradigm. To complicate matters further, the case studies also reveal that a policy that is conventionally classed as an investment may simultaneously have a consumption function. Lee points out in Chapter 3 that housing has a strong investment function but that it simultaneously meets the consumption need for shelter. This is also the case in South Africa, where Patel notes in Chapter 6 that the Child Support Grant is designed to supplement the incomes of poor families but that it also fosters social investment. She observes that it also promotes caring and has major implications for gender equity. Conley Wright (Chapter 2) points out that the Australian government's comprehensive early childhood policy comprises a variety of interventions of which some, such as cash transfers, play a significant role. This issue is also raised by Halvorsen and his colleagues in Chapter 10, who point out that child care programmes can be configured to serve different functions. They make a plea for child care in Norway to place less emphasis on preparing children for future careers and more on facilitating enjoyment and personal growth.

Their discussion also raises questions about the normative derivation of social investment. As Midgley observes in Chapter 1, various views on this issue have been expressed and it is unclear whether social investment is rooted in social democratic or neoliberal ideology or in a combination of the two. Dahl and Lorentzen address this issue in Chapter 5 by examining employment policy in Norway, a traditional social democratic country with a strong commitment to social investment. Although several reforms affecting cash transfers and labour activation have been adopted, they conclude that these changes do not negate the way social investment ideas have been implemented within a wider social democratic framework. Their conclusions in Chapter 5 and the other chapters in the book suggest that a much more nuanced interpretation of social investment that transcends simplistic categories is required. This also suggests that much more research into the complex issues raised in this book is needed.

FUTURE DIRECTIONS

As mentioned earlier, several of the book's chapters discuss the way cash benefits promote social investment and challenge the widely accepted view that they are typical of consumption transfers. In Chapter 6, Patel examines the investment impact of South Africa's Child Support Grant; and in Chapter 8, Hall critically assesses Brazil's *Bolsa Família* programme which invests in children by promoting human capital development. Similarly, in their discussion of pension policy in China, Leung and Xu (Chapter 9) examine how the government is promoting social investment through pensions in the context of wider policy reforms. However, it cannot simply be assumed that all social protection programmes have a social investment function. Clearly, meagre, stigmatizing and coercive cash transfers to passive welfare recipients differ significantly from those such as the Brazilian *Bolsa Família* programme which are purposefully designed to promote social investment. Midgley (2008) contends that policy design is a crucial factor and that to promote social investment, these programmes should be configured and implemented in ways that generate social returns. A future direction for research is to study how governments and nonprofits can use social protection cash transfers for this purpose.

Another direction for future research concerns the cash versus investments issue which has featured prominently in social investment debates in Europe. Several scholars have claimed that there has been too strong an emphasis on social investment services (such as early childhood education, job training and family leave programmes) which, they contend, have been implemented at the cost of cash transfers. As a result of this emphasis on social investment services, poverty rates have not declined even though employment has increased. Cantillon (2011) argues that, at least partly, social investment policies with an emphasis on services are to blame, since services tend to be less redistributive than cash benefits. However, this view is contested by Vandenbroucke and Vleminckx (2011) and Hudson and Kühner (2012).

Several chapters in the book touch on this issue and suggest that the widespread use of cash transfers to meet welfare goals in countries such as Brazil and South Africa has placed pressure on health, basic education, housing, sanitation and social welfare services. In Brazil, *Bolsa Família* has been a success because it has lifted millions out of poverty and contributed to lower income inequality, and as Hall observes in Chapter 8, the programme has become a victim of its own success. Due to its widespread popularity no politicians dare to question it, and consequently it is hard to secure adequate funding for conventional services. Patel makes a similar observation in her account of cash transfer programmes in South Africa (Chapter 6). This suggests that the balance between cash and social investment services differs between Europe and the Global South. In the former, there seems to be an excessive emphasis on investment services, while in the latter there is too strong a reliance on cash transfers. It is hard to find the right balance between cash transfers and investment services, and clearly there is a need for a well-designed mix of transfers and services (Ahn and Kim, 2015). Future research should investigate the most appropriate way of balancing the two. It is interesting, as Hall reports in Chapter 8, that the Brazilian government is aware of the problem and has adopted a more integrated approach with its *Brasil Sem Miséria* policy. Policy-makers in other countries will benefit from more extensive research into this issue.

Another topic for future inquiry concerns the supply- and demand-side approaches to social investment. Most, if not all, theoretical accounts of the social investment perspective have a supply-side bias. Empirically, this is also the case even in celebrated social investment states such as the Nordic countries. As shown in the book's chapters, demand-side issues are largely ignored in their discussion of social and labour market policies. This is understandable, given the preoccupation and concern with the capabilities of individuals to adapt to and be active players in the global marketplace. On the other hand, the one-sided focus on the supply side does not resonate with the concern expressed by some social investment advocates for the importance of quality jobs, jobs with a good work environment and jobs that pay decent wages (Morel et al., 2012). It could be argued that a better-educated and higher-skilled workforce would indirectly lead to the creation of better jobs (Nelson and Stephens, 2012), but such a strategy would be indirect and hardly optimal. Also, it would not in itself be effective in mobilizing and preserving skills among the (potentially) employed population; and in addition, as shown by Dahl and Lorentzen in Chapter 5, it has difficulty providing jobs for disadvantaged groups. Finding an appropriate balance between the supply- and demand-side approaches in social investment is clearly another important direction for future research.

Another, but neglected issue which requires more research is the asymmetrical power relations that people experience in their working lives, and the increasing gap in power resources as indicated by a general decline in unionization all over the world. If a prominent aim of social investment is to further labour force participation among disadvantaged groups, this issue should be higher on the agenda. The social investment perspective would benefit from a more thorough consideration of at least three aspects of this issue. First, focus should be given to strategies that proactively support the relationship between employees and employers. In this regard, the integration of theories on disability management and corporate social responsibility in social investment may be helpful. Second, since high quality work may have salutogenic effects on health, individuals' residual work capacity and the possibilities for recovery, coping and social inclusion may be more effectively developed through direct work participation than through traditional pre-vocational schemes such as conventional active labour market programmes. Third, interventions aimed at training and providing credentials should take place in ordinary workplaces under the provision of customized support to the job seeker and advice to employers. This is demonstrated in various forms of supported employment guided by a 'place, then train' strategy. Here, supported treatment and work inclusion are performed simultaneously, not sequentially.

Finally, it is clear that future debates on social investment should address the need for a comprehensive conceptual basis which can integrate the disparate approaches which, as Midgley shows in Chapter 1, continue to be used in the field. While the European social investment literature is conceptually well developed, this is not the case in other academic fields, where social investment is not viewed in paradigmatic or stadial terms but rather as discrete and fluid interventions. Similarly, the statist approach which dominates the European literature can be contrasted with the pluralist inclinations of those in development studies and other fields. Although it will not be easy to forge an approach which encompasses different academic and national contexts, closer collaboration between scholars from diverse disciplinary and interdisciplinary fields as well as diverse cultural and social origins can produce a One World perspective of global relevance.

It is equally important that future scholarship into social investment explicitly address the question of values. At the moment, values are either glossed over or assumed to be self-evident, but they are central to a normatively viable social investment approach. Among these values, equality is of central importance but has attracted relatively little attention, and there is no agreement over what kind of equality should be pursued. While some writers stress the need for equality of opportunity, others maintain that equality of outcome is crucially important. Several of the book's chapters, such as Chapter 5 on Norway and Chapter 6 on South Africa, address this issue but they also reveal its complexity since the two approaches are interlinked. To complicate matters further, policies aiming at furthering equality may create the dilemma of improving conditions for one vulnerable group while one or more other vulnerable groups may be left disadvantaged. Other key values such as participation, solidarity and collective responsibility also need much more scrutiny. Together with a wider collaborative effort to formulate a universally relevant conceptual basis for social investment, a thorough analysis of values will be needed if social investment policies and programmes are to enhance the welfare of all the world's people.

REFERENCES

Ahn, S.H. and Kim, S.W. (2015). Social Investment, Social Service and the Economic Performance of Welfare States. *International Journal of Social Welfare*, 24, 109–119.

Cantillon, B. (2011). The Paradox of the Social Investment State: Growth, Employment and Poverty in the Lisbon Era. *Journal of European Social Policy*, 21 (5), 432–449.

Deacon, B. (2007). *Global Social Policy and Governance*. London: Sage Publications.

Deacon, B. and Stubbs, P. (2013). Global Social Policy Studies: Conceptual and Analytical Reflections. *Global Social Policy*, 13 (1), 5–23.

Garritzmann, J.L., Häusermann, S., Palier, B. and Zollinger, C. (2016). WoPSI – The World Politics of Social Investment. Background Paper. Available at http://ssrn.com/abstract=2795451.

Hudson, J. and Kühner, S. (2012). Analyzing the Productive and Protective Dimensions of Welfare: Looking Beyond the OECD. *Social Policy and Administration*, 46 (1), 35–60.

Midgley, J. (2008). Social Security and the Economy: Key Perspectives. In J. Midgley and K.L. Tang (eds), *Social Security, the Economy and Development*. New York: Palgrave Macmillan, pp. 51–84.

Midgley, J. (2014). *Social Development: Theory and Practice*. London: Sage Publications.

Midgley, J. (2017). *Social Welfare for a Global Era: International Perspectives on Policy and Practice*. Los Angeles, CA: Sage Publications.

Morel, N., Pallier, B. and Palme, J. (2012). Social Investment: A Paradigm in Search of a New Economic Model and Political Mobilization. In Morel, N., Pallier, B. and Palme, J. (eds), *Towards a Social Investment Welfare State? Ideas, Policies and Challenges*. Bristol: Policy Press, pp. 353–376.

Nelson, M. and Stephens, J.D. (2012). Do Social Investment Policies Produce More and Better Jobs?. In Morel, N., Pallier, B. and Palme, J. (eds), *Towards a Social Investment Welfare State? Ideas, Policies and Challenges*. Bristol: Policy Press, pp. 205–234.

Vandenbroucke, F. and Vleminckx, K. (2011). Disappointing Poverty Trends: Is the Social Investment State to Blame?. *Journal of European Social Policy*, 21 (5), 450–471.

Index